READING TUTOR

고등 독해의
절대 자신감

수능 PLUS

고등 독해의 절대 자신감
리딩튜터 〈수능 PLUS〉

지은이	NE능률 영어교육연구소
선임 연구원	신유승
연구원	이은주, 신이례
영문 교열	August Niederhaus, Nathaniel Galletta
디자인	박정진, 김명진
내지 일러스트	박정원, 혜란, 김영미, 홍승표
내지 사진	www.shutterstock.com, www.istockphoto.com, www.hellophoto.kr
맥편집	김재민
영업	한기영, 이경구, 박인규, 정철교, 김남준, 김남형, 이우현
마케팅	박혜선, 고유진, 김여진

SECTION 01

☐	lodging	숙박
☐	head	가다[향하다]
☐	renovate	개조하다
☐	notorious	악명 높은
☐	convert	개조하다, 전환시키다
☐	jail	감옥
☐	structure	구조; 구조물, 건물
☐	combine	결합하다
☐	confine	국한시키다
☐	historic	역사적으로 중요한
☐	historical	역사상의
☐	architecture	건축
☐	feature	특징; …을 특색으로 삼다
☐	landmark	주요 지형지물; 역사적인 건물
☐	transfer	이송하다
☐	transmit	전송하다
☐	prisoner	죄수
☐	carriage	마차, 운송 수단
☐	cell	감방
☐	transform	변모시키다, 변형시키다
☐	authentic	진짜의
☐	awkward	어색한
☐	electronics	전자제품
☐	approach	…에 다가가다
☐	sales clerk	점원, 판매원

☐	sigh	한숨 쉬다
☐	reluctantly	마지못해
☐	recommendation	추천
☐	employ	고용하다; 쓰다, 이용하다
☐	measure	측정하다; 평가하다
☐	retail store	소매점
☐	instruct	지시하다
☐	analyze	분석하다
☐	rate	평가하다
☐	criticism	비판, 비평
☐	ethical	윤리적인
☐	aspect	측면
☐	concern	우려, 걱정
☐	deceive	속이다
☐	except for	…을 제외하고는
☐	flaw	결함
☐	melt	녹다
☐	rate	속도
☐	interestingly	흥미롭게도
☐	discovery	발견
☐	accidental	우연한
☐	intentional	의도적인
☐	liquid	액체
☐	instantly	즉시, 즉각
☐	solid	단단한, 견고한
☐	separate	분리되다
☐	stay	(특정 상태를) 유지하다, …인 채로 있다
☐	firm	딱딱한, 단단한

☐	realize	깨닫다, 알아차리다
☐	effect	효과
☐	substance	물질
☐	product	상품, 제품
☐	claim	주장
☐	excuse	변명, 이유
☐	last	오래가다, 지속되다
☐	currently	현재
☐	teamwork	팀워크, 협동 작업
☐	company retreat	회사 야유회
☐	put ... in a circle	…을 원형으로 둘러 세우다
☐	particular	특정한
☐	hand	건네주다, 넘겨주다
☐	equal	같다, …이다
☐	equally	똑같이, 동일하게
☐	maximum	최대의, 최고의
☐	have ... in motion	…을 움직이게 하다
☐	demonstrate	입증하다; 보여주다, 설명하다
☐	individual	개인
☐	be concerned about	…에 관심을 가지다, …을 걱정하다
☐	ultimately	결국

SECTION 02

☐	climate	기후
☐	level	정도, 수준

☐	mineral	광물; 무기물, 미네랄
☐	contain	포함하다
☐	nutrient	영양소, 영양분
☐	increase	증가
☐	require	필요로 하다
☐	have a negative effect on	…에 부정적인 영향을 미치다
☐	demonstrate	입증하다, 실증하다
☐	experiment	실험
☐	indoor	실내의
☐	take place	일어나다
☐	category	범주
☐	reduce	줄이다
☐	reduction	감소
☐	potentially	잠재적으로
☐	lead to	…로 이어지다
☐	struggle	투쟁[고투]하다, 몸부림치다
☐	nutrition	영양
☐	rapid	빠른
☐	influence	영향
☐	natural	자연의; 타고난
☐	apply	신청하다; 적용하다, 응용하다
☐	curiosity	호기심
☐	laboratory	실험실
☐	pause	잠시 멈추다
☐	magnetron	마그네트론, 전자관
☐	device	장치
☐	melt	녹다
☐	panic	당황하다

☐	suspect	의심쩍어하다, 짐작하다
☐	explode	폭발하다
☐	fluffy	솜털 같은
☐	enormous	거대한
☐	decade	10년
☐	improvement	향상, 개선
☐	addition	추가된 것, 부가물
☐	average	평균의; 보통의
☐	accidental	우연한
☐	household	가정
☐	complex	복잡한
☐	approach	접근; 접근법
☐	backwards	거꾸로
☐	involve	수반하다; 필요로 하다
☐	maintain	유지하다
☐	maintenance	유지, 보수 관리
☐	deteriorate	악화되다, 나빠지다
☐	exterior	외부[외면]의
☐	adjust	조절하다, 맞추다
☐	dusk	황혼, 땅거미
☐	swell	증가, 팽창
☐	thorough	철저한
☐	formulate	만들어내다
☐	problem-solving	문제 해결
☐	disadvantage	불리한 점, 약점
☐	strengthen	강화하다
☐	decay	부식하다, 썩다
☐	dropping	pl. (새 · 짐승의) 배설물

☐	prey on	…을 잡아먹다
☐	fiancé	약혼자(남자)
☐	military	군대
☐	forward	앞으로
☐	accommodate	공간을 제공하다; (요구 등에) 부응하다
☐	aspect	측면
☐	elegance	우아, 고상
☐	grace	…을 빛내다[영예롭게 하다]
☐	presence	참석, 존재
☐	arrangement	준비, 마련

SECTION 03

☐	composer	작곡가
☐	composition	작곡법
☐	dice	주사위
☐	popularize	대중화하다
☐	by chance	우연히
☐	measure	측정하다; (음악) 소절
☐	assign	배정하다
☐	sequence	연속; 순서
☐	experimental	실험적인
☐	coin tossing	동전 던지기
☐	critical	비판적인
☐	extraordinary	기이한, 놀라운

□	catch fire	불붙다, 타오르다
□	spectacular	장관을 이루는, 화려한
□	feast day	축일
□	puppet	인형, 꼭두각시
□	cardboard	판지
□	plaster	회반죽, 석고반죽
□	depict	묘사하다
□	current event	시사, 시사 문제
□	corrupt	부패한, 타락한
□	lifelike	실물과 똑같은
□	crane	크레인, 기중기
□	transportation	수송, 운송
□	chop	썰다[다지다], (장작 같은 것을) 패다
□	stuff	속을 채우다
□	streetlight	가로등
□	alongside	… 옆에, …와 나란히
□	pardon	용서하다; 사면하다
□	previous	이전의
□	affordable	이용할 수 있는, 알맞은
□	ironically	역설적으로
□	deal with	…에 대처하다, …을 해결하다
□	nonprofit	비영리의
□	estimate	추정하다
□	have access to	…에 접근할 수 있다
□	seed	씨앗
□	windowsill	창턱, 창 아래틀
□	assure	보장하다
□	accessible	접근[이용] 가능한

☐	worn-out	닳아서 해진
☐	offend	기분을 상하게 하다
☐	humiliate	수치심을 느끼게 하다
☐	charity	자선, 구호
☐	case	대상자
☐	upset	화나게 하다
☐	youngster	아이, 청소년
☐	within one's grasp	…가 이해할 수 있는
☐	recess	휴식 (시간)
☐	proficiency	숙달, 능숙
☐	instruct	지시하다

SECTION 04

☐	suspect	…라고 여기다, 짐작하다
☐	domestic	국내의; (동물이) 길든
☐	leopard	표범
☐	lack	…이 없다
☐	receptor	수용기, 감각기
☐	gene	유전자
☐	genetic	유전의
☐	detect	인지하다, 감지하다
☐	stimulus	자극
☐	evolution	진화
☐	nutrition	영양(물)
☐	nutritional	영양상의

☐	mammal	포유류
☐	signal	신호
☐	taste bud	미뢰
☐	be made up of	…로 구성되다
☐	represent	대표하다
☐	bitter	쓴
☐	die out	멸종되다
☐	perceive	감지하다, 인지하다
☐	intelligence	지능
☐	motorsports	모터스포츠
☐	rear	뒤쪽
☐	vehicle	차량, 탈것
☐	serve	…에 도움이 되다, 쓸모가 있다
☐	practical	실용적인
☐	precise	정확한
☐	law	(과학 · 철학상의) 법칙
☐	physics	물리학
☐	in effect	사실상, 실제로는
☐	mass	덩어리; 질량
☐	friction	마찰, 마찰 저항
☐	double	두 배로 되다
☐	calculate	계산하다, 추정하다
☐	crash	충돌하다
☐	sun protection factor	자외선 차단 지수
☐	sunscreen	자외선 차단제
☐	measure	조치; 척도
☐	time	시간을 측정하다
☐	tingle	따끔거리다

□	estimate	추정하다
□	statistics	통계
□	approximately	대략, 거의
□	multiply	곱하다
□	golden rule	황금률
□	take a dip	잠깐 수영을 하다
□	reapply	다시 바르다
□	ray	광선
□	shine	빛나다
□	silky	비단 같은
□	hind	뒤의
□	lower	낮추다
□	roll	굴러가다, 구르듯이 가다
□	delicately	섬세하게
□	stem	줄기
□	stick	붙이다
□	tip	끝
□	make sense	의미가 통하다, 이해가 되다
□	disbelief	믿기지 않음, 불신감
□	shiver	(몸을) 떨다
□	attack	공격하다
□	terrified	무서워[두려워]하는
□	indifferent	무관심한
□	ashamed	부끄러운, 창피한
□	essential	필수적인
□	lifesaving	구명(용)의, 구조의; 수난[인명] 구조(법)
□	enthusiastic	열렬한, 열광적인

☐	countryside	시골 지역
☐	unexpected	예기치 않은, 뜻밖의
☐	encounter	만남

SECTION 05

☐	one-of-a-kind	독특한, 단 하나뿐인
☐	distant	거리가 먼
☐	access	입장; 접근권, 접촉 기회
☐	far-off	(시간 · 거리 등이) 먼, 멀리 떨어진
☐	mobile	이동하는, 이동식의
☐	maintain	유지하다; 정비하다
☐	transportation	수송, 운송
☐	vehicle	탈것, 운송 수단
☐	reliable	믿을 수 있는, 의지가 되는
☐	suited	적합한
☐	source	원천
☐	material	재료; 자료
☐	gathering	모임, 집회
☐	take place	개최되다
☐	similar	비슷한
☐	differentiate	구별하다
☐	appearance	(겉)모습, 외모
☐	identical	동일한, 똑같은
☐	odd	이상한, 특이한
☐	donate	기증하다

☐	deal	거래
☐	bury	묻다, 매장하다
☐	grave	무덤
☐	erect	세우다
☐	in exchange for	… 대신에, …와 교환으로
☐	claim	주장하다
☐	phenomenon	현상
☐	perceive	인지[인식]하다
☐	vague	흐릿한, 모호한
☐	significant	중요한
☐	trait	특성, 특징
☐	evolution	진화
☐	recognize	알아보다, 인식하다
☐	bond	유대, 끈
☐	identify	확인하다, 식별하다
☐	minimal	아주 적은, 최소의
☐	interpret	이해하다, 판단하다
☐	panic	당황하다
☐	unreliable	믿을[신뢰할] 수 없는
☐	precise	정확한
☐	overabundance	과잉, 과다
☐	option	선택(권), 옵션
☐	marketplace	시장
☐	price	가격; 대가
☐	in terms of	…의 관점에서
☐	psychologist	심리학자
☐	factor	요인, 요소
☐	influence	영향을 미치다

☐	surprisingly	놀랍게도
☐	selection	선택
☐	purchase	구입하다
☐	a wide range of	광범위한, 다양한
☐	ironic	반어적인, 비꼬는; 역설[모순]적인
☐	relieved	안도하는
☐	prompt	촉구하다, 부추기다
☐	consumer	소비자
☐	paradox	역설

SECTION 06

☐	natural phenomenon	자연 현상
☐	occur	일어나다, 발생하다
☐	occurrence	발생; 사건, 생긴 일
☐	invade	침략하다
☐	witness	목격하다
☐	incredibly	놀랍게도
☐	species	종(種)
☐	interval	간격
☐	calculation	계산
☐	predator	포식자, 포식 동물
☐	life cycle	생활 주기
☐	ensure	반드시 …하게 하다, 보장하다
☐	encounter	마주치다
☐	remind A of B	A에게 B를 생각나게 하다

☐ comfort	위안하다, 위로하다
☐ adjust	조절하다
☐ preserve	보호하다; 보존하다
☐ get along with	…와 잘 지내다
☐ prey on	…을 잡아먹다
☐ refer to A as B	A를 B라고 부르다
☐ term	용어
☐ operation	작전
☐ carry out	…을 수행하다
☐ Allied forces	연합군
☐ land	상륙하다
☐ mainland	본토
☐ designate	지정하다
☐ celebrate	기념하다, 축하하다
☐ anniversary	기념일
☐ invasion	침입, 침공
☐ commemorate	기념하다
☐ keep track of	…을 기록하다
☐ shrink	줄어들다
☐ indicate	나타내다, 보여주다
☐ projection	예상, 추정
☐ little more than	…에 지나지 않는
☐ puddle	물웅덩이
☐ be responsible for	…을 책임지고 있다; …의 원인이 되다
☐ consistent	거듭되는, 변함없는
☐ rainfall	강우(량)
☐ particular	특정한; 특유의
☐ geographical	지리(학)적인

☐	contribute to	…에 기여하다; …의 한 원인이 되다
☐	shallow	얕은
☐	evaporate	증발하다
☐	excessive	지나친, 과도한
☐	rely on	…에 의지[의존]하다
☐	optimistic	낙관적인, 낙관하는
☐	competition	경쟁
☐	intense	극심한; 치열한
☐	sustain	지속시키다; (생명을) 유지하다, 부양하다
☐	die out	멸종되다
☐	habitat	서식지
☐	tourist attraction	관광 명소
☐	physical	신체적인
☐	limit	한계
☐	engage in	…에 참여하다
☐	physical strength	체력
☐	majority	다수
☐	compete	경쟁하다
☐	compare	비교하다
☐	participate in	…에 참가[참여]하다
☐	anticipate	기대하다
☐	frequent	빈번한
☐	collision	충돌
☐	risk	위험성
☐	injury	부상
☐	get involved in	…에 참가하다
☐	individual	개인적인
☐	recognize	알아보다, 인식하다

SECTION 07

□	mysticism	신비주의
□	be composed of	…으로 구성되어 있다
□	element	요소, 원소
□	combination	조합
□	substance	물질
□	precious metal	귀금속
□	remedy	치료(약)
□	prolong	연장시키다
□	originate	시작되다, 생기다
□	evolve	발달하다; 진화하다
□	ultimately	마침내, 결국
□	degenerate	퇴화[쇠퇴]하다
□	superstition	미신
□	migrate	이주하다; 이동하다
□	scholarly	학문상의, 전문적인
□	discipline	훈련; 학과, 학문
□	medieval	중세의
□	revive	되살리다; 부활[부흥]시키다
□	foundation	기초, 토대
□	breakthrough	돌파구; 새로운 발견, 큰 발전
□	struggle	애쓰다
□	effective	효과적인
□	overweight	과체중의, 비만의
□	capacity	수용력; 능력
□	indicate	나타내다, 보여주다

☐	surgical	외과의
☐	operation	수술
☐	digestive	소화의
☐	appetite	식욕
☐	stimulant	흥분제, 자극제
☐	obese	비만인
☐	workable	운용[실행] 가능한
☐	relieve	경감[완화]시키다
☐	notable	눈에 띄는, 주목할 만한
☐	feature	특징
☐	visibility	눈에 잘 보임, 가시성
☐	interior	내부(의)
☐	unobstructed	가로막는 것이 없는
☐	virtuous	도덕적인, 고결한
☐	prove	입증[증명]하다
☐	install	설치하다
☐	vertical	수직의
☐	blind	블라인드
☐	flood	물에 잠기게 하다; (빛 등이) …을 가득 채우다
☐	share	나누다, 공유하다
☐	write down	…을 적다, 기록하다
☐	bottled	병에 든
☐	announce	알리다, 통보하다
☐	discovery	발견
☐	catch	잡다; (예상 밖의 상황에) 처하게 하다
☐	toss	던지다

SECTION 08

☐	unlikely	…일 것 같지 않은; 예상 밖의
☐	circumstance	상황
☐	hippopotamus	하마
☐	tortoise	거북
☐	bond	유대
☐	devastating	파괴적인, 엄청난
☐	tsunami	쓰나미
☐	orphan	고아로 만들다
☐	rescue	구조하다
☐	enclosure	울타리를 친 장소
☐	cohabitant	동거인
☐	be wary of	…을 경계하다
☐	imitate	모방하다
☐	inseparable	떨어질 수 없는
☐	companion	동료, 친구
☐	astonishing	놀라운
☐	celebrity	유명인
☐	feature	(배우를) 주연시키다
☐	translate	번역하다
☐	patient	참을성 있는
☐	sympathetic	동정 어린
☐	intensely	강렬하게; 열심히
☐	realize	깨닫다; 실현[달성]하다
☐	be stricken with	(병)에 걸리다
☐	for life	평생

□	crutch	목발
□	instant	즉각적인
□	composer	작곡가
□	onstage	무대 위의
□	presence	존재
□	eloquently	웅변으로; 감동적으로
□	on behalf of	…을 대신해서, 대표해서
□	commitment	헌신
□	welfare	복지
□	astronaut	우주비행사
□	float	(물 위나 공중에) 뜨다, 떠돌다
□	ship	운송[수송]하다
□	artificial	인공의
□	substance	물질
□	yield	생산하다
□	content	내용물; 함량
□	nutrition	영양
□	obviously	확실히
□	fund	자금을 대다
□	enhance	향상시키다
□	initial	처음의
□	out of this world	너무도 훌륭한
□	cultivate	경작하다, 재배하다
□	eliminate	없애다, 제거하다
□	manpower	인력
□	favoritism	편애
□	attractive	매력적인
□	attractiveness	매력

☐	demonstrate	보여주다, 입증하다
☐	follow-up	뒤따르는, 후속의
☐	be unaware of	…을 알지 못하다
☐	bias	편견
☐	automatically	자동적으로, 무의식적으로
☐	assign	맡기다; 부여하다
☐	favorable	호의적인; 유리한, 좋은
☐	trait	특성
☐	unconscious	무의식적인
☐	assumption	추정, 가정
☐	consequence	결과
☐	federal	연방의, 연방 정부의
☐	candidate	후보자
☐	deny	부인[부정]하다
☐	acknowledge	인정하다
☐	electability	선출 가능성
☐	troubling	성가신, 곤혹스러운
☐	prejudice	편견
☐	satisfaction	만족

SECTION 09

☐	once in a lifetime	일생에 한 번뿐인
☐	saying	속담
☐	association	협회, 단체
☐	aim	목표, 목적

□	sight-disabled	시각 장애가 있는
□	greet	맞이하다, 환영하다
□	belonging	pl. 소지품
□	illuminated	조명 장식을 한
□	tricky	힘든, 까다로운
□	locate	찾아내다
□	nuclear power	원자력
□	industry	산업
□	publish	출판하다; 게재하다
□	go forward	진행하다, 나아가다
□	examine	조사하다, 검토하다
□	power plant	발전소
□	threat	위협
□	deadly	치명적인
□	consumption	소비
□	investment	투자
□	conservation	보존
□	measure	pl. 수단, 대책
□	insulation	단열(재)
□	energy-efficient	에너지 효율적인
□	appliance	pl. 가전제품
□	renewable	재생 가능한
□	recommendation	추천
□	come up with	…을 생각해내다
□	chemist	화학자
□	will	의지; 유언장
□	mathematician	수학자
□	field	들판; 분야

□	regardless of	…에 상관없이
□	absence	결석; 부재
□	inspire	고무하다, 격려하다
□	inspiration	영감
□	attain	이루다, 획득하다
□	restrict	제한하다, 한정하다
□	vary	다르다; 달라지다
□	congress	회의; 학술 대회
□	acclaim	찬사, 칭찬
□	prestigious	권위 있는, 명성 있는
□	spotlight	스포트라이트; 주목
□	enhance	높이다, 향상시키다
□	employee	종업원, 고용인
□	satisfaction	만족(감)
□	productivity	생산성
□	produce	생산하다
□	organization	조직, 단체
□	directly	곧장, 똑바로
□	attitude	태도
□	affect	영향을 미치다
□	matter	중요하다, 문제되다
□	performance	공연; 실적, 성과
□	suffer	고통받다; 더 나빠지다
□	acceptable	용인되는, 받아들여지는
□	improve	개선하다, 향상시키다
□	stick to	…을 고수하다[지키다]
□	independent	독립적인
□	discontented	불만족한, 불만스러워하는

SECTION 10

□	attempt	시도하다
□	alpine	알프스의
□	mountaineer	등산가
□	peak	절정; 봉우리, 정상
□	freeze to death	얼어 죽다
□	altitude	(해발) 고도
□	tragedy	비극
□	scale	오르다
□	conquer	정복하다
□	steep	가파른, 경사가 급한
□	loose	헐거운
□	unpredictable	예측할 수 없는
□	obstacle	장애(물)
□	vow	맹세, 서약
□	defeat	패배시키다, 이기다
□	once in a lifetime	평생 단 한 번뿐인
□	aimlessly	목적 없이
□	unaltered	변하지 않은
□	average	보통의
□	option	선택사항
□	decoy	유인하는 장치, 미끼
□	undesirable	바람직하지 않은, 달갑지 않은
□	weak point	약점
□	minor	작은, 가벼운
□	flaw	결함

☐	in comparison	비교해 보면
☐	previous	이전의
☐	reduction	감소
☐	elimination	제거
☐	adoption	채택
☐	affordable	(가격이) 알맞은
☐	break up	헤어지다; 해체하다
☐	have an effect on	…에 영향을 미치다
☐	generation	세대
☐	establish	설립하다, 개설하다
☐	youngster	청소년
☐	a handful of	한줌의; 소수의
☐	mobile	이동하는, 이동식의
☐	mix	믹싱 녹음하다
☐	vocal	pl. 보컬, 노래 부분
☐	compose	구성하다; 작곡하다
☐	original	본래의; 독창적인
☐	target	목표로 삼다; 대상으로 삼다
☐	struggle	분투[고투]하다; 힘겹게 나아가다
☐	budget cut	예산 삭감
☐	stick with	…을 계속하다
☐	accomplish	완수하다, 성취하다
☐	thrilled	황홀해 하는, 아주 신이 난
☐	in the first place	우선, 먼저
☐	resolution	다짐[결심]
☐	rather than	… 보다는[대신에]
☐	matter	중요하다, 문제되다
☐	consider	고려하다

☐	figure out	이해하다, 알아내다
☐	deadline	기한, 마감 시간
☐	guidance	지도, 안내

SECTION 11

☐	slippery	미끄러운
☐	slip	미끄러지다
☐	material	물질, 재료
☐	friction	마찰
☐	molecule	분자
☐	adapt	맞추다; 적응하다
☐	adaptation	적응
☐	contact	접촉
☐	sweat	땀
☐	involve	수반하다
☐	outer	외부의, 바깥의
☐	fingerprint	지문
☐	locate	두다, 설치하다
☐	rough	거친
☐	release	방출하다
☐	flatten	납작해지다; 납작하게 만들다
☐	firm	단단한, 견고한
☐	grip	꽉 붙잡음
☐	unusual	특이한
☐	process	과정

☐	immediately	즉시, 즉각
☐	individual	개인
☐	sensory cell	감각 세포
☐	definition	정의
☐	surgery	수술
☐	retina	망막
☐	receptor	수용체
☐	sensitive	민감한
☐	sense	감지하다
☐	interpret	해석하다, 이해하다
☐	fatigued	지친, 피곤한
☐	afterimage	잔상
☐	complementary color	보색
☐	accompany	…을 수반하다, 동반하다
☐	bleeding	출혈
☐	vision	시력; 시야
☐	concentration	집중(력)
☐	prevent	예방하다, 방지하다
☐	symbolic	상징적인
☐	political scientist	정치학자
☐	analysis	분석
☐	phenomenon	현상
☐	put forward	(의견을) 내다, 제기하다
☐	nutrition	영양
☐	compelling	흥미를 돋우는; 설득력 있는
☐	constant	끊임없는; 변함없는
☐	impairment	장애
☐	significant	상당한, 현저한

☐	boost	신장시키다, 북돋우다
☐	gadget	장치, 기계
☐	abstract	추상적인, 관념적인
☐	sophistication	세련; 복잡화, 정교화
☐	stimulate	자극[격려]하다, 활발하게 하다
☐	work out	…을 해결하다
☐	extended	길어진, 늘어난
☐	enhanced	증대한, 향상된
☐	manage	처리하다
☐	management	처리
☐	solid	고체의
☐	waste	폐기물
☐	recycling	재활용
☐	recycle	재활용하다
☐	bury	묻다
☐	landfill	쓰레기 매립지
☐	commonly	흔히, 보통
☐	technique	기법, 기술
☐	disposal	처리
☐	take up	…을 차지하다
☐	respectively	각각
☐	think of A as B	A를 B로 생각하다[여기다]
☐	explanation	해명, 설명

SECTION 12

□	approach	다가가다
□	interruption	중단, 방해
□	replace	대체하다
□	conduct	(특정한 활동을) 하다
□	phenomenon	현상
□	blindness	맹목, 무지
□	process	처리하다
□	detect	감지하다
□	pass by	…을 스쳐 지나가다
□	suffer from	…로 고통받다
□	nasal	코의
□	congestion	혼잡; 막힘
□	respiratory	호흡의, 호흡 기관의
□	chemical	화학물질
□	pollen	꽃가루
□	device	장치
□	passageway	통로
□	filter	여과하다, 거르다
□	pollutant	오염 물질
□	clog	막다
□	saltwater	소금물
□	relief	안도; 경감[완화]
□	tract	(생물) 관
□	infection	감염
□	stop by	…에 들르다

□	pharmacy	약국
□	reinforce	강화하다
□	side effect	부작용
□	construct	건설하다; 구성하다
□	fiber	섬유질
□	arrange	처리하다; 배열하다
□	pack	(짐을) 싸다; (물건으로) 빽빽이 채우다
□	stalk	(식물의) 줄기
□	surface	표면[표층]
□	absorb	흡수하다
□	vibration	진동
□	impact	충격
□	available	이용할 수 있는
□	resource	자원; 재료
□	profit	이익, 수익
□	benefit from	…로부터 이득을 보다
□	smooth	매끈한, 부드러운
□	appreciate	진가를 알아보다
□	special effect	특수 효과
□	specialize in	…을 전문으로 하다
□	realistic	사실적인
□	budget	예산
□	insist	고집하다, 주장하다
□	original	원래의; 원본의
□	filming	(영화의) 촬영
□	believable	그럴듯한
□	shoot	쏘다; 촬영하다
□	aircraft	비행기

MEMO

MEMO

MEMO

The future belongs to those who believe in the beauty of their dreams.

미래는 꿈의 아름다움을 믿는 사람의 것이다.

– 엘리너 루즈벨트 (Eleanor Roosevelt) –

영어를 잘하고 싶은데, 지루하고 어렵게 느껴지나요?

다양한 주제의 흥미로운 글을 영어로 읽어 보세요. 문법, 문장구조, 어려운 어휘, 이런 것들에 너무 얽매이지 말고, 전체적인 내용에만 집중하세요. 그렇게 읽다 보면, 조금 더 자세히, 정확히 알고 싶은 부분이 생기고, 그런 것들을 알기 위해 공부하고자 하는 마음이 들 것입니다. 완벽하게 해석이 되지 않는다고 스트레스받지 마세요. 글을 읽으며 자신에게 필요한 학습 요소가 무엇인지 파악하고 차근차근 더해 나가면 됩니다.

이렇게 영어 공부에 대한 스트레스는 줄이고, 재미와 상식을 더하는 영어 독해!

리딩튜터 시리즈와 함께 하면 됩니다.

새로운 정보와 흥미로운 이야기가 담긴 지문들을 읽으면서 재미있게 공부할 수 있고, 자연스럽게 다양한 분야와 주제에 대한 배경지식을 넓힐 수 있을 것입니다. 또한 글을 꼼꼼하게 이해하고 파악하는 데 도움이 되는 양질의 문제들을 풀면서 독해 실력도 향상시킬 수 있을 것입니다.

리딩튜터를 통해 여러분이 목표하는 영어 실력을 얻고, 나아가 여러분이 이루고자 하는 꿈에 조금 더 가까이 다가갈 수 있기를 바랍니다.

저자 일동

영어 독해가 재미있어지는 리딩튜터만의 매력

Welcome to Reading Tutor

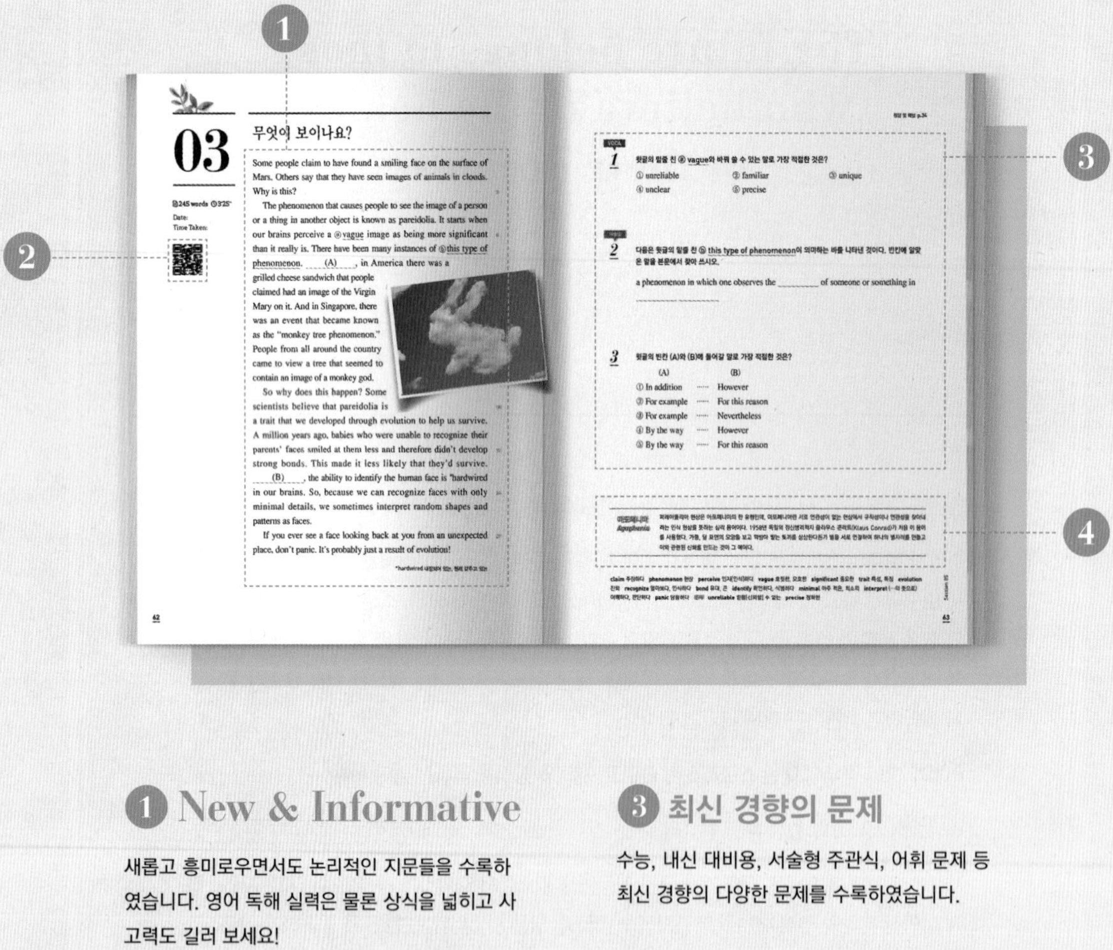

❶ New & Informative

새롭고 흥미로우면서도 논리적인 지문들을 수록하였습니다. 영어 독해 실력은 물론 상식을 넓히고 사고력도 길러 보세요!

❷ Smart Learning

원어민이 녹음한 지문 MP3 파일을 QR 코드 스캔 한 번으로 바로 들을 수 있게 하였습니다.

❸ 최신 경향의 문제

수능, 내신 대비용, 서술형 주관식, 어휘 문제 등 최신 경향의 다양한 문제를 수록하였습니다.

❹ 배경지식

지문 내용과 관련된 배경지식을 수록하여, 지문을 보다 흥미롭고 깊이 있게 읽을 수 있게 하였습니다.

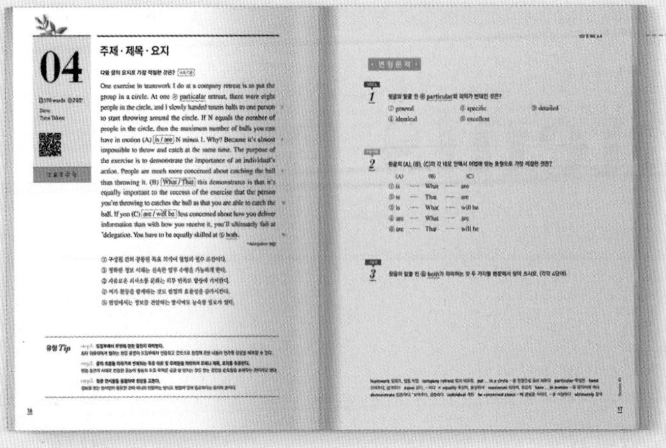

TRY 수능

수능 및 모의학력평가 문제 중에서 유형별 대표 문제를 선별하여 수능 유형을 연습해 볼 수 있도록 하였습니다. 또한, 추가 변형 문제를 제시하여 기출 지문을 활용한 다양한 독해 문제를 연습해 볼 수 있도록 하였습니다.

Review Test

각 섹션에서 배운 단어와 숙어, 주요 구문들을 다양한 유형의 문제를 통해 확인하고 정리해 보세요.

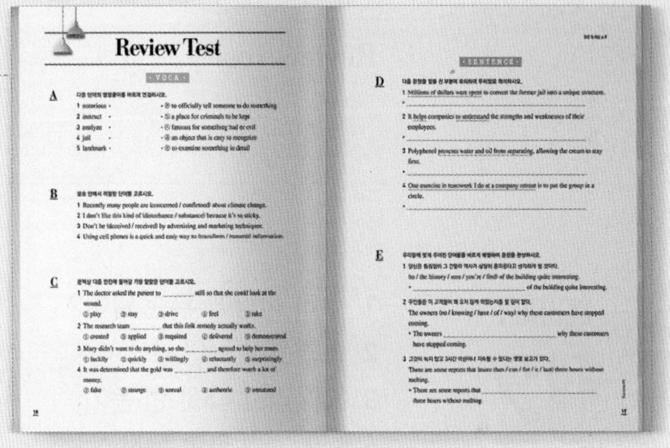

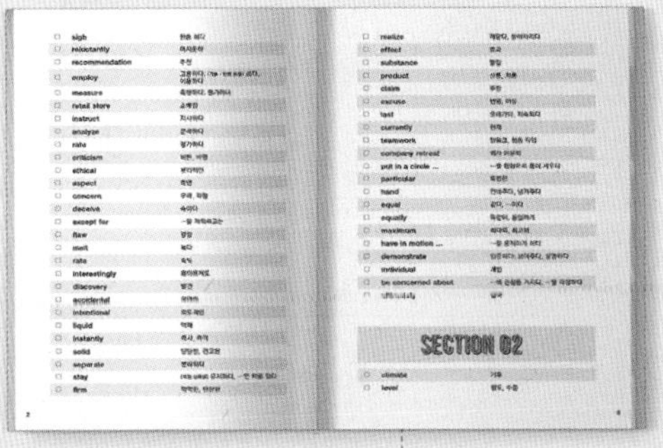

Special Corners

경제 용어와 세계의 이색 도서관을 소개하는 재미있는 쉬어가기 코너를 준비하였습니다. 공부에 지친 몸과 마음에 잠시 휴식을 주는 건 어떨까요?

어휘 암기장

본문에서 쓰인 주요 어휘들을 부록으로 별도 제공하여 휴대하면서 틈틈이 어휘 학습을 할 수 있도록 하였습니다.

Contents

SECTION 01

01

감옥에서 하룻밤을

172 words 2'35"

Date:

Time Taken:

If you're looking for a unique lodging experience during your tour of New England, head to the Liberty Hotel in Boston. You're sure to find the history of the building quite interesting. Before it ⓐ (renovate), it was the notorious Charles Street Jail. Millions of dollars ⓑ (spend) to convert the former jail into a unique structure that (A) [combines / confines] historic architecture with the luxury features of a modern hotel.

The original *granite structure, built in 1851, was a National Historical Landmark. Today, careful planning has made the Liberty Hotel an interesting mix of public spaces, historical features, and guestrooms. The area where the guards used to (B) [transfer / transmit] prisoners from the police carriages to their cells was transformed into the entrance of a restaurant called Scampo, which means "escape" in Italian. Another restaurant in the hotel features original bars from the old cell doors and windows, and the waiters and waitresses wear shirts with prison numbers on them. Everything feels very (C) [authentic / awkward], but don't worry — you'll be able to leave whenever you want!

*granite 화강암

교도소에서 호텔로

유럽에는 오래된 교도소를 개조한 이색 호텔이 많다. 슬로베니아 류블랴나의 셀리카 호스텔은 19세기 말 오스트리아 헝가리 제국의 군사 감옥을 현대에 와서 호스텔로 개조한 것이다. 19세기 핀란드의 헬싱키 교도소도 현재 베스트웨스턴 호텔로 변신했다. 교도소였을 때 지어졌던 붉은 벽돌의 높은 담장은 여전히 존재하고 있다. 한편 과거 이스탄불 교도소였던 포시즌 호텔도 눈길을 끄는데, 이 교도소는 영화 *미드나이트 익스프레스*에 등장하기도 했다.

1 Liberty Hotel에 관한 윗글의 내용과 일치하지 않는 것은?

① 원래 Charles Street Jail이었다.
② 감옥을 호텔로 바꾸는 데 수백만 달러가 들었다.
③ 1851년에 감옥에서 호텔로 개조되었다.
④ 죄수들이 들어오던 입구는 현재 식당의 입구로 바뀌었다.
⑤ 이 호텔 안에 있는 한 식당의 종업원들은 죄수의 복장을 하고 있다.

서술형

2 윗글의 ⓐ와 ⓑ에 주어진 동사를 어법에 알맞은 형태로 쓰시오.

ⓐ ________________ ⓑ ________________

VOCA

3 윗글의 (A), (B), (C)의 각 네모 안에서 문맥에 맞는 낱말로 가장 적절한 것은?

	(A)		(B)		(C)
①	combines	……	transfer	……	authentic
②	combines	……	transfer	……	awkward
③	combines	……	transmit	……	awkward
④	confines	……	transfer	……	authentic
⑤	confines	……	transmit	……	awkward

lodging 숙박 **head** (특정 방향으로) 가다[향하다] **renovate** 개조하다 **notorious** 악명 높은 **convert** 개조하다, 전환시키다 **jail** 감옥 **structure** 구조; *구조물, 건물 **combine** 결합하다 **confine** 국한시키다 **historic** 역사적으로 중요한 ※ **historical** 역사상의 **architecture** 건축 **feature** 특징; …을 특색으로 삼다 **landmark** 주요 지형지물; *역사적인 건물 **transfer** 이송하다 **transmit** 전송하다 **prisoner** 죄수 **carriage** 마차, 운송 수단 **cell** 감방 **transform** 변모시키다, 변형시키다 **authentic** 진짜의 **awkward** 어색한

02

당신은 가짜 손님

190 words 3'00"

Date:

Time Taken:

You've decided to buy a new laptop at a big electronics store. (waiting, ten minutes, to help, after, for someone, you), you finally approach a sales clerk. He sighs and reluctantly agrees ① <u>to help</u> you. After he makes a quick recommendation, he walks away and leaves you alone. Normally, when customers experience this kind of bad service, they ② <u>stop going</u> to that store. However, the store's owners have no way of knowing why these customers have stopped coming. That's ③ <u>why</u> some stores use "mystery shoppers."

Market researchers employ mystery shoppers to measure the quality of employee service at retail stores. (A) Mystery shoppers are instructed to behave in a certain way and ask the sales clerks specific questions. (B) The data they collect is then analyzed by the market researchers. (C) They record the responses they receive and rate the quality of the customer service. Information provided by mystery shoppers can help companies ④ <u>understanding</u> the strengths and weaknesses of their employees. Some criticism has been raised about the ethical aspects of this system ⑤ <u>because of</u> concerns about deceiving the sales clerks, but it can be a useful tool for ______________________.

다양한 분야에서 활약하는 미스터리 쇼퍼

최근 미스터리 쇼퍼의 활동 영역은 음식점, 금융회사, 병원뿐만 아니라 공공 기관까지 그 범위가 확대되고 있다. 서울시에서 최근 선발한 시민 감시원들은 미스터리 쇼퍼로 활동하며 서울 소재 정육점, 정육식당에서 한우로 둔갑한 수입 쇠고기를 적발하는 일에 투입되었다. 이들이 소비자로 가장해 고기를 구매한 후, 보건환경연구원으로 보내 한우 확인 검사인 유전자 검사를 진행했다. 서울의 한 구청에서는 최근 해마다 대학생들을 미스터리 쇼퍼로 선발해 구청의 친절 업무평가를 실시하고 있다. 이 활동으로 대학생들은 공직 경험을 쌓으면서 학비 마련의 기회를 얻고, 구청에서는 서비스의 개선 효과를 얻고 있다.

서술형

1 윗글의 괄호 안에 주어진 단어들을 다음 우리말에 맞게 배열하시오.

누군가가 당신을 도와주기를 10분간 기다린 후에

→ ______________________________

수능 어법

2 윗글의 밑줄 친 ①~⑤ 중, 어법상 틀린 것은?

3 윗글의 (A)~(C)를 글의 흐름에 맞게 배열한 것으로 가장 적절한 것은?

① (A) – (B) – (C)
② (A) – (C) – (B)
③ (B) – (C) – (A)
④ (C) – (A) – (B)
⑤ (C) – (B) – (A)

4 윗글의 빈칸에 들어갈 말로 가장 적절한 것은?

① improving customer service
② researching target customers
③ receiving useful data about products
④ interviewing people about ethical issues
⑤ suggesting the best way to sell products

electronics 전자제품 **approach** …에 다가가다 **sales clerk** 점원, 판매원 **sigh** 한숨 쉬다 **reluctantly** 마지못해 **recommendation** 추천 **employ** 고용하다; *(기술·방법 등을) 쓰다, 이용하다 **measure** 측정하다; *평가하다 **retail store** 소매점 **instruct** 지시하다 **analyze** 분석하다 **rate** 평가하다 **criticism** 비판, 비평 **ethical** 윤리적인 **aspect** 측면 **concern** 우려, 걱정 **deceive** 속이다

03

이런 아이스크림 보셨나요?

211 words 3'00"

Date:

Time Taken:

Ice cream is the perfect summertime snack, except for one big (A) flaw / flow — it melts. Thanks to science, however, this problem may soon be a thing of the past.

There is already some ice cream that melts at a slower rate, but Japanese researchers have now created a type of ice cream that doesn't seem to melt at all. Interestingly, this discovery was (B) accidental / intentional — they had been using a liquid taken from strawberries, called polyphenol, to make a dessert. However, when the polyphenol was added to the dessert's cream, the cream instantly became solid. This occurred because polyphenol prevents water and oil from separating, allowing the cream to stay firm and keep its shape. Realizing that polyphenol would have the same effect on other substances, the researchers began using it to make ice cream products that don't melt.

In order to test their (C) claims / excuses, a reporter purchased some of the ice cream and left it outside in 28 °C weather. After five minutes, it was still cold and had not begun to melt. There are even some reports that it can last for more than three hours without melting. Currently, it is not being sold outside of Japan, so you'll have to go there if you want to find out for yourself.

아이스크림의 역사 아이스크림의 기원에 관한 유력한 가설은 기원전 3000년경 중국인들이 과일이나 꿀에 눈이나 얼음을 넣어 먹기 시작한 데서 비롯했다는 것이다. 이후 1292년, 중국 각지를 여행했던 마르코 폴로가 원나라로부터 냉동 우유를 만드는 방법을 베네치아로 가지고 가 이탈리아에 전파했다. 아이스크림의 현대적 대량 생산은 1851년 미국에서 시작되었다. 우유 상인인 제이콥 푸셀이 볼티모어에 아이스크림 공장을 세운 이후로 아이스크림이 전 세계에 보급되기 시작했다. 그는 이 업적으로 인하여 '미국 아이스크림 산업의 아버지'라고 불린다.

VOCA

1

윗글의 (A), (B), (C)의 각 네모 안에서 문맥에 맞는 낱말로 가장 적절한 것은?

	(A)		(B)		(C)
①	flaw	……	accidental	……	claims
②	flaw	……	intentional	……	excuses
③	flaw	……	accidental	……	excuses
④	flow	……	accidental	……	claims
⑤	flow	……	intentional	……	claims

2

윗글의 내용을 다음과 같이 요약할 때, 빈칸 (A)와 (B)에 들어갈 말로 가장 적절한 것은?

> Japanese researchers have found a way to keep ice cream ____(A)____ for a long time by using ____(B)____.

	(A)		(B)
①	cold	……	ice
②	frozen	……	cream
③	solid	……	polyphenol
④	soft	……	strawberries
⑤	firm	……	water and oil

3

윗글의 내용과 일치하면 T에, 일치하지 않으면 F에 표시하시오.

	T	F
(1) Ice cream that doesn't melt is made with an ingredient obtained from a fruit.	□	□
(2) Polyphenol stops water and oil from dividing.	□	□
(3) Ice cream that doesn't melt stays solid only at temperatures of 20 ℃ or lower.	□	□

except for …을 제외하고는 **flaw** 결함 **melt** 녹다 **rate** 속도 **interestingly** 흥미롭게도 **discovery** 발견 **accidental** 우연한 **intentional** 의도적인 **liquid** 액체 **instantly** 즉시, 즉각 **solid** 단단한, 견고한 **separate** 분리되다 **stay** (특정 상태를) 유지하다, …인 채로 있다 **firm** 딱딱한, 단단한 **realize** 깨닫다, 알아차리다 **effect** 효과 **substance** 물질 **product** 상품, 제품 **claim** 주장 **excuse** 변명, 이유 **last** 오래가다, 지속되다 **currently** 현재

04

170 words 2'35"

Date:

Time Taken:

TRY 수능

주제 · 제목 · 요지

다음 글의 요지로 가장 적절한 것은? 수능기출

One exercise in teamwork I do at a company retreat is to put the group in a circle. At one ⓐ particular retreat, there were eight people in the circle, and I slowly handed tennis balls to one person to start throwing around the circle. If N equals the number of people in the circle, then the maximum number of balls you can have in motion (A) [is / are] N minus 1. Why? Because it's almost impossible to throw and catch at the same time. The purpose of the exercise is to demonstrate the importance of an individual's action. People are much more concerned about catching the ball than throwing it. (B) [What / That] this demonstrates is that it's equally important to the success of the exercise that the person you're throwing to catches the ball as that you are able to catch the ball. If you (C) [are / will be] less concerned about how you deliver information than with how you receive it, you'll ultimately fail at *delegation. You have to be equally skilled at ⓑ both.

*delegation 위임

① 구성원 간의 공통된 목표 의식이 협업의 필수 조건이다.

② 정확한 정보 이해는 신속한 업무 수행을 가능하게 한다.

③ 자유로운 의사소통 문화는 직무 만족도 향상에 기여한다.

④ 여가 활동을 함께하는 것도 협업의 효율성을 증가시킨다.

⑤ 협업에서는 정보를 전달하는 방식에도 능숙할 필요가 있다.

유형 *Tip*

step1. **도입부에서 무엇에 관한 글인지 파악한다.**
회사 야유회에서 행하는 협업 훈련이 도입부에서 언급되고 있으므로 협업에 관한 내용이 전개될 것임을 예측할 수 있다.

step2. **글의 흐름을 따라가며 반복되는 주요 어휘 및 주제문을 파악하여 주제나 제목, 요지를 추론한다.**
협업 훈련의 사례로 언급된 공놀이 활동의 주요 목적은 공을 잘 던지는 것도 받는 것만큼 중요함을 보여주는 것이라고 했다.

step3. **찾은 단서들을 종합하여 정답을 고른다.**
정보를 얻는 방식만이 중요한 것이 아니라 전달하는 방식도 협업에 있어 중요하다는 요지의 글이다.

정답 및 해설 p.6

• 변형문제 •

VOCA

1 윗글의 밑줄 친 ⓐ particular와 의미가 반대인 것은?

① general ② specific ③ detailed
④ identical ⑤ excellent

수능 어법

2 윗글의 (A), (B), (C)의 각 네모 안에서 어법에 맞는 표현으로 가장 적절한 것은?

	(A)	(B)	(C)
①	is	What	are
②	is	That	are
③	is	What	will be
④	are	What	are
⑤	are	That	will be

서술형

3 윗글의 밑줄 친 ⓑ both가 의미하는 것 두 가지를 본문에서 찾아 쓰시오. (각각 4단어)

teamwork 팀워크, 협동 작업 **company retreat** 회사 야유회 **put ... in a circle** …을 원형으로 둘러 세우다 **particular** 특정한 **hand** 건네주다, 넘겨주다 **equal** 같다, …이다 ※ **equally** 똑같이, 동일하게 **maximum** 최대의, 최고의 **have ... in motion** …을 움직이게 하다 **demonstrate** 입증하다; *보여주다, 설명하다 **individual** 개인 **be concerned about** …에 관심을 가지다, …을 걱정하다 **ultimately** 결국

Review Test

• VOCA •

A

다음 단어의 영영풀이를 바르게 연결하시오.

1 notorious •	• ⓐ to officially tell someone to do something
2 instruct •	• ⓑ a place for criminals to be kept
3 analyze •	• ⓒ famous for something bad or evil
4 jail •	• ⓓ an object that is easy to recognize
5 landmark •	• ⓔ to examine something in detail

B

괄호 안에서 적절한 단어를 고르시오.

1 Recently many people are (concerned / confirmed) about climate change.

2 I don't like this kind of (disturbance / substance) because it's so sticky.

3 Don't be (deceived / received) by advertising and marketing techniques.

4 Using cell phones is a quick and easy way to (transform / transmit) information.

C

문맥상 다음 빈칸에 들어갈 가장 알맞은 단어를 고르시오.

1 The doctor asked the patient to __________ still so that she could look at the wound.

① play ② stay ③ drive ④ feel ⑤ take

2 The research team __________ that this folk remedy actually works.

① created ② applied ③ required ④ delivered ⑤ demonstrated

3 Mary didn't want to do anything, so she __________ agreed to help her mom.

① luckily ② quickly ③ willingly ④ reluctantly ⑤ surprisingly

4 It was determined that the gold was __________ and therefore worth a lot of money.

① fake ② strange ③ unreal ④ authentic ⑤ unnatural

정답 및 해설 p.8

· SENTENCE ·

D 다음 문장을 밑줄 친 부분에 유의하여 우리말로 해석하시오.

1 Millions of dollars were spent to convert the former jail into a unique structure.

▸ ______________________________

2 It helps companies to understand the strengths and weaknesses of their employees.

▸ ______________________________

3 Polyphenol prevents water and oil from separating, allowing the cream to stay firm.

▸ ______________________________

4 One exercise in teamwork I do at a company retreat is to put the group in a circle.

▸ ______________________________

E 우리말에 맞게 주어진 단어들을 바르게 배열하여 문장을 완성하시오.

1 당신은 틀림없이 그 건물의 역사가 상당히 흥미롭다고 생각하게 될 것이다.

(to / the history / sure / you're / find) of the building quite interesting.

▸ ______________________ of the building quite interesting.

2 주인들은 이 고객들이 왜 오지 않게 되었는지를 알 길이 없다.

The owners (no / knowing / have / of / way) why these customers have stopped coming.

▸ The owners ______________________ why these customers have stopped coming.

3 그것이 녹지 않고 3시간 이상이나 지속될 수 있다는 몇몇 보고가 있다.

There are some reports that (more than / can / for / it / last) three hours without melting.

▸ There are some reports that ______________________ three hours without melting.

Talk Like an Economist

FRENEMY

01.

프레너미(Frenemy)란?

'프레너미(frenemy)'는 친구(friend)와 적(enemy)의 합성어로, 사랑과 미움 사이를 오가며 유지되는 친구 관계를 의미한다. 최근에는 두 기업이 서로 협력하는 동시에 경쟁하는 관계를 뜻하는 데 자주 사용되고 있다.

이 용어를 최초로 사용한 사람은 세계 최대의 다국적 광고회사인 WWP 그룹에서 오랜 기간 CEO로 재직했던 마틴 소렐(Martin Sorrell)이다. 그는 자신이 운영했던 WWP 그룹이 구글 사의 경쟁자인 동시에, 구글 사의 최대 고객인 상황을 빗대어 '한편으로는 친구 관계이지만 다른 한편으로는 적 관계'를 나타내는 '프레너미'라는 단어를 사용했다.

프레너미와 같은 맥락으로, 경쟁 관계에 있는 기업들이 서로의 이익을 위해 협력하는 행위를 '코피티션(copetition)'이라고 하는데, 이는 협력을 뜻하는 'cooperation'과 경쟁을 뜻하는 'competition'의 합성어로, 이러한 표현들은 최근 변화무쌍한 기업 환경을 반영하고 있다.

SECTION 02

1 우리 식량에 무슨 일이?
2 초콜릿이 녹아서…
3 '왜?'라고 다섯 번 묻기
4 TRY수능 글의 목적

01

우리 식량에 무슨 일이?

196 words 3'00"

Date:

Time Taken:

Can climate change make the food you eat less ① healthy? As strange as it may sound, it could be possible.

Studies have shown that the levels of minerals, vitamins, and proteins in food crops have been dropping over the past 50 to 70 years. Some scientists believe this is related to the use of crops that produce more food but contain fewer ② nutrients. However, others suggest it has been caused by the increase of carbon dioxide (CO_2) in the air over the same period. Although plants require CO_2 to grow, a large increase in CO_2 seems to have a negative ③ effect on them.

This has been demonstrated in experiments in which plants were grown in an indoor space with ④ low CO_2 levels. The results of the experiments showed that important changes took place in a wide category of plants that ⑤ includes wheat, rice, potatoes, and other food crops we depend on. In each case, important minerals such as calcium, *potassium, *zinc, and iron were reduced.

Although more studies need to be done, this could potentially lead to an environmental disaster, as many people around the world already struggle to get enough nutrition in their daily diets.

*potassium 칼륨
*zinc 아연

탄소 발자국
Carbon Footprint

탄소 발자국이란 지구 온난화의 주범으로 인식되는 이산화탄소 배출량을 줄이기 위해 사용하기 시작한 개념으로, 사람의 활동 혹은 기업의 제품 생산에서 소비까지의 전 과정에서 발생되는 이산화탄소의 총량을 의미한다. 탄소 발자국은 kg으로 표시하거나, 광합성으로 감소시킬 수 있는 이산화탄소의 양을 나무의 수로 환산하여 표시한다. 국내에서도 한국기후·환경네트워크 홈페이지(www.kcen.kr)를 통해 탄소 발자국을 계산할 수 있는데, 일정 기간 동안 자신이 사용한 가스와 전기, 수도의 양을 입력하면 된다. 최근 친환경기업에 대한 관심과 선호도가 높아지면서, 많은 나라들이 적극적으로 이 개념을 받아들이고 있으며, 우리나라에서도 2009년부터 이산화탄소 배출량을 제품에 표기하고 있다.

1 윗글의 주제로 가장 적절한 것은?

① reasons for rapid climate change
② the influence of increased CO_2 on food
③ a species of food crops with few nutrients
④ daily essential nutrients for modern people
⑤ the perfect environment for growing plants

서술형

2 윗글의 밑줄 친 it이 의미하는 바를 나타낸 것이다. 빈칸에 들어갈 알맞은 말을 본문에서 찾아 쓰시오.

The levels of nutrients, such as minerals, vitamins, and ______________, in food crops have been ______________ for the past several decades.

VOCA

3 윗글의 밑줄 친 ①~⑤ 중, 문맥상 낱말의 쓰임이 적절하지 않은 것은?

4 윗글의 내용과 일치하면 T에, 일치하지 않으면 F에 표시하시오.

	T	F
(1) CO_2 is not necessary for plants to grow properly.	□	□
(2) Too much CO_2 may result in the reduction of important minerals in plants.	□	□

climate 기후 **level** 정도, 수준 **mineral** 광물; *무기물, 미네랄 **contain** 포함하다 **nutrient** 영양소, 영양분 **increase** 증가 **require** 필요로 하다 **have a negative effect on** …에 부정적인 영향을 미치다 **demonstrate** 입증하다, 실증하다 **experiment** 실험 **indoor** 실내의 **take place** 일어나다 **category** 범주 **reduce** 줄이다 ※ **reduction** 감소 **potentially** 잠재적으로 **lead to** …로 이어지다 **struggle** 투쟁[고투]하다, 몸부림치다 **nutrition** 영양 문제 **rapid** 빠른 **influence** 영향

02

초콜릿이 녹아서…

191 words 3'00"

Date:

Time Taken:

Percy Spencer was a natural inventor who knew ① how to apply his curiosity. Shortly after World War II, he was walking through his laboratory when he paused in front of a magnetron, a device ② used to power radar systems. Suddenly, he realized that a chocolate bar in his pocket was melting. But Spencer didn't panic. Instead, he put some unpopped popcorn in a bag and held it in front of the magnetron. As Spencer ③ had suspected, the small hard popcorn soon exploded, becoming fluffy and white. This simple experiment eventually led to the invention of the microwave oven. The first of these devices was enormous — it was 167 centimeters tall and weighed 340 kilograms. Because of this, it was only used in restaurants (to cook, a lot of, in a short time, needed, chefs, food, where). There were also other problems. Meat didn't turn brown, and French fries turned white. But, over decades, improvements were made, and eventually the microwave oven reached the point ④ which it was the perfect addition to the average family's kitchen. Today, people around the world use these ovens ⑤ to melt their chocolate and pop their popcorn.

퍼시 스펜서 퍼시 스펜서(Percy Spencer, 1894~1970)는 미국 출신의 공학자이자 발명가이다. 그는 어려운 가정환경으로 인해 초등학교 5학년 수준의 교육밖에 받지 못했지만, 매일 제지공장에서 일하면서도 밤이면 기계에 대해 공부하는 열정을 잃지 않았다. 후에 해군에 입대한 퍼시 스펜서는 그곳에서 삼각함수, 화학, 물리학, 미적분 등을 배우게 되었다. 군대를 제대한 후에 그는 무전장비 회사인 레이시온에 취직하게 되었고, 이곳에서 그는 전자레인지의 프로토타입을 발명했다. 퍼시 스펜서의 동료들은 그를 '불가능을 모르는 사람'이라고 평가했다.

정답 및 해설 p.11

1 윗글의 제목으로 가장 적절한 것은?

① An Accidental Invention
② Percy Spencer: Super Chef
③ What Makes Popcorn Pop?
④ The Danger of Microwaves
⑤ Radar: Changing the World

수능 어법

2 윗글의 밑줄 친 ①~⑤ 중, 어법상 틀린 것은?

3 윗글을 읽고 microwave oven에 대해 답할 수 없는 질문은?

① Who invented it?
② How big was it at first?
③ Why was it only used in restaurants at first?
④ What problems did the first version have?
⑤ When was it first used in households?

서술형

4 윗글의 괄호 안에 주어진 단어들을 다음 우리말에 맞게 배열하시오.

(그것은) 요리사들이 짧은 시간에 많은 음식을 요리해야 하는 (식당에서만 사용되었다)

→ it was only used in restaurants ______________________________

natural 자연의; *타고난 **apply** 신청하다; *적용하다, 응용하다 **curiosity** 호기심 **laboratory** 실험실 **pause** 잠시 멈추다 **magnetron** 마그네트론, 전자관 **device** 장치 **melt** 녹다 **panic** 당황하다 **suspect** 의심쩍어하다, 짐작하다 **explode** 폭발하다 **fluffy** 솜털 같은 **enormous** 거대한 **decade** 10년 **improvement** 향상, 개선 **addition** 추가된 것, 부가물 **average** 평균의; *보통의 문제 **accidental** 우연한 **household** 가정

03

'왜?'라고 다섯 번 묻기

250 words 3'45"

Date:

Time Taken:

What would you do if you ⓐ (be) given a problem that seemed too complex to solve? Guess? Give up? A better trick to try is the 5 Whys technique. To use this approach, you start with the end result and work backwards. This simply involves asking "why?" at each stage.

Recently, a team of workers responsible for maintaining the Jefferson Memorial in Washington, D.C., applied the 5 Whys to come up with a solution to a problem they were facing.

Problem: The surface of the Jefferson Memorial was <u>deteriorating</u> rapidly.

1. Why?: They had recently switched to stronger cleaners for the memorial's exterior surface.
2. Why?: ______________ (A) ______________
3. Why?: ______________ (B) ______________
4. Why?: ______________ (C) ______________
5. Why?: The lights surrounding the memorial had been adjusted to turn on at dusk a few months ago, ⓑ (cause) a swell in the population of insects which are most active at dusk.

Solution: Readjust the timing of the lights so that they come on later in the evening.

This story shows the importance of getting to the root of a problem in a thorough and organized manner, rather than simply rushing to judgment. If you fail to ask enough questions, you may misunderstand the real reason for the problem and never formulate an effective solution.

"5 Whys" 기술의 시작

"5 Whys" 기술은 도요타 자동차의 창업자인 도요타 사키치 회장이 최초로 고안한 아이디어이다. 그는 5번 "왜?"라고 물어야만 어떤 문제의 근본 원인을 파악하고, 개선 방법 또한 알 수 있다고 생각했다. 도요타는 이러한 경영 방식과 철학을 유지하며 현재 세계에서 가장 높은 생산량과 판매량을 내고 있는 회사 중 하나이다. 2017년 브랜드 전문 회사 미국 인터브랜드가 발표한 『베스트 글로벌 100대 브랜드』 중 자동차 브랜드 부문에서 가장 높은 가치의 브랜드로 평가받은 바 있다.

정답 및 해설 p.12

1 윗글의 주제로 가장 적절한 것은?

① practical skills to answer questions
② the influence of the timing of lights
③ an effective problem-solving technique
④ disadvantages of the 5 Whys technique
⑤ maintenance problems at the Jefferson Memorial

서술형

2 윗글의 ⓐ와 ⓑ에 주어진 동사를 어법에 알맞은 형태로 쓰시오.

ⓐ ______________ ⓑ ______________

VOCA

3 윗글의 밑줄 친 deteriorating과 바꿔 쓸 수 있는 말로 가장 적절한 것은?

① improving ② shaking ③ moving
④ strengthening ⑤ decaying

4 윗글의 빈칸 (A), (B), (C)에 들어갈 적절한 말을 〈보기〉에서 고르시오.

〈보기〉
ⓐ There was an increase in the amount of pigeon droppings on the memorial.
ⓑ Spiders had moved there to prey on the increasing number of insects in the area.
ⓒ More pigeons were coming to the memorial to feed on the growing number of spiders there.

(A) ______________ (B) ______________ (C) ______________

complex 복잡한 **approach** 접근; *접근법 **backwards** 거꾸로 **involve** 수반하다; *필요로 하다 **maintain** 유지하다 ※ **maintenance** 유지, 보수 관리 **deteriorate** (질 등이) 악화되다, 나빠지다 **exterior** 외부[외면]의 **adjust** 조절하다, 맞추다 **dusk** 황혼, 땅거미 **swell** 증가, 팽창 **thorough** 철저한 **formulate** 만들어내다 **문제** **problem-solving** 문제 해결 **disadvantage** 불리한 점, 약점 **strengthen** 강화하다 **decay** 부식하다, 썩다 **dropping** 《*pl.*》 (새·짐승의) 배설물 **prey on** …을 잡아먹다

04

130 words 2'10"

Date:

Time Taken:

TRY 수능

글의 목적

다음 글의 목적으로 가장 적절한 것은? [모의기출]

Dear Lauren Baker,

We thank you for agreeing to play the music for my daughter's wedding on September 17. Unfortunately, her fiancé, who is in the military, (which, orders, impossible, this date, make, has received), so we are moving the wedding date forward two weeks to September 3. Would it be possible for you to <u>accommodate</u> us on this date instead? All the other aspects of our agreement will remain the same. We would be most grateful if you could make this change and I really hope to see the extra touch of elegance added to my daughter's wedding. Will you be gracing us with your presence? If you are unable to, please let us know as soon as possible so that we can make other arrangements.

Sincerely,
Bill Gibson

① 결혼식 장소가 변경되었음을 공지하려고
② 상사의 지시에 따를 수 없음을 사과하려고
③ 멋진 공연을 보여준 것에 대해 감사하려고
④ 행사에 사용될 곡을 바꿔줄 것을 요청하려고
⑤ 연주 날짜를 앞당겨 줄 수 있는지 문의하려고

유형 *Tip*

step1. **글의 도입부에서 중심 소재를 파악한다.**
글의 앞부분에 언급된 play the music for my daughter's wedding으로 보아 결혼식 음악 연주와 관련된 내용임을 알 수 있다.

step2. **글쓴이와 독자를 파악하는 것도 정답을 유추하는 단서가 된다.**
이 글은 편지로, 첫 번째 문장에서 발신인은 신부의 부모, 수신인은 음악 연주자임을 알 수 있다.

step3. **글의 중반부나 후반부에서 글의 목적이 직접적으로 제시되는 경우가 많다.**
중반부의 'Would it be possible for you ... ?'에서, 변경된 결혼식 날짜에 맞추어 연주를 해달라고 직접 요청하고 있다.

• 변형문제 •

1 윗글의 내용과 일치하지 않는 것은?

① 약혼자는 군에 복무 중이다.
② 결혼식은 9월 3일에 있을 예정이다.
③ 결혼식은 예정보다 2주 앞당겨졌다.
④ 날짜 외에, 연주자와의 계약에 다른 변화가 있다.
⑤ 글쓴이는 연주자의 답변을 들은 후 대안을 마련할 계획이다.

서술형

2 윗글의 괄호 안에 주어진 단어들을 다음 우리말에 맞게 배열하시오.

이 날짜를 불가능하게 하는 명령을 받았습니다

→ ____________________

VOCA

3 윗글의 밑줄 친 accommodate의 의미로 가장 적절한 것은?

① to join the group
② to make room for
③ to get used to a new situation
④ to meet the needs of someone
⑤ to provide someone with a place to stay

fiancé 약혼자(남자) **military** 군대 **forward** 앞으로 **accommodate** 공간을 제공하다; *(요구 등에) 부응하다 **aspect** 측면 **elegance** 우아, 고상 **grace** …을 빛내다[영예롭게 하다] **presence** 참석, 존재 **arrangement** 준비, 마련

Review Test

· VOCA ·

A

다음 중 단어의 뜻풀이가 잘못된 것을 고르시오.

① explode: to violently burst or shatter
② enormous: very small in size or quantity
③ potentially: possibly but not yet actually
④ curiosity: a strong desire to know about something
⑤ strengthen: to make something stronger and more powerful

B

괄호 안에서 적절한 단어를 고르시오.

1 Sue (respected / suspected) that her son might be lying to her.
2 Every vehicle undergoes a (rough / thorough) and careful test.
3 (Improvement / Importance) in the car's design led to increased fuel efficiency.
4 The experiment (demonstrated / concentrated) that water freezes at 0 °C.

C

문맥상 다음 빈칸에 들어갈 가장 알맞은 단어를 고르시오.

1 There has been a(n) __________ in the number of visitors to Seoul thanks to the Korean Wave.
① category ② pause ③ swell ④ level ⑤ approach

2 If you prefer a mild flavor, __________ the amount of chili powder.
① add ② reduce ③ cook ④ include ⑤ prepare

3 She always tries to find the positive __________ of a situation.
① plan ② device ③ aspect ④ shortage ⑤ elegance

4 Many underdeveloped African countries __________ to provide a constant supply of electricity.
① lead ② help ③ adapt ④ struggle ⑤ remain

정답 및 해설 p.16

· SENTENCE ·

D

다음 문장을 밑줄 친 부분에 유의하여 우리말로 해석하시오.

1 Can climate change make the food you eat less healthy?

▸ ______________________________

2 The lights surrounding the memorial had been adjusted to turn on at dusk.

▸ ______________________________

3 Please let us know as soon as possible so that we can make other arrangements.

▸ ______________________________

4 What would you do if you were given a problem that seemed too complex to solve?

▸ ______________________________

E

우리말에 맞게 주어진 단어들을 바르게 배열하여 문장을 완성하시오.

1 퍼시 스펜서는 자신의 호기심을 응용하는 방법을 아는 타고난 발명가였다.

Percy Spencer was a natural inventor (how / knew / his curiosity / who / apply / to).

▸ Percy Spencer was a natural inventor ______________________.

2 이것은 더 많은 식량을 생산하지만 더 적은 영양분을 포함하는 식용 작물의 사용과 관련이 있다.

This is related to the use of crops that (fewer nutrients / but / contain / more food / produce).

▸ This is related to the use of crops that ______________________.

3 만약 당신이 충분한 질문을 하지 못한다면, 당신은 그 문제에 대한 이유를 잘못 이해할 수 있다.

If you (enough / fail / ask / to / questions), you may misunderstand the reason for the problem.

▸ If you ______________________, you may misunderstand the reason for the problem.

LIBRARIES AROUND THE WORLD

Kansas City Public Library

3층 높이의 책 속으로 들어가는 기분, 캔자스 시립 도서관

미국 캔자스에서는 건물 3층 높이에 달하는 커다란 책들이 줄지어 서 있는 도서관을 볼 수 있다.

사실 이 책들은 진짜 책이 아니라 책등의 모습을 한 주차장 외벽으로, 도서관의 상징물로 자리잡았다. 벽을 장식한 22권의 책들은 캔자스 주민들이 가장 사랑하는 도서들을 선정한 것이다.

주차장 외벽뿐만 아니라, 도서관 내부의 디자인도 독특하다. 어린이 도서가 있는 공간의 입구는 펼친 책의 모양을 하고 있어 아이들의 호기심을 유발한다. 은행에 온 기분을 느끼게 해주는, 지하 상영관의 35톤짜리 철제 금고문 또한 이 도서관의 볼거리이다.

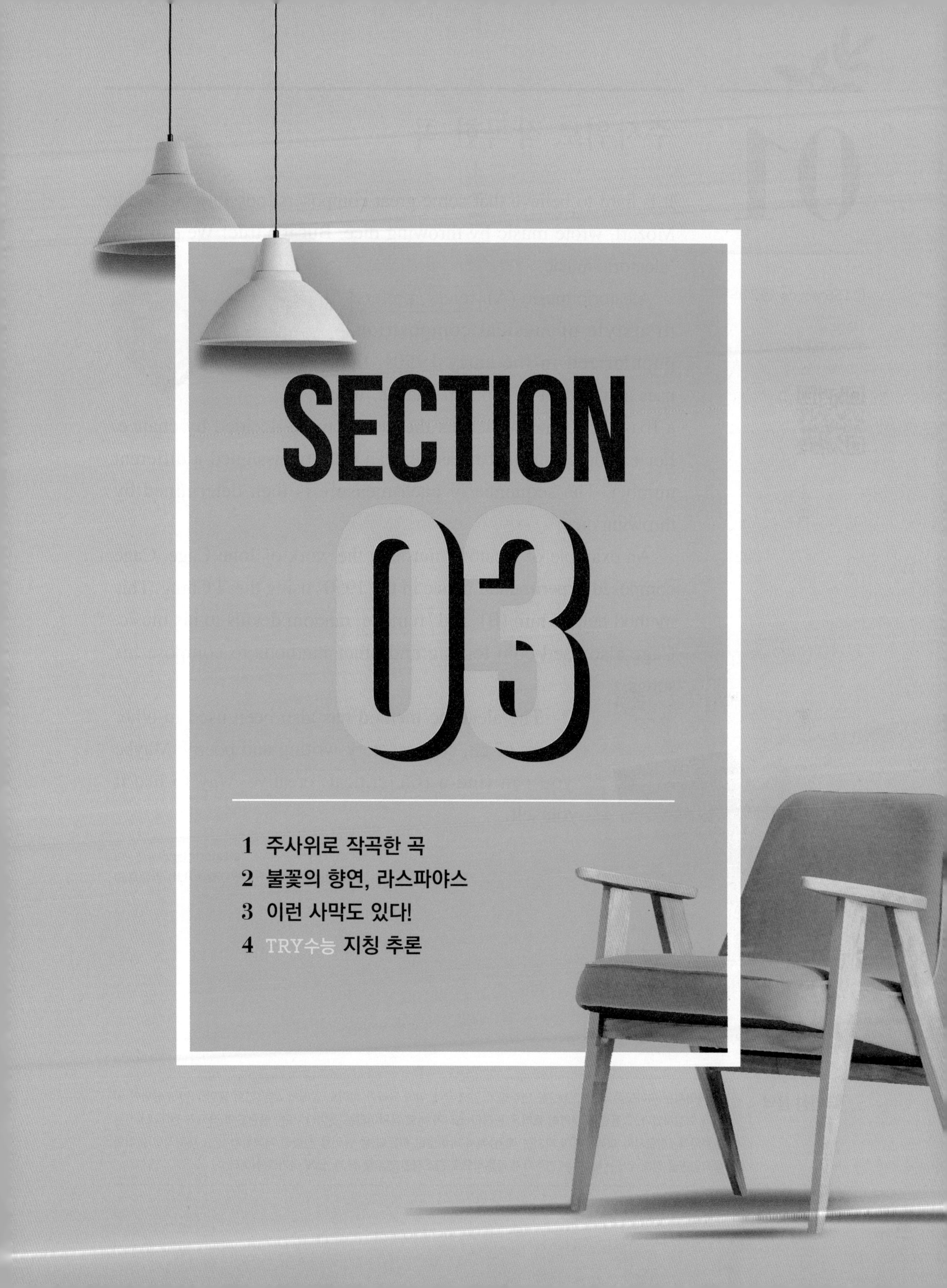

SECTION 03

01

📄155 words ⏱2'35"

Date:

Time Taken:

주사위로 작곡한 곡

It is hard to believe that some great composers, possibly including Mozart, wrote music by throwing dice. But it's true! We call this *aleatoric music.

Aleatoric music (A) [refers / prefers] to a style of musical composition, popularized in the early 1950s, that uses some form of random chance. It has a fixed structure but leaves the details to be decided by chance. For example, musical measures can each be assigned a different number. The sequence of each measure is then determined by throwing dice.

An example of aleatoric music is the work of John Cage. Cage composed experimental music in the 1950s using the *I Ching. This method helped him (B) [add / remove] random details to his music. Cage also used coin tossing and other methods to compose his songs.

The aleatoric method has also been used in other forms of art, such as story writing and poetry. Maybe you can find a (C) [critical / creative] way to use it yourself.

*aleatoric (음악) 우연성의

*I Ching (길흉을 판단하는) 팔괘(八卦), 역점(易占)

우연성 음악 존 케이지는 피아노곡 〈4분 33초〉를 연주하기 위해 무대 위에 올라가 피아노 앞에서 4분 33초 동안 가만히 앉아만 있다가 퇴장하였다. 그동안에 우연히 들려온 관객의 소리가 바로 음악이라는 것이다. 또한 폴란드의 작곡가 펜데레츠키는 관현악곡 〈히로시마 희생자에게 바치는 애가〉에서 바이올린 파트의 음 높이를 정확히 지정하지 않고 대략적인 높이와 움직임만을 정해 두었는데, 이는 연주자가 즉흥적으로 창조적인 연주를 할 수 있게 하기 위함이다.

정답 및 해설 p.17

1 윗글의 제목으로 가장 적절한 것은?

① Aleatoric Music: What Is It?
② The World's First Aleatoric Music
③ How to Throw Dice to Write a Poem
④ Various Methods of Composing Music
⑤ Mozart, the Inventor of Aleatoric Music

2 aleatoric method에 관한 윗글의 내용과 일치하지 않는 것은?

① 주사위를 활용하여 작곡을 하기도 한다.
② 1950년대에 많은 사람들에게 알려졌다.
③ 곡의 세부적인 부분들은 작곡가의 의지에 따라 작곡되었다.
④ 존 케이지는 동전을 던져 음악을 작곡하기도 했다.
⑤ 시를 짓거나 글을 쓸 때도 사용된다.

VOCA

3 윗글의 (A), (B), (C)의 각 네모 안에서 문맥에 맞는 낱말로 가장 적절한 것은?

	(A)		(B)		(C)
①	refers	……	add	……	critical
②	refers	……	remove	……	creative
③	refers	……	add	……	creative
④	prefers	……	add	……	creative
⑤	prefers	……	remove	……	critical

서술형

4 윗글의 내용과 일치하도록, 빈칸에 알맞은 말을 본문에서 찾아 쓰시오.

Some famous musicians composed their work using the __________ results of throwing __________.

composer 작곡가 ※**composition** 작곡법 **dice** 주사위 **popularize** 대중화하다 **by chance** 우연히 **measure** 측정하다; *(음악) 소절 **assign** 배정하다 **sequence** 연속; *순서 **experimental** 실험적인 **coin tossing** 동전 던지기 **critical** 비판적인

02

불꽃의 향연, 라스파야스

217 words 3'00"

Date:
Time Taken:

Perhaps the most extraordinary part of my trip to Spain was when the city of Valencia seemed to catch fire during a loud, smoky, and exciting party! This was during a spectacular festival known as *Las Fallas*, or "the fires."

Las Fallas is one of the most unique festivals in Spain. Though it started as a feast day for St. Joseph, it has become a wonderful five-day celebration that is very popular. Valencia is normally home to 1 million people, but during *Las Fallas* the population grows to 3 million!

The festival involved creating and ① destroying *ninots*, which are like puppets or dolls. Made out of cardboard, wood, plaster or *papier-mache, the *ninots* depicted current events, featuring corrupt politicians and other Spanish celebrities. I was impressed at ② how lifelike they were. They had been made by local organizations, (some of them, to complete, taking, almost a year). Many *ninots* were very tall and thus needed cranes for transportation on the day of *la planta* (the rising).

The *ninots* ③ were put in place until *la crema* (the burning), when young men chopped holes in the *ninots* and stuffed them full of fireworks. At midnight, I ④ joined a crowd of people outside. The streetlights were turned off. Then the *ninots* were set on fire, and a spectacular fireworks display began! Only one *ninot*, ⑤ that was saved by popular vote, was not burned. It was taken to the local Museum of the Ninot to sit alongside *ninot indultats* (the pardoned puppets) of previous years.

It was an incredible experience I'll never forget. Any tourist who wants a wild, exciting experience should try to attend!

*papier-mache 종이 반죽

니노트를 불태우는 이유

라스파야스 축제의 마지막 날에 니노트들을 불태우는 것은 한 해 동안 있었던 모든 안 좋은 일들을 불태워 없애고 다가오는 봄을 새롭게 맞이하자는 의미를 담고 있다. 이때 화려한 불꽃놀이와 흥겨운 음악이 더해져서 축제의 대미를 장식한다. 수백 년 동안 내려오는 이 축제는 이제 스페인 발렌시아의 상징이 되었다.

1 *Las Fallas*에 관한 윗글의 내용과 일치하지 않는 것은?

① *Las Fallas*는 스페인의 발렌시아에서 열리는 축제이다.
② *Las Fallas*는 화재로 사망한 St. Joseph을 추모하기 위해 시작되었다.
③ *ninot*는 꼭두각시나 인형 같은 것들을 말한다.
④ *la crema* 때 *ninot*들은 불태워진다.
⑤ 사람들의 투표로 선택된 *ninot* 하나는 지역 박물관에 전시된다.

수능 어법

2 윗글의 밑줄 친 ①~⑤ 중, 어법상 틀린 것은?

서술형

3 윗글의 괄호 안에 주어진 단어들을 다음 우리말에 맞게 배열하시오.

(그것들은 지역 단체들에 의해 만들어졌는데,) 그것들 중 일부는 완성하는 데 거의 1년이 걸렸다.

→ They had been made by local organizations, ______________________________.

Las Fallas

extraordinary 기이한, 놀라운 **catch fire** 불붙다, 타오르다 **spectacular** 장관을 이루는, 화려한 **feast day** (기독교의) 축일 **puppet** 인형, 꼭두각시 **cardboard** 판지 **plaster** 회반죽, 석고반죽 **depict** 묘사하다 **current event** 시사, 시사 문제 **corrupt** 부패한, 타락한 **lifelike** 실물과 똑같은 **crane** 크레인, 기중기 **transportation** 수송, 운송 **chop** 썰다[다지다], (장작 같은 것을) 패다 **stuff** 속을 채우다 **streetlight** 가로등 **alongside** … 옆에, …와 나란히 **pardon** 용서하다; *사면하다 **previous** 이전의

03

이런 사막도 있다!

232 words 3'35"

Date:
Time Taken:

A desert is an area where there is little rain and almost nothing grows. But there is also another kind of desert — a food desert. This is an area where there are (A) [few / little] affordable places for people to shop for food. Ironically, in America, these food deserts are often found in the places where (B) [almost / most] of the nation's food is grown. To deal with this situation, a government-supported nonprofit supermarket was created. Called Fare & Square, it is located in Chester, a small city in Pennsylvania that (C) [doesn't have / hadn't had] a grocery store for more than 10 years. (①) Before Fare & Square opened, it was estimated that more than half of the city's families had to travel long distances to purchase food. (②) Now, however, all of the city's residents have easy access to the food they need. (③) The One Seed Chicago Project helps people living in the city by giving them seeds so they can start their own small vegetable gardens. (④) These seeds can be planted in yards, local community gardens or even windowsills. (⑤) By growing their own vegetables, people can eat fresh, healthy food without driving long distances to supermarkets. Although these two projects won't solve the problem of food deserts, they are the first step to assuring that all people can get healthy food, no matter where they live.

식량 정의 운동
Food Justice Movement

식량 정의 운동은 사람들이 인종, 사회적 지위 및 수입과 관계없이 건강에 좋고 영양가 높은 지역 식품을 구매할 수 있어야 한다는 생각에서 비롯한 운동이다. 이 운동은 미국 등지에서 발생하는 식품 사막 문제를 해결하고자 하는 데서 시작되어, 식량의 생산, 가공, 유통, 소비 과정에서 나타나는 불평등을 해결하는 데까지 그 목표가 확대되었다. 뿐만 아니라 자연 생태 및 생물 다양성 보호, 농업 및 산업계에 종사하는 노동자들의 인권과 복지, 동물복지, 전 세계 기아 문제에 대한 관심과 개선, 공정무역 장려 등을 위한 운동들도 함께 펼쳐지고 있다.

1 윗글의 제목으로 가장 적절한 것은?

① Fight Food Deserts with Gardens
② Learn How To Choose Healthy Food
③ Finding Ways To Make Food Accessible
④ A Small City with a Big Farming Project
⑤ Growing Food in Deserts: Is It Possible?

수능어법

2 윗글의 (A), (B), (C)의 각 네모 안에서 어법에 맞는 표현으로 가장 적절한 것은?

	(A)		(B)		(C)
①	few	……	almost	……	doesn't have
②	few	……	most	……	hadn't had
③	few	……	most	……	doesn't have
④	little	……	most	……	hadn't had
⑤	little	……	almost	……	doesn't have

3 윗글의 흐름으로 보아, 주어진 문장이 들어가기에 가장 적절한 곳은?

> The fight against food deserts is also taking place in another city.

서술형

4 윗글의 밑줄 친 this situation이 의미하는 바를 나타낸 것이다. 빈칸에 들어갈 알맞은 말을 본문에서 찾아 쓰시오.

People can't easily find affordable places to __________ __________ __________.

affordable 이용할 수 있는, 알맞은 **ironically** 역설적으로 **deal with** …에 대처하다, …을 해결하다 **nonprofit** 비영리의 **estimate** 추정하다 **have access to** …에 접근할 수 있다 **seed** 씨앗 **windowsill** 창턱, 창 아래틀 **assure** 보장하다 **문제** **accessible** 접근[이용] 가능한

04

162 words 2'45"

Date:

Time Taken:

TRY 수능

지칭 추론

밑줄 친 부분이 가리키는 대상이 나머지 넷과 다른 것은? 모의기출 응용

One day, Mr. Smith saw a young boy walking to school in old, worn-out shoes. ① He was clearly in need of new ones, but Mr. Smith knew the boy's father was a proud man who would be offended and humiliated if ② his son were treated like a charity case. So Mr. Smith came up with a plan to provide the boy with shoes without upsetting his father. (A) When the boy answered them correctly, Mr. Smith said "Wonderful!" and gave ③ the youngster two written messages. (B) He then asked the boy several easy questions that were very much within the youth's grasp. (C) During the morning recess, he called the boy into his office, saying he had to test ④ him on his English proficiency. The first was for a local shoemaker, instructing him to give a good pair of shoes to the boy, for which Mr. Smith would pay. The second was for the boy's father, telling ⑤ him about the "prize" won by his son.

유형 *Tip*

step1. **첫 번째 선택지인 ①이 지칭하는 대상을 먼저 파악한다.**
첫 문장에서 스미스 선생님과 낡은 신발을 신은 소년이 등장하는데, ①의 He는 새 신발이 필요하다고 했으므로 ①은 소년을 가리킨다.

step2. **새로운 대상이 등장하는 부분에 주목한다.**
두 번째 문장에서 소년의 아버지가 새롭게 등장하므로 그 이후로 사용되는 지시대명사에 유의해야 한다.

step3. **주요 인물을 중심으로 각각의 대명사가 가리키는 대상을 확인한다.**
스미스 선생님이 쓴 두 번째 메시지는 소년의 아버지를 위한 것이므로, ⑤의 him은 소년의 아버지를 가리킨다. 나머지는 모두 소년을 가리킨다.

정답 및 해설 p.21

· 변 형 문 제 ·

1 윗글의 제목으로 가장 적절한 것은?

① A Clever Man's Good Deed
② A Father's Love for His Son
③ The Negative Effects of Pride
④ The World's Kindest Shoemaker
⑤ The Best English Speaker in School

2 윗글의 (A)~(C)를 글의 흐름에 맞게 배열한 것으로 가장 적절한 것은?

① (A) – (B) – (C)　② (A) – (C) – (B)　③ (B) – (C) – (A)
④ (C) – (A) – (B)　⑤ (C) – (B) – (A)

서술형
3 윗글의 밑줄 친 the "prize"가 가리키는 것을 본문에서 찾아 쓰시오. (5단어)

worn-out 닳아서 해진　**offend** 기분을 상하게 하다　**humiliate** 수치심을 느끼게 하다　**charity** 자선, 구호　**case** (구제 등의) 대상자　**upset** 화나게 하다　**youngster** 아이, 청소년　**within one's grasp** …가 이해할 수 있는　**recess** 휴식 (시간)　**proficiency** 숙달, 능숙　**instruct** 지시하다

Review Test

• VOCA •

A

다음 단어의 영영풀이를 바르게 연결하시오.

1 composer •	• ⓐ a person who writes a piece of music
2 popularize •	• ⓑ a high degree of ability or skill
3 corrupt •	• ⓒ to represent something in a picture, story, etc.
4 proficiency •	• ⓓ to cause something to become well-known
5 depict •	• ⓔ acting dishonestly and immorally

B

괄호 안에서 적절한 단어를 고르시오.

1 Each student was (assigned / assessed) a room in the dormitory.

2 The scenery on the way to the castle was (particular / spectacular).

3 It is (estimated / esteemed) that the world population will reach 9 billion by 2050.

4 Jack (stuffed / stuck) his backpack with sunglasses, a flashlight, and some food.

C

문맥상 다음 빈칸에 들어갈 가장 알맞은 단어를 고르시오.

1 The doctor __________ his patient that the operation was safe.

① warned ② pardoned ③ assured ④ instructed ⑤ complained

2 This best-selling novel shows the author's __________ talent for storytelling.

① average ② strange ③ inferior ④ pleasant ⑤ extraordinary

3 Many people were __________ by his rude behavior.

① calmed ② excited ③ offended ④ encouraged ⑤ inspired

4 Only a few employees have __________ to the confidential files.

① recess ② access ③ sequence ④ knowledge ⑤ possibility

정답 및 해설 p.23

· SENTENCE ·

D

다음 문장을 밑줄 친 부분에 유의하여 우리말로 해석하시오.

1 Cage used coin tossing and other methods to compose his songs.

▸ ______________________________

2 Only one *ninot*, which was saved by popular vote, was not burned.

▸ ______________________________

3 More than half of the city's families had to travel long distances to purchase food.

▸ ______________________________

4 Mr. Smith came up with a plan to provide the boy with shoes without upsetting his father.

▸ ______________________________

E

우리말에 맞게 주어진 단어들을 바르게 배열하여 문장을 완성하시오.

1 축제는 *니노트*들을 만드는 것과 파괴하는 것을 포함하는데, *니노트*들은 꼭두각시나 인형 같은 것들이다.

The festival involved creating and destroying *ninots*, (are / puppets / which / dolls / like / or).

▸ The festival involved creating and destroying *ninots*, ______________.

2 사막은 비가 거의 오지 않고 거의 아무것도 자라지 않는 곳이다.

A desert is (there / an area / little / where / rain / is) and almost nothing grows.

▸ A desert is ______________ and almost nothing grows.

3 두 번째 것은 소년의 아버지를 위한 것으로, 아들이 받은 상에 관해 알려주는 것이었다.

The second was for the boy's father, (him / telling / about / won / the "prize") by his son.

▸ The second was for the boy's father, ______________ by his son.

Talk Like an Economist

TWINSUMER

02.

트윈슈머 (Twinsumer)란?

인터넷 쇼핑을 할 때 다른 구매자들의 후기를 꼼꼼히 읽어본 뒤 구매 여부를 결정하는 편인가? 그렇다면 당신은 트윈슈머에 가깝다. '트윈슈머(twinsumer)'란 쌍둥이(twin)와 소비자(consumer)의 합성어로, 소비 패턴, 취향, 상품에 대한 반응 등이 서로 비슷한 소비자를 가리키는 용어이다. 트윈슈머는 다른 사람들의 구매 경험을 중요하게 생각하고, 그들의 제품 사용 후기 등을 토대로 제품이나 서비스를 구매한다. 트윈슈머는 온라인 상품 구매가 많아지면서 나타난 새로운 소비자 유형이다. 인터넷에서 판매되는 상품은 사진으로 볼 수는 있지만 실제로 체험해볼 수 없기 때문에 이전 구매자들의 상품 후기가 상품 구매 결정의 판단 기준으로 작용한다. 트윈슈머는 기존 소비자의 의견을 참고할 뿐만 아니라 본인 역시 적극적으로 제품 사용 후기를 인터넷에 올리기도 한다.

SECTION 04

01

161 words 2'55"

Date:

Time Taken:

고양이 혀의 비밀

It has long been suspected that ① domestic cats, along with lions, tigers, and leopards, prefer eating meat because they cannot taste sweet foods. Now there's proof! According to a study, cats lack a key taste receptor gene that is needed to ② detect sweet stimuli. This missing gene is likely responsible for the evolution of cats' *carnivorous behavior.

In the process of evolution, genetic influences on taste might have played an important role in food selection and nutrition in both humans and animals. The brains of all mammals ③ give taste signals from the tongue's receptor cells. These cells are joined together to form taste buds. In humans, each taste bud is made up of 50 to 100 receptor cells ④ representing the five major tastes: salty, sour, sweet, bitter and *umami. Scientists believe that, for some reason, ancient cats that ⑤ lacked sweetness taste buds had ________________ than other cats. Over time, these meat-eating cats remained while others died out.

*carnivorous 육식성의
*umami 감칠맛

고양이 혀의 또 다른 비밀 고양이의 혓바닥에는 약 300~400개의 가시 모양 돌기(사상유두)들이 있는데, 이것들은 사람의 손가락이 하는 것과 유사한 역할을 한다. 고양이는 이 돌기들을 사용하여 사냥한 먹이의 뼈와 살을 발라낼 수 있으며 스스로 털 단장을 할 수도 있다.

정답 및 해설 p.24

1 윗글의 주제로 가장 적절한 것은?

① the way the brain perceives taste
② why cats live longer than other animals
③ the roles of different taste receptor genes
④ how cat's genes are different from human's
⑤ genetic reason that cats can't taste sweet foods

VOCA

2 윗글의 밑줄 친 ①~⑤ 중, 문맥상 낱말의 쓰임이 적절하지 않은 것은?

3 윗글의 빈칸에 들어갈 말로 가장 적절한 것은?

① bigger brains
② lower intelligence
③ smaller body frames
④ a higher survival rate
⑤ a poorer nutritional state

서술형

4 윗글의 내용과 일치하도록 빈칸에 알맞은 말을 본문에서 찾아 쓰시오.

Cats prefer eating meat because they lack a taste receptor gene which senses ________ ________.

suspect …라고 여기다, 짐작하다 **domestic** 국내의; *(동물이) 길든 **leopard** 표범 **lack** …이 없다 **receptor** 수용기, 감각기 **gene** 유전자 ※ **genetic** 유전의 **detect** 인지하다, 감지하다 **stimulus** 자극 (*pl.* stimuli) **evolution** 진화 **nutrition** 영양(물) ※ **nutritional** 영양상의 **mammal** 포유류 **signal** 신호 **taste bud** 미뢰 **be made up of** …로 구성되다 **represent** 대표하다 **bitter** 쓴 **die out** 멸종되다
문제 **perceive** 감지하다, 인지하다 **intelligence** 지능

02

차에도 날개가 필요해요

214 words 3'10"

Date:

Time Taken:

Fans of motorsports are probably aware that race cars usually have a kind of wing, called a *spoiler, on both the front and the rear of the vehicle. It might seem like they are only used to (A) [make / making] the car look cool, but they actually serve a practical purpose.

These spoilers are set at a precise angle in order to force passing air up and through them. One of the basic laws of physics is that for every force there is an equal and opposite force; therefore spoilers, by forcing air upward, create a force that pushes the car downward. In effect, this force, (B) [knowing / known] as *downforce, increases the automobile's weight without increasing its mass. This is important when racing at high speeds, as downforce increases the friction between the car's tires and the track, (C) [which / that] prevents the car from sliding.

As a race car's speed increases, so does the downforce created by its spoilers. Downforce, however, increases at a faster rate. If the car's speed doubles, its downforce will become four times stronger. This is important information for race car drivers. In a Formula One race car going through a turn at 300 kilometers per hour, correctly calculating the downforce can mean the difference between winning the race and crashing into a wall.

*spoiler (자동차의) 스포일러

*downforce 다운포스 (공기역학적으로 차체를 밑으로 누르는 힘)

포뮬러 원 Formula One

레이스 전용차로 하는 경기 중 세계 최고 수준의 대회로, 1950년에 시작되었다. 본래 '포뮬러 원'은 FIA(국제자동차연맹)가 규정한 경주용 자동차를 뜻한다. 이 경기는 가장 큰 광고 효과를 내는 스포츠 종목으로도 유명한데, 연간 보통 300만 명 이상의 관중과 20억 명 이상의 전 세계 TV 시청자들을 사로잡고 있다. 매년 여러 번의 경기가 개최되며, 각 경기를 '그랑프리'라고 부른다. 그랑프리당 10~12개 팀(1팀 2명)이 출전하며, 1위부터 8위까지 각각 10, 8, 6, 5, 4, 3, 2, 1점을 주어 한 해 동안의 점수를 집계하여 최종 순위를 산출한다. 시상은 참가 운전자와 경주용 자동차 제작팀 부문으로 나누어 이루어진다.

정답 및 해설 p.25

1

윗글의 내용과 일치하지 않는 것은?

① 스포일러는 차량의 전방과 후방에 모두 위치한다.
② 스포일러는 공기를 위로 밀어 올리는 역할을 한다.
③ 스포일러는 공기가 통과할 수 있게 만들어진다.
④ 다운포스는 타이어와 도로 간의 마찰력을 증가시킨다.
⑤ 자동차의 속도와 다운포스는 같은 비율로 증가한다.

수능어법

2

윗글의 (A), (B), (C)의 각 네모 안에서 어법에 맞는 표현으로 가장 적절한 것은?

	(A)		(B)		(C)
①	make	……	knowing	……	which
②	make	……	known	……	that
③	make	……	known	……	which
④	making	……	knowing	……	which
⑤	making	……	known	……	that

서술형

3

다음은 윗글의 밑줄 친 a practical purpose가 의미하는 바를 나타낸 것이다. 빈칸에 들어갈 알맞은 말을 본문에서 찾아 쓰시오.

Spoilers keep cars from __________ by creating __________, which increases friction.

motorsports 모터스포츠(자동차·오토바이 등을 사용하는 경주) **rear** 뒤쪽 **vehicle** 차량, 탈것 **serve** …에 도움이 되다, 쓸모가 있다 **practical** 실용적인 **precise** 정확한 **law** (과학·철학상의) 법칙 **physics** 물리학 **in effect** 사실상, 실제로는 **mass** 덩어리; *질량 **friction** 마찰, 마찰 저항 **double** 두 배로 되다 **calculate** 계산하다, 추정하다 **crash** 충돌하다

03

태양으로부터 피부를 보호하세요!

193 words 3'10"

Date:

Time Taken:

Have you ever wondered ① what "sun protection factor (SPF)" really means? And how is it calculated?

To begin with, the SPF of a sunscreen is a measure of ________ ________________. This time period is also based on something ② called your *minimal erythemal dose (MED). How can you calculate your personal MED? You can stay out in the sun and time how long it takes before your skin begins ③ to tingle and burn. You can also estimate this time based on statistics. Light-skinned people tend to have an MED of approximately 10 minutes. People with medium to dark skin tend to have an MED of about 15 minutes. ④ Multiplying your MED by your sunscreen's SPF, you can calculate how long you'll be protected before burning. So, if you're wearing a sunscreen with an SPF of 15 and your MED is 10 minutes, you are protected for 150 minutes (15 times 10).

Remember the two golden rules of SPF: If you feel yourself burning, run for cover. And if you take a dip in the pool or ocean, reapply your sunscreen and let the countdown ⑤ to begin again!

*minimal erythemal dose (MED) 최소 홍반량 (피부에 홍반을 일으키는 최소 자외선 양)

자외선과 자외선 차단제

자외선에는 UV-C, UV-B, UV-A 세 종류가 있으며, 이 중 UV-C는 오존층에 완전히 흡수되어 지구상의 사람에게는 영향을 미치지 않는다. 피부를 그을리게 하거나 노화시키는 것은 UV-A와 UV-B로, UV-A는 멜라닌 색소를 자극하여 피부에 기미, 주근깨 등을 유발하는 광노화의 주범으로 꼽힌다. 햇볕이 강한 여름철에 가장 많이 나타나는 UV-B는 피부에 화상을 입히거나 피부 조직에 깊이 침투한다. 자외선 차단제의 SPF 지수는 UV-B를 차단하는 효과를 나타내는 단위이고, PA(Protection Grade of UVA) 지수는 UV-A를 차단하는 효과를 나타내는 단위이므로, 자외선 차단제를 고를 때에는 두 자외선 모두 차단이 되는지 확인할 필요가 있다.

1 윗글의 빈칸에 들어갈 말로 가장 적절한 것은?

① how strong the sun rays are
② how light or dark your skin is
③ what types of rays should be avoided
④ how much sunscreen you should apply at a time
⑤ how long you can stay in the sun without burning

2 윗글의 내용을 바르게 이해한 사람으로 짝지어진 것은?

미진: 내 피부는 흰 편이니, 약 15분간 자외선에 노출되면 피부가 타기 시작하겠군.
인혜: SPF 지수가 같은 선크림을 바른다면 어두운 피부를 가진 사람이 햇볕으로부터 더 오래 보호되겠군.
지훈: SPF 지수보다는 MED가 높은 것이 햇볕 아래에서 피부를 더 오래 보호하는 데 중요하군.
나연: MED가 같다면 SPF 지수가 더 높은 선크림을 바른 사람이 햇볕 아래에서 피부를 더 오래 보호할 수 있겠군.

① 미진, 지훈 ② 인혜, 지훈 ③ 인혜, 나연 ④ 미진, 나연 ⑤ 지훈, 나연

수능 어법

3 윗글의 밑줄 친 ①~⑤ 중, 어법상 틀린 것은?

서술형

4 윗글의 내용과 일치하도록 빈칸에 알맞은 말을 쓰시오.

If you're wearing a sunscreen with an SPF of 15 and your MED is 15 minutes, you are protected for __________ minutes.

sun protection factor 자외선 차단 지수 **sunscreen** 자외선 차단제 **measure** 조치; *척도 **time** 시간을 측정하다 **tingle** 따끔거리다 **estimate** 추정하다 **statistics** 통계 **approximately** 대략, 거의 **multiply** 곱하다 **golden rule** 황금률 **take a dip** 잠깐 수영을 하다 **reapply** 다시 바르다 **문제** **ray** 광선

04

137 words 2'10"

Date:
Time Taken:

TRY 수능

심경

다음 글에 드러난 Brian의 심경으로 가장 적절한 것은? 모의기출

The sun caught the ends of the hairs along the bear's back. (A) Shining / Shone black and silky, ① it stood on its hind legs, half up, and studied Brian, just studied him. Then it lowered ② itself and moved slowly to the left, eating berries as it rolled along, delicately using ③ its mouth to lift each berry from the stem. In seconds ④ it was gone. Gone, and Brian still had not moved. His tongue was stuck to the top of his mouth, the tip half out, and his eyes were wide. Then Brian made a low sound, "Nnnnnnnggg." It made no sense. ⑤ It was just a sound of fear, of his disbelief (B) that / which something that large could have come so close to him without his knowing. Brian couldn't stop (C) shivering / to shiver, thinking that the bear could return and attack him anytime.

① scared and terrified
② calm and relaxed
③ bored and indifferent
④ proud and satisfied
⑤ ashamed and depressed

유형 *Tip*

step1. **인물이 처한 상황을 파악한다.**
글의 도입에서 중반까지 곰이 브라이언을 살펴보다 가버린 상황을 서술하고 있다.

step2. **심경을 직·간접적으로 드러내는 표현에 주목한다.**
'his eyes were wide', 'a sound of fear', 'couldn't stop shivering' 등의 표현에서 브라이언의 심경을 유추할 수 있다.

step3. **글의 전체적인 상황과 심경의 단서가 되는 표현을 종합하여 정답을 고른다.**
곰이 나타났다가 가버린 것, 그 후 인물의 행동과 생각을 나타내는 표현들을 통해 인물의 심경을 추론할 수 있다.

정답 및 해설 p.28

· 변형문제 ·

1 윗글의 제목으로 가장 적절한 것은?

① An Essential Lifesaving Tip
② Black Bears: Enthusiastic Berry Lovers
③ A Wonderful Experience in the Countryside
④ A Young Boy Smarter Than an Old Bear
⑤ An Unexpected Encounter with Danger

2 윗글의 밑줄 친 ①~⑤ 중, 가리키는 대상이 나머지 넷과 다른 것은?

수능 어법

3 윗글의 (A), (B), (C)의 각 네모 안에서 어법에 맞는 표현으로 가장 적절한 것은?

	(A)		(B)		(C)
①	Shining	......	that	......	shivering
②	Shining	......	which	......	to shiver
③	Shining	......	that	......	to shiver
④	Shone	......	which	......	to shiver
⑤	Shone	......	that	......	shivering

shine 빛나다 **silky** 비단 같은 **hind** 뒤의 **lower** 낮추다 **roll** 굴러가다, 구르듯이 가다 **delicately** 섬세하게 **stem** 줄기 **stick** 붙이다 (stuck/stuck) **tip** 끝 **make sense** 의미가 통하다, 이해가 되다 **disbelief** 믿기지 않음, 불신감 **shiver** (몸을) 떨다 **attack** 공격하다
문제 **terrified** 무서워[두려워]하는 **indifferent** 무관심한 **ashamed** 부끄러운, 창피한 **essential** 필수적인 **lifesaving** 구명(용)의, 구조의; 수난[인명] 구조(법) **enthusiastic** 열렬한, 열광적인 **countryside** 시골 지역 **unexpected** 예기치 않은, 뜻밖의 **encounter** 만남

Review Test

· VOCA ·

A

다음 단어의 영영풀이를 바르게 연결하시오.

1 domestic •	• ⓐ tame and kept as a pet
2 detect •	• ⓑ appropriate for actual use
3 evolution •	• ⓒ the development of something over time
4 practical •	• ⓓ to discover the presence of something
5 shiver •	• ⓔ to shake slightly with cold or fear

B

괄호 안에서 적절한 단어를 고르시오.

1 Proper (nutrition / evolution) is important if you want to stay healthy.

2 It's fragile, so you need to handle it (delicately / roughly).

3 Electric (vehicles / frictions) are becoming more and more popular.

4 The application allows you to (manipulate / calculate) exchange rates easily and quickly.

C

문맥상 다음 빈칸에 들어갈 가장 알맞은 단어를 고르시오.

1 When I'm exhausted, I like to see stars __________ at night.

① serve ② shine ③ lack ④ create ⑤ disappear

2 The pottery is __________ to be more than 5,000 years old.

① designed ② composed ③ appointed ④ estimated ⑤ represented

3 BMI(Body Mass Index) is a __________ of body fat based on an individual's height and mass.

① receptor ② measure ③ signal ④ friction ⑤ stimulus

4 Don't forget to __________ sunscreen every two hours to your face.

① assist ② carry ③ reapply ④ purchase ⑤ exchange

• SENTENCE •

D

다음 문장을 밑줄 친 부분에 유의하여 우리말로 해석하시오.

1 You can calculate how long you'll be protected before burning.

▸ ______________________________

2 It lowered itself and moved slowly to the left, eating berries as it rolled along.

▸ ______________________________

3 Genetic influences on taste might have played an important role in food selection.

▸ ______________________________

4 This force, known as downforce, increases the automobile's weight without increasing its mass.

▸ ______________________________

E

우리말에 맞게 주어진 단어들을 바르게 배열하여 문장을 완성하시오.

1 경주용 자동차의 속도가 증가함에 따라, 자동차의 스포일러에 의해 만들어지는 다운포스 또한 증가한다.

As a race car's speed increases, (created / the downforce / by / does / so) its spoilers.

▸ As a race car's speed increases, ______________ its spoilers.

2 피부가 따가워지고 타기 시작하기 전까지 얼마나 걸리는지 시간을 재면 된다.

(takes / can / you / how long / time / it) before your skin begins to tingle and burn.

▸ ______________ before your skin begins to tingle and burn.

3 그것은 그렇게나 커다란 것이 그에게 가까이 다가올 수도 있었다는 것이 믿기지 않는다는 소리였다.

It was a sound of his disbelief that (could have come / that / something / large) close to him.

▸ It was a sound of his disbelief that ______________ close to him.

LIBRARIES AROUND THE WORLD

Stuttgart Public Library

독일 땅 위에 자랑스러운 한국인의 작품, 슈투트가르트 중앙도서관

2011년 독일 슈투트가르트에서는 한 한국인 건축가의 작품이 유럽인들의 이목을 사로잡았다. 그의 이름은 바로 이은영이다. 무명 건축가였던 그는 1999년 슈투트가르트 도서관 설계 공모에서 234개의 경쟁 작품들을 물리치고 1등으로 당선되었다. 완공하는 데 12년이 걸린 이 도서관은 동서양 문화를 아름답게 결합시킨 건축물로 극찬을 받았다. 건물은 정육면체 형태로 각 외벽에 한국어, 독일어, 영어, 아랍어로 '도서관'을 의미하는 글씨가 새겨져 있다. 온통 하얀색으로 이루어진 내부는 다양한 책들의 색채와 어우러져 환상적인 분위기를 연출한다. 1층부터 4층까지 뻥 뚫려 있는 공간은 자아 성찰을 위해 마련되었고, 도서관의 핵심이라는 의미에서 '심장'이라고 이름 붙여졌다. 이 도서관은 '가장 아름다운 7대 도서관'(CNN), '독일 올해의 도서관'(독일도서관협회) 등으로 선정되며 세계적인 주목을 받아왔다.

SECTION 05

1 책을 가져오는 낙타
2 여기는 쌍둥이들의 천국!
3 무엇이 보이나요?
4 TRY수능 어휘

01

책을 가져오는 낙타

200 words 3'10"

Date:

Time Taken:

Although it has books that people can borrow, just like any other library, the “Camel Library” is one-of-a-kind. It brings books to villages on the backs of camels!

In the past, distant villages in northern Kenya had little or no access to books. There were no libraries nearby, and people could not travel to far-off libraries in cities. You might think that trucks or cars would be better than camels for a mobile library, but not in Kenya. Poorly maintained roads make transportation by vehicle very difficult, so camels are more reliable and better suited to the local conditions. Camels are very strong and can go for a long time without water.

(①) Recently, the Camel Library had 12 camels that worked from Monday to Thursday and carried about 7,000 books to 12 different sites. (②) The library visits each village once every two weeks, spending an entire day there. (③) Villagers can borrow books to read and return them the next time the Camel Library arrives. (④) Even though the people of Kenya speak *Swahili, most of the books are in English. (⑤) That’s because it is their only source of new reading material.

*Swahili 스와힐리어 (동부 아프리카·콩고의 공용어)

소설 『낙타 이동도서관』 케냐의 낙타 이동도서관은 소설에도 등장한다. 미국 작가 마샤 해밀턴(Masha Hamilton)의 소설 『낙타 이동도서관(*The Camel Bookmobile*)』이 바로 이 도서관에서 영감을 받아 쓰인 작품이다. 저자는 소설의 집필을 위해 직접 케냐에 가서 낙타 도서관이 운영되는 모습을 보았다고 한다. 그녀는 낙타 등에 실린 책을 반갑게 맞이하는 오지 마을 주민들의 모습에서 감동을 받았으며, 낙타 도서관이 재정적인 어려움을 겪고 있다는 것을 알게 된 후 사람들에게 이 도서관을 알리고 도움을 호소했다. “Camel Book Drive”로 알려진 이 프로젝트는 많은 사람들의 관심과 지원을 받아 성공적으로 운영되고 있다.

1 윗글의 흐름으로 보아, 주어진 문장이 들어가기에 가장 적절한 곳은?

Despite this, many people borrow books from the Camel Library.

2 Camel Library에 관한 윗글의 내용과 일치하면 T에, 일치하지 않으면 F에 표시하시오.

	T	F
(1) It travels through some parts of northern Kenya regularly.	□	□
(2) Its camels work on weekends.	□	□
(3) It carries thousands of books people can borrow.	□	□

서술형

3 주어진 질문에 대한 답을 할 때, 빈칸에 들어갈 알맞은 말을 본문에서 찾아 쓰시오.

Why are camels more suited than cars as transportation in Kenya?

→ Camels are very strong and can travel more easily on __________ __________ __________ than cars.

one-of-a-kind 독특한, 단 하나뿐인 **distant** 거리가 먼 **access** 입장; *접근권, 접촉 기회 **far-off** (시간·거리 등이) 먼, 멀리 떨어진 **mobile** 이동하는, 이동식의 **maintain** 유지하다; *정비하다 **transportation** 수송, 운송 **vehicle** 탈것, 운송 수단 **reliable** 믿을 수 있는, 의지가 되는 **suited** 적합한 **source** 원천 **material** 재료; *자료

02

여기는 쌍둥이들의 천국!

171 words 2'35"

Date:
Time Taken:

Each year in Twinsburg, Ohio, the world's largest gathering of twins takes place. Thousands of sets of twins attend the festival (A) held / holding in memory of Moses and Aaron Wilcox, the pair of twin brothers who gave Twinsburg its name.

Moses and Aaron were born in Killingworth, Connecticut, on May 18, 1772. They looked (B) so / such similar that even their friends and family couldn't differentiate between them. Not only were their appearances identical, but their lives followed similar courses as well. They (C) married / married with a pair of sisters and each had nine children. Together, the families moved to a town in Ohio, where they made an odd proposal — they would donate land for a public park if the town would change its name to Twinsburg. The town agreed, and the deal was done.

A few years later, the twins died on the same day and were buried together in a single grave. A *plaque was erected in the park to honor the Wilcox twins and everything that they had done for the town.

*plaque (사건·인물을 기념하는 금속·석제의) 명판(銘板)

Twins Days 미국 오하이오의 트윈스버그에서 1976년부터 열리고 있는 세계 최대의 쌍둥이들의 모임이다. 매년 8월 첫 주말에 열리며 매년 전 세계의 수천 쌍의 쌍둥이들이 참여하고 있다. 이 축제에는 매년 축제를 대표할 한 쌍의 왕, 여왕, 왕자, 공주를 뽑는 행사, 대학 등록금이 필요한 한 쌍의 쌍둥이를 선발해 소정의 장학금을 전달하는 등의 행사가 있다. 이외에도, 미술 공예 부스, 어린 아이들을 위한 게임과 놀이기구, 어른들을 위한 맥주 텐트 등 여러 활동을 즐길 수 있다. 하지만 사람들이 가장 즐겨 하는 활동은 바로 다른 쌍둥이들을 만나 이야기하고 사진을 찍는 일이다!

정답 및 해설 p.32

1 **Wilcox 형제에 관한 윗글의 내용과 일치하지 않는 것은?**

① 같은 수의 자녀들을 두었다.
② Ohio에 있는 도시로 이주했다.
③ 쌍둥이들을 위한 축제를 만들자고 제안했다.
④ 같은 날 사망하여 한 무덤에 같이 묻혔다.
⑤ 이들을 기리는 명판이 세워졌다.

수능어법

2 **윗글의 (A), (B), (C)의 각 네모 안에서 어법에 맞는 표현으로 가장 적절한 것은?**

	(A)		(B)		(C)
①	held	……	so	……	married
②	held	……	so	……	married with
③	held	……	such	……	married
④	holding	……	so	……	married with
⑤	holding	……	such	……	married

서술형

3 **윗글의 내용과 일치하도록 빈칸에 알맞은 말을 본문에서 찾아 쓰시오.**

The town changed its name to Twinsburg in exchange for receiving __________ for __________ __________ __________ from the Wilcox brothers' families.

gathering 모임, 집회 **take place** 개최되다 **similar** 비슷한 **differentiate** 구별하다 **appearance** (겉)모습, 외모 **identical** 동일한, 똑같은 **odd** 이상한, 특이한 **donate** 기증하다 **deal** 거래 **bury** 묻다, 매장하다 **grave** 무덤 **erect** 세우다 **문제** **in exchange for** … 대신에, …와 교환으로

03

245 words 3'25"

Date:

Time Taken:

무엇이 보이나요?

Some people claim to have found a smiling face on the surface of Mars. Others say that they have seen images of animals in clouds. Why is this?

The phenomenon that causes people to see the image of a person or a thing in another object is known as pareidolia. It starts when our brains perceive a ⓐ vague image as being more significant than it really is. There have been many instances of ⓑ this type of phenomenon. _____(A)_____, in America there was a grilled cheese sandwich that people claimed had an image of the Virgin Mary on it. And in Singapore, there was an event that became known as the "monkey tree phenomenon." People from all around the country came to view a tree that seemed to contain an image of a monkey god.

So why does this happen? Some scientists believe that pareidolia is a trait that we developed through evolution to help us survive. A million years ago, babies who were unable to recognize their parents' faces smiled at them less and therefore didn't develop strong bonds. This made it less likely that they'd survive. _____(B)_____, the ability to identify the human face is *hardwired in our brains. So, because we can recognize faces with only minimal details, we sometimes interpret random shapes and patterns as faces.

If you ever see a face looking back at you from an unexpected place, don't panic. It's probably just a result of evolution!

*hardwired 내장되어 있는, 원래 갖추고 있는

정답 및 해설 p.34

VOCA

1 윗글의 밑줄 친 ⓐ vague와 바꿔 쓸 수 있는 말로 가장 적절한 것은?

① unreliable ② familiar ③ unique
④ unclear ⑤ precise

서술형

2 다음은 윗글의 밑줄 친 ⓑ this type of phenomenon이 의미하는 바를 나타낸 것이다. 빈칸에 알맞은 말을 본문에서 찾아 쓰시오.

a phenomenon in which one observes the __________ of someone or something in __________ __________

3 윗글의 빈칸 (A)와 (B)에 들어갈 말로 가장 적절한 것은?

	(A)		(B)
①	In addition	……	However
②	For example	……	For this reason
③	For example	……	Nevertheless
④	By thc way	……	Howcver
⑤	By the way	……	For this reason

아포페니아 Apophenia 파레이돌리아 현상은 아포페니아의 한 유형인데, 아포페니아란 서로 연관성이 없는 현상에서 규칙성이나 연관성을 찾아내려는 인식 현상을 뜻하는 심리 용어이다. 1958년 독일의 정신병리학자 클라우스 콘라트(Klaus Conrad)가 처음 이 용어를 사용했다. 가령, 달 표면의 모양을 보고 떡방아 찧는 토끼를 상상한다든가 별을 서로 연결하여 하나의 별자리를 만들고 이와 관련된 신화를 만드는 것이 그 예이다.

claim 주장하다 **phenomenon** 현상 **perceive** 인지[인식]하다 **vague** 흐릿한, 모호한 **significant** 중요한 **trait** 특성, 특징 **evolution** 진화 **recognize** 알아보다, 인식하다 **bond** 유대, 끈 **identify** 확인하다, 식별하다 **minimal** 아주 적은, 최소의 **interpret** (…의 뜻으로) 이해하다, 판단하다 **panic** 당황하다 **문제** **unreliable** 믿을[신뢰할] 수 없는 **precise** 정확한

04

161 words 2'35"

Date:

Time Taken:

TRY 수능

어휘

다음 글의 밑줄 친 부분 중, 문맥상 낱말의 쓰임이 적절하지 <u>않은</u> 것은? 모의기출

The overabundance of options in today's marketplace gives you more freedom of choice. However, there may be a price to pay in terms of happiness. ⓐ According to research by psychologists David Myers and Robert Lane, all this choice often makes people ① <u>depressed</u>. ⓑ They were followed by Barry Schwartz, who found other factors that influence people's emotions. ⓒ Researchers gave some shoppers 24 choices of jams to taste and others only 6 choices. ⓓ Those who had ② <u>fewer</u> choices were happier with the tasting. ⓔ Even more surprisingly, the ones with a smaller selection purchased jam 31% of the time, while those with a wider range of choices only purchased jam 3% of the time. The ironic thing about this is that people nearly always say they want ③ <u>more</u> choices. Yet, the more options they have, the more ④ <u>relieved</u> they become. *Savvy restaurant owners provide fewer choices. This allows customers to feel more relaxed, ⑤ <u>prompting</u> them to choose easily and leave more satisfied with their choices.

*savvy 사리에 밝은

유형 *Tip*

step1. **글의 중심 소재와 전체적인 흐름을 파악한다.**
도입부에서 선택 항목의 과잉이 행복의 관점에서는 부정적일 수도 있다는 암시를 통해, 선택 항목의 과잉과 행복감의 관계에 대한 내용임을 알 수 있다.

step2. **해당 어휘가 전체적인 글의 흐름에 적절한지를 파악한다.**
잼 쇼핑 실험에 따르면 상품 가짓수가 적었을 때 사람들이 더 만족감을 느꼈고 구매율도 높았으므로, 선택 항목이 많을수록 더 안도감을 느낀다고 하는 것은 적절하지 않다.

step3. **반의어가 존재하는 선택지에 유의하여 정답을 찾는다.**
문맥상 부적절한 어휘를 찾는 유형의 경우 적절한 어휘의 반의어가 답으로 제시되어 있을 가능성이 높다는 점에 유의한다.

· 변형문제 ·

1 윗글의 제목으로 가장 적절한 것은?

① Being a Smart Consumer
② The Paradox of Expanded Choices
③ The Psychology Behind Free Samples
④ Why People Want More Options in Their Lives
⑤ The More Options You Have, The Happier You Feel

2 윗글의 ⓐ ~ ⓔ 중, 전체 흐름과 관계 없는 문장은?

서술형

3 윗글의 내용과 일치하도록 빈칸에 알맞은 말을 본문에서 찾아 쓰시오.

Though people seem to want many options to choose from, having them doesn't always bring ________.

overabundance 과잉, 과다 **option** 선택(권), 옵션 **marketplace** 시장 **price** 가격; *대가 **in terms of** …의 관점에서 **psychologist** 심리학자 **factor** 요인, 요소 **influence** 영향을 미치다 **surprisingly** 놀랍게도 **selection** 선택 **purchase** 구입하다 **a wide range of** 광범위한, 다양한 **ironic** 반어적인, 비꼬는; *역설[모순]적인 **relieved** 안도하는 **prompt** 촉구하다, 부추기다 **문제** **consumer** 소비자 **paradox** 역설

Review Test

· VOCA ·

A

다음 단어의 영영풀이를 바르게 연결하시오.

1 vague •	• ⓐ an agreement, often for mutual advantage
2 deal •	• ⓑ not clearly stated, seen, or felt
3 material •	• ⓒ an act of choosing something from a group
4 phenomenon •	• ⓓ facts, information, or ideas used when creating a book
5 selection •	• ⓔ something that can be observed

B

괄호 안에서 적절한 단어를 고르시오.

1 After the composer's death, a statue was (erected / elected) in his honor.

2 Engineers are trying to (testify / identify) the cause of the network failure.

3 Babies begin to (deceive / perceive) sensory information before they are born.

4 How do you (differentiate / negotiate) between those two bird species?

C

문맥상 다음 빈칸에 들어갈 가장 알맞은 단어를 고르시오.

1 Wearing a seat belt is a __________ factor in reducing your chance of injury in a car crash.

① precise ② unknown ③ favorable ④ mobile ⑤ significant

2 The mission of the spacecraft is to explore __________ planets and collect data on them.

① untrue ② constant ③ direct ④ distant ⑤ immediate

3 We are looking for someone __________ and intelligent for the position.

① minor ② negative ③ reliable ④ ironic ⑤ odd

4 Because of modern communication and __________ systems, the world is getting smaller.

① source ② transportation ③ recognition ④ interpretation ⑤ evolution

정답 및 해설 p.37

• SENTENCE •

D

다음 문장을 밑줄 친 부분에 유의하여 우리말로 해석하시오.

1 This made it less likely that they'd survive.

▸ ______________________________

2 The more options they have, the more paralyzed they become.

▸ ______________________________

3 Not only were their appearances identical, but their lives followed similar courses.

▸ ______________________________

4 Villagers can borrow books to read and return them the next time the library arrives.

▸ ______________________________

E

우리말에 맞게 주어진 단어들을 바르게 배열하여 문장을 완성하시오.

1 이것은 고객들이 더 편안함을 느끼게 하고, 그들이 쉽게 선택하도록 한다.

This allows customers to feel more relaxed, (to / prompting / easily / choose / them).

▸ This allows customers to feel more relaxed, ______________________.

2 사람들이 원숭이 신의 이미지를 담고 있는 것처럼 보이는 나무를 구경하기 위해 왔다.

People came to view (contain / that / a tree / to / seemed) an image of a monkey god.

▸ People came to view ______________________ an image of a monkey god.

3 그 도시가 이름을 트윈스버그로 바꾼다면 그들은 공원을 위한 땅을 기증할 것이었다.

They would donate land for a public park (its name / if / change / would / the town) to Twinsburg.

▸ They would donate land for a public park ______________________ to Twinsburg.

Talk Like an Economist

LEMON MARKET

03.

레몬마켓 (Lemon Market)이란?

미국에서 레몬은 불량품을 의미하는 말로도 쓰인다. 이는 레몬이 처음 미국에 들어왔을 때 쓰고 시어서 맛없는 과일이라고 여겨진 데에서 비롯되었다. 같은 맥락으로, 질적으로 떨어지는 상품이 거래되는 시장을 '레몬마켓(lemon market)'이라고 부른다. 레몬마켓이 생겨나는 원인은 소비자와 판매자 간의 정보 불균형 때문이다. 정보 불균형은 판매자는 제품에 대해 많은 정보가 있지만 소비자들은 그렇지 못할 때 발생한다. 예를 들어 중고차 시장에서 딜러는 중고차에 대해 구매자보다 훨씬 많은 정보를 갖고 있다. 따라서 구매자는 손해를 보지 않기 위해 되도록 저렴한 비용에 차를 구매하려 하고, 딜러 또한 손해를 보지 않기 위해 레몬, 즉 상품 가치가 떨어지는 중고차만을 내놓게 된다. 결과적으로는 품질이 낮은 상품만이 넘치는 시장이 되는 것이다. 이와 반대로, 질적으로 우수한 상품이 거래되는 시장은 '피치마켓(peach market)'이라고 한다.

SECTION 06

1 17년마다 나타나요
2 그날은 일급비밀!
3 아프리카의 줄어드는 호수
4 TRY수능 요약문 완성

01

17년마다 나타나요

202 words 3'10"

Date:

Time Taken:

Every 17 years in the eastern United States, an amazing natural phenomenon occurs — the area is invaded by billions of insects (A) [knowing / known] as "17-year *cicadas." A similar occurrence can be witnessed in the southern part of the country, where "13-year cicadas" and "7-year cicadas" are found.

Incredibly, these cicada species all fit into the pattern of *prime numbers. So, why do cicadas appear all at once at prime-numbered intervals? This is actually the cicada's way of ________________. First, with the calculation that natural predators cannot eat billions of cicadas at once, cicadas appear all at the same time.

Also, by basing their life cycles on prime numbers, they ensure that their life cycles are different from those of their natural predators. This allows cicadas to avoid (B) [to encounter / encountering] predators for long periods of time. For instance, if the cycle of the cicada is 17 years and that of a natural predator is 3 years, they can only meet once every 51 years.

The sound of billions of cicadas singing at once reminds some people (C) [from / of] a horror movie. But in some parts of North America, people are comforted by the fact that they won't have to hear them again for another 17 years.

*cicada 매미

*prime number 소수(素數) (1과 자기 자신만으로 나누어지는 1보다 큰 양의 정수)

소수 주기로 사는 매미

매미는 종에 따라 5년, 7년, 13년 등의 다양한 소수의 생활 주기를 가지는데, 그 이유로는 먹이 경쟁을 피하기 위해서라는 가설이 가장 유력하다. 여러 종의 매미가 동시에 출현하게 되면 먹이 경쟁이 치열해진다. 따라서 가능하면 서로 만나지 않도록 진화했다는 것이다.

정답 및 해설 p.38

수능 어법

1 윗글의 (A), (B), (C)의 각 네모 안에서 어법에 맞는 표현으로 가장 적절한 것은?

	(A)		(B)		(C)
①	knowing	……	to encounter	……	from
②	knowing	……	to encounter	……	of
③	known	……	encountering	……	from
④	known	……	to encounter	……	of
⑤	known	……	encountering	……	of

2 윗글의 빈칸에 들어갈 말로 가장 적절한 것은?

① meeting its predators
② adjusting its body size
③ preserving its own species
④ getting along with its enemies
⑤ preying on its natural predators

서술형

3 윗글의 내용을 다음과 같이 요약할 때, 빈칸에 알맞은 말을 본문에서 찾아 쓰시오.

In some parts of the U.S., cicadas have ____________ life cycles in order to protect themselves from their ____________ ____________.

natural phenomenon 자연 현상 **occur** 일어나다, 발생하다 ※ **occurrence** 발생; *사건, 생긴 일 **invade** 침략하다 **witness** 목격하다 **incredibly** 놀랍게도 **species** 종(種) **interval** 간격 **calculation** 계산 **predator** 포식자, 포식 동물 **life cycle** 생활 주기 **ensure** 반드시 …하게 하다, 보장하다 **encounter** 마주치다 **remind A of B** A에게 B를 생각나게 하다 **comfort** 위안하다, 위로하다
문제 **adjust** 조절하다 **preserve** 보호하다; *보존하다 **get along with** …와 잘 지내다 **prey on** …을 잡아먹다

02

그날은 일급비밀!

192 words 3'00"

Date:

Time Taken:

When an important event is being planned, the day on which it is scheduled to occur is sometimes referred to as "D-Day." In the military, this term refers to the day on which a certain operation will be carried out. The most famous D-Day took place during World War II. On June 6, 1944, Allied forces landed at Normandy, France, to free mainland Europe from the Nazis. However, this was (A) the first (B) the last military operation to be designated as D-Day. ① To celebrate the anniversary of the invasion, Normandy is organizing a program of events commemorating D-Day. ② In addition, the term is commonly used outside of the military whenever the date of an event needs to be kept a secret. ③ It is also sometimes used if the date has not yet been decided. ④ Along with "D-Day," the term "H-Hour" is used to refer to the exact hour at which the event will take place. ⑤ Numbers with plus or minus signs can be used to refer to certain times before or after D-Day or H-Hour. For example, H-4 means four hours before H-Hour, while D+5 means five days after D-Day. By using these terms, the timing of an event can be talked about both easily and secretly.

노르망디 상륙작전 제2차 세계대전 중이던 1944년 6월 6일 미국과 영국군이 주력이 된 연합군은 독일이 점령하고 있던 프랑스의 노르망디 해안에 사상 최대 규모의 상륙작전을 실시한다. 이 상륙작전의 목적은 전쟁 초기 독일군과의 싸움에서 패배해 유럽 대륙에서 퇴각할 수밖에 없었던 연합군이 독일 본토를 공격하기 위한 발판을 마련하고자 함이었다. 노르망디 상륙작전에서 연합군은 전략적 기습 작전을 펼쳤고, 이에 당황한 독일군은 제대로 대처하지 못했다. 결국, 이 작전의 성공이 제2차 세계대전에서 연합군이 승리하는 결정적인 계기로 작용하게 된다.

1 윗글의 주제로 가장 적절한 것은?

① how the term D-Day is used
② the allied invasion of Normandy
③ different methods of telling time
④ the first time the term D-Day was used
⑤ the importance of keeping track of the time

서술형

2 윗글의 밑줄 친 문장이 주어진 우리말과 일치하도록 빈칸 (A)와 (B)에 알맞은 말을 쓰시오.

그러나, 이것은 디데이로 지정된 첫 번째 (군사 작전)도 마지막 군사 작전도 아니었다.

(A) ________________ (B) ________________

3 윗글의 ①~⑤ 중, 전체 흐름과 관계 <u>없는</u> 문장은?

refer to A as B A를 B라고 부르다 **term** 용어 **operation** 작전 **carry out** …을 수행하다 **Allied forces** 연합군 **land** 상륙하다 **mainland** 본토 **designate** 지정하다 **celebrate** 기념하다, 축하하다 **anniversary** 기념일 **invasion** 침입, 침공 **commemorate** 기념하다
문제 **keep track of** …을 기록하다

03

274 words 3'45"

Date:

Time Taken:

June 17, 2018

Africa's Shrinking Lake

Reports from NASA researchers indicate that Lake Chad has shrunk by nearly 95 percent since 1963. Once the fourth-largest body of water in Africa, it stretched across 9,650 square miles; now it covers a surface area of just 520 square miles. What's worse, projections show that this trend will continue, leaving the lake as little more than a "puddle" in a few years.

The reports explain that a range of factors are most likely responsible for <u>the change</u>. First of all, global warming over the last few decades has played a part, with the region where the lake is located experiencing consistent drops in rainfall levels over this time. Secondly, the particular geographical features of the lake have contributed to the problem. The fact that the lake is very shallow means that its water has evaporated more quickly than that of deeper lakes. The final reason is excessive use of water for drinking and farming. The population in the region has increased dramatically in recent years, meaning many more people are relying on the lake to fill their water needs. The lake has traditionally been ____________ ____________ across six countries — Sudan, Chad, Niger, Nigeria, Cameroon and the Central African Republic. Today, it is believed to be depended on by around 20 million people.

Unfortunately, the researchers are not optimistic about the future. They expect global warming to get worse and believe competition over water resources will become more intense. Moreover, while the lake may be able to sustain human populations for a while longer, the rich wildlife surrounding the lake is expected to die out in the near future.

정답 및 해설 p.40

1 윗글을 읽고 답할 수 <u>없는</u> 질문은?

① How much has Lake Chad shrunk so far?
② How large is Lake Chad now?
③ What are the main reasons Lake Chad is shrinking?
④ How much rainfall does the Lake Chad region get every year?
⑤ What are Lake Chad's geographical features?

서술형

2 윗글의 밑줄 친 <u>the change</u>가 의미하는 바를 본문에서 찾아 쓰시오. (10단어)

3 윗글의 빈칸에 들어갈 말로 가장 적절한 것은?

① a perfect holiday place for foreigners
② a precious source of water for people
③ an important natural habitat for wildlife
④ a useful way for people to make a profit
⑤ a famous tourist attraction for local business

차드 호수 아프리카 대륙에 위치한 차드 호수는 1960년대에 약 26,000제곱킬로미터의 면적을 자랑했지만, 2000년대에 들어서는 약 2,400제곱킬로미터로 줄어들었다. 차드 호수는 수심이 최고 7미터에 불과하여 호수의 물이 약간만 줄어도 외관상 금세 표가 난다고 한다. 지역 주민들의 생존을 책임지는 수원일 뿐만 아니라, 140종이 넘는 풍부한 어류가 이 호수에 서식하고 있기 때문에 차드 호수의 면적 감소는 심각한 문제로 대두되고 있다.

shrink 줄어들다(shrank-shrunk) **indicate** 나타내다, 보여주다 **projection** 예상, 추정 **little more than** …에 지나지 않는 **puddle** 물웅덩이 **be responsible for** …을 책임지고 있다; *…의 원인이 되다 **consistent** 거듭되는, 변함없는 **rainfall** 강우(량) **particular** 특정한; *특유의 **geographical** 지리(학)적인 **contribute to** …에 기여하다; *…의 한 원인이 되다 **shallow** 얕은 **evaporate** 증발하다 **excessive** 지나친, 과도한 **rely on** …에 의지[의존]하다 **optimistic** 낙관적인, 낙관하는 **competition** 경쟁 **intense** 극심한; *치열한 **sustain** 지속시키다; *(생명을) 유지하다, 부양하다 **die out** 멸종되다 **문제** **habitat** 서식지 **tourist attraction** 관광 명소

04

142 words 2'45"

Date:

Time Taken:

TRY 수능

요약문 완성

다음 글의 내용을 한 문장으로 요약하고자 한다. 빈칸 (A)와 (B)에 들어갈 말로 가장 적절한 것은? 모의기출 응용

Our childhood years are often spent testing our physical limits through all kinds of team sports. By the time we reach high school, we may even engage in two or three different team sports at once. At that age, (so, physical strength, enough, have, to do, we). But by the time we become adults, even though the majority of us still enjoy playing sports, very few of us have the ability to ⓐ compete / compare at the elite level. We find that we don't have the physical strength that we used to. Naturally, we stop ⓑ participating / anticipating in team sports with frequent collisions, such as football, basketball, and soccer, and we move towards sports that involve less stress on the body and risk of physical injury. Many adults get involved in individual sports, instead. Thus, it becomes more difficult to ⓒ recognize / organize team sports for adults.

⇩

Adults tend to ____(A)____ team sports, because their level of ____(B)____ changes with age.

	(A)		(B)
①	avoid	···	physical fitness
②	avoid	···	emotional experience
③	organize	···	emotional experience
④	value	···	physical fitness
⑤	value	···	communication ability

유형 *Tip*

step1. **제시된 요약문을 먼저 읽고 글의 내용을 유추한다.**
요약문의 'Adults', 'team sports', 'age' 등의 단어를 통해 나이와 팀 스포츠에 관한 글이라는 것을 유추할 수 있다.

step2. **핵심 어휘를 찾아보고 글의 요지를 파악한다.**
'don't have the physical strength', 'less stress on the body and risk of physical injury' 등의 어구를 통해 성인들의 신체 상태가 팀 스포츠에 적합하지 않다는 내용임을 알 수 있다.

step3. **선택지를 요약문에 대입해 보고 글의 내용과 어울리는지 확인한다.**
이 글은 성인이 되면 체력이 저하되어 팀 스포츠보다 부담과 부상의 위험이 덜한 개인 스포츠를 선호하게 된다는 내용이다.

정답 및 해설 p.42

· 변형문제 ·

1 윗글의 주제로 가장 적절한 것은?

① health benefits of exercise for adults
② ways to encourage children to play sports
③ changes that happen to the body over time
④ why most adults don't enjoy playing sports
⑤ how age affects people's involvement in sports

서술형

2 윗글의 괄호 안에 주어진 단어들을 다음 우리말에 맞게 배열하시오.

(그 나이 때에는), 우리는 그렇게 할 수 있는 충분한 체력을 가지고 있다.

→ At that age, ______________________________

VOCA

3 윗글의 ⓐ, ⓑ, ⓒ의 각 네모 안에서 문맥에 맞는 낱말로 가장 적절한 것은?

	ⓐ		ⓑ		ⓒ
①	compete	……	participating	……	recognize
②	compete	……	participating	……	organize
③	compete	……	anticipating	……	organize
④	compare	……	participating	……	organize
⑤	compare	……	anticipating	……	recognize

physical 신체적인 **limit** 한계 **engage in** …에 참여하다 **physical strength** 체력 **majority** 다수 **compete** 경쟁하다 **compare** 비교하다 **participate in** …에 참가[참여]하다 **anticipate** 기대하다 **frequent** 빈번한 **collision** 충돌 **risk** 위험성 **injury** 부상 **get involved in** …에 참가하다 **individual** 개인적인 **recognize** 알아보다, 인식하다

Review Test

· VOCA ·

A

다음 중 단어의 뜻풀이가 잘못된 것을 고르시오.

① shallow: extremely deep

② witness: to see something happen

③ shrink: to become smaller in size or amount

④ limit: a point beyond which something does not exist

⑤ compete: to try to win an activity or contest

B

괄호 안에서 적절한 단어를 고르시오.

1 The graph (dictates / indicates) that women tend to live longer than men.

2 The soccer player hurt his forehead in a (collision / division) with another player.

3 The organization is committed to (preserving / reserving) endangered species.

4 She always (comforted / confirmed) herself with music when she was lonely.

C

문맥상 다음 빈칸에 들어갈 가장 알맞은 단어를 고르시오.

1 It is very important to define __________ clearly in the field of law.

① intervals ② preys ③ terms ④ anniversaries ⑤ operations

2 The __________ rise in the city's crime rate made people worried.

① hidden ② variable ③ obsessive ④ consistent ⑤ competitive

3 The receptionist at the hospital called me to __________ me of the medical check-up.

① cause ② remind ③ observe ④ invade ⑤ interrupt

4 Players whose teams do not win will still get a medal for __________ in the tournament.

① supporting ② providing ③ delaying ④ managing ⑤ participating

· SENTENCE ·

D

다음 문장을 밑줄 친 부분에 유의하여 우리말로 해석하시오.

1 The particular geographical features of the lake have contributed to the problem.

▸ ______________________________

2 By using these terms, the timing of an event can be talked about both easily and secretly.

▸ ______________________________

3 The rich wildlife surrounding the lake is expected to die out in the near future.

▸ ______________________________

4 By the time we reach high school, we may even engage in two or three different team sports at once.

▸ ______________________________

E

우리말에 맞게 주어진 단어들을 바르게 배열하여 문장을 완성하시오.

1 그것이 발생할 예정인 날짜는 때때로 '디데이'라고 말해진다.

The day on which (scheduled / is / occur / it / to) is sometimes referred to as "D-Day."

▸ The day on which ______________ is sometimes referred to as "D-Day."

2 이러한 추세가 계속되어, 몇 년 안에 호수는 '물웅덩이'에 지나지 않게 될 것으로 추정된다.

Projections show that this trend will continue, leaving (little / a "puddle" / as / than / the lake / more) in a few years.

▸ Projections show that this trend will continue, leaving ______________ ______________ in a few years.

3 이것은 매미들이 오랜 기간 동안 포식자들을 마주치지 않게 해준다.

(allows / avoid / this / to / cicadas) encountering predators for long periods of time.

▸ ______________ encountering predators for long periods of time.

LIBRARIES AROUND THE WORLD

Geisel Library

영화 속 전투 기지, UCSD 가이젤 도서관

미국의 캘리포니아 대학교 샌디에이고 캠퍼스(University California of San Diego)에는 SF영화에 나오는 관제탑처럼 생긴 건물이 있다. 바로 가이젤 도서관이다. 두 손으로 지식을 떠받드는 모습을 형상화한 이 건물은 유명 건축가 윌리엄 레오나드 페레이라(William Leonard Pereira)에 의해 설계되었다. 1970년에 완공되었으며, 가이젤이라는 이름은 미국의 유명 그림책 작가인 닥터 수스(Dr. Seuss)를 기리기 위해 그의 성(姓)인 가이젤(Geisel)에서 따온 것이다.

이 도서관은 UCSD 캠퍼스의 중앙에 위치해 있고, 대학뿐만 아니라 샌디에이고 주를 대표하는 주요 지형지물로 자리 잡았다. 워낙 유명한 건물이라 '책의 무게로 인해 도서관이 가라앉고 있다'는 등의 캠퍼스 괴담도 종종 들을 수 있으며, 영화 '인셉션'에서는 설원 속 전투 기지의 모티브가 되기도 했다.

SECTION 07

1 미신일까? 과학일까?
2 당신이 배고픈 이유
3 활짝 열린 창문
4 TRY수능 이어질 글의 순서

01

미신일까? 과학일까?

173 words 2'45"

Date:

Time Taken:

*Alchemy in the Middle Ages was a mixture of science, philosophy, and mysticism. It was based on the belief that all matter ① is composed of four elements: earth, air, fire, and water. It was thought that with the right combination of these elements, any substance might be formed, including precious metals and remedies ② to cure diseases and prolong life. The dream of alchemists was to find the "philosopher's stone," a mysterious substance (into gold, that, could turn, they believed, any metal).

Alchemy originated in ancient times, ③ evolving independently in China, India, and Greece. In each of these places, the practice ultimately degenerated into superstition, but it migrated to Egypt and survived there as a scholarly discipline. In medieval Europe, alchemy ④ was revived when 12th-century scholars translated Arabic works into Latin. The rediscovered writings of Aristotle also played a role. By the end of the 13th century, it was discussed seriously by leading philosophers, scientists, and *theologians. Eventually, the practice of alchemy ⑤ lay the foundation for the development of chemistry as a scientific discipline.

*alchemy 연금술
*theologian 신학자

연금술사들이 얻고자 했던 것

중세 유럽의 많은 사람들은 금이 부와 명예뿐만 아니라, 영원한 생명력도 준다고 믿었다. 연금술사들은 이런 금을 만들기 위해 노력했으나 금이 잘 만들어지지 않자, 어떤 금속이든 금으로 바꿀 수 있는 신비로운 물질이 있을 거라고 믿게 된다. 연금술사들은 그 물질을 '현자의 돌(philosopher's stone)'이라고 부르고, 이후 현자의 돌을 찾기 위해 노력한다. 금속을 금으로 바꾸려 했던 중세 유럽의 연금술사들과 달리, 동양의 연금술사들은 불로장생약을 만드는 것이 목표였다. 이들은 열을 가하거나 땅에 묻어도 변함이 없는 금을 영원한 생명력을 주는 신비의 약으로 생각했다.

1 **윗글의 주제로 가장 적절한 것은?**

① the history of alchemy
② various uses of alchemy
③ what a philosopher's stone is
④ why scientists don't believe in alchemy
⑤ how chemistry is different from alchemy

수능어법

2 **윗글의 밑줄 친 ①~⑤ 중, 어법상 틀린 것은?**

서술형

3 **윗글의 괄호 안에 주어진 단어들을 다음 우리말에 맞게 배열하시오.**

어떤 금속이든 금으로 바꿀 수 있다고 그들이 믿었던 (신비한 물질)

→ a mysterious substance ______________________________

4 **alchemy에 관한 윗글의 내용과 일치하지 않는 것은?**

① 4원소의 조합을 통해 어떤 물질이든 만들 수 있다고 여겨졌다.
② 고대에 생겨나 여러 나라에서 각기 독립적으로 발달했다.
③ 그리스에서만 전문적인 학문으로 살아남았다.
④ 12세기 중세 유럽에서 학자들에 의해 부흥했다.
⑤ 화학이 과학의 한 부문으로 발달하는 데 토대를 마련했다.

mysticism 신비주의 **be composed of** …으로 구성되어 있다 **element** 요소, 원소 **combination** 조합 **substance** 물질 **precious metal** 귀금속 **remedy** 치료(약) **prolong** 연장시키다 **originate** 시작되다, 생기다 **evolve** *발달하다; 진화하다 **ultimately** 마침내, 결국 **degenerate** 퇴화[쇠퇴]하다 **superstition** 미신 **migrate** 이주하다; *이동하다 **scholarly** 학문상의, 전문적인 **discipline** 훈련; *학과, 학문 **medieval** 중세의 **revive** 되살리다; *부활[부흥]시키다 **foundation** 기초, 토대

02

당신이 배고픈 이유

223 words 3'35"

Date:

Time Taken:

A new scientific breakthrough may explain why people get hungry at mealtimes, why dieters struggle to maintain weight loss, and why stomach surgery is an ① effective treatment for dangerously overweight patients. The answer is ghrelin, a naturally occurring hormone that causes hunger and slows the body's fat-burning capacity. New research indicates that dieters experience increased production of ghrelin when they ② lose weight. This drives them to eat, forcing them to put the weight back on. In patients who have received a surgical operation called a *gastric bypass, however, ghrelin levels remain low, so they do not have the same hunger pains.

Ghrelin is one of many substances produced ③ naturally in the body that pass messages between the brain and the digestive system. But it is the first natural appetite stimulant found to be produced outside the brain — it is produced by specialized cells in the stomach. Since it occurs outside the brain, it may be an ④ easier target for scientists searching for a way to control appetite.

The hope is that drugs that ⑤ increase or block ghrelin may be developed, which would help obese people to lose weight and keep it off. Likewise, drugs that boost ghrelin levels may lead dangerously thin cancer patients to recover their appetite. In short, ghrelin could be the key to finding ________________________.

*gastric bypass 위장 접합술

식욕 억제 호르몬 렙틴 Leptin

식욕을 증진시키는 그렐린과 반대의 역할을 하는 호르몬으로 렙틴이 있다. 렙틴은 지방 세포에서 분비되는 물질로, '마른, 얇은'이라는 뜻의 그리스어 leptos에서 유래된 말이다. 렙틴이 뇌에 도달하면 식욕을 억제하고 포만감을 느끼게 하며 더 많은 칼로리를 소모하게 하는 역할을 한다. 렙틴과 그렐린은 식욕을 비롯하여 에너지 섭취와 신진대사를 조절하기 때문에 우리 몸에 중요한 호르몬이다.

정답 및 해설 p.46

1 윗글에서 ghrelin에 관해 언급되지 않은 것은?

① its relationship to hunger
② when it increases
③ its effect on appetite
④ the place it is produced
⑤ the possibility of it curing diseases

VOCA

2 윗글의 밑줄 친 ①~⑤ 중, 문맥상 낱말의 쓰임이 적절하지 않은 것은?

3 윗글의 빈칸에 들어갈 말로 가장 적절한 것은?

① natural stimulants produced outside the brain
② workable solutions to weight control problems
③ an effective way to help obese people lose weight
④ helpful drugs to relieve the pain of cancer patients
⑤ the answer for people who have had a gastric bypass

서술형

4 윗글의 내용과 일치하도록 빈칸에 알맞은 말을 본문에서 찾아 쓰시오.

People who struggle to lose weight suffer from __________ levels of ghrelin, a natural hormone that causes __________.

breakthrough 돌파구; *새로운 발견, 큰 발전 **struggle** (…하려고) 애쓰다 **effective** 효과적인 **overweight** 과체중의, 비만의 **capacity** 수용력; *능력 **indicate** 나타내다, 보여주다 **surgical** 외과의 **operation** 수술 **digestive** 소화의 **appetite** 식욕 **stimulant** 흥분제, 자극제 **obese** 비만인 문제 **workable** 운용[실행] 가능한 **relieve** 경감[완화]시키다

03

활짝 열린 창문

229 words 3'15"

Date:
Time Taken:

(①) The most notable feature of Dutch homes is their large windows, which are traditionally left uncovered both during the day and through the night. (②) More interestingly, they also create an unusually high level of visibility between the people inside of the house and those passing by outside. (③) At night, with the interior lights (A) turned / turning on, anyone standing on the street can enjoy an unobstructed view of the rooms within. (④) And a person standing inside can press his or her nose against the window and see (B) how / what is going on outside. (⑤)

The reason for these uncovered windows can be traced back to the influence of *Puritanism on Dutch culture. Virtuous people, in their eyes, have nothing to hide and therefore have no reason to draw their curtains. Large, uncovered windows, in other words, show exactly what's happening inside the home and prove (C) that / what there is nothing wrong going on.

These days, many things are changing in the Netherlands, including windows. Some people are installing vertical blinds that make it difficult for outsiders to look in. However, there are plenty of places in the country where uncovered windows are still popular. So, if you ever visit the Netherlands, keep your eyes open. You may get an interesting look at the private lives of the Dutch.

*Puritanism 청교도주의

1 윗글의 흐름으로 보아, 주어진 문장이 들어가기에 가장 적절한 곳은?

One advantage of these windows is that they allow homes to be flooded with natural light.

수능 어법

2 윗글의 (A), (B), (C)의 각 네모 안에서 어법에 맞는 표현으로 가장 적절한 것은?

	(A)		(B)		(C)
①	turned	……	how	……	that
②	turned	……	what	……	that
③	turned	……	what	……	what
④	turning	……	how	……	what
⑤	turning	……	what	……	that

서술형

3 주어진 질문에 대한 답을 할 때, 빈칸에 들어갈 알맞은 말을 본문에서 찾아 쓰시오. (7단어)

Why do Dutch homes have large, uncovered windows?

→ It is due to ________________________________.

네덜란드 집의 또 다른 특징

네덜란드에 가보면 도로 주변에 좁게 다닥다닥 붙어 있는 여러 주택들의 모습이 눈에 띈다. 실제로 네덜란드 주택은 좁고 긴 구조가 특징이다. 집안에는 1층에서 2, 3층으로 연결되는 계단이 있는데, 이는 한 사람이 겨우 지나갈 정도로 좁고 가파르다. 이런 집의 구조는 옛 네덜란드의 주택법과 관련이 있다. 과거 네덜란드에서는 주택이 도로에 접하는 면적에 따라 세금을 부과했기 때문에, 사람들은 절세를 위해 층별 면적은 좁게 하고 높이는 2, 3층까지 높여 집을 지었다. 암스테르담에 있는 관광 명소인 안네 프랑크의 집에서도 가파른 계단을 찾아볼 수 있다.

notable 눈에 띄는, 주목할 만한 **feature** 특징 **visibility** 눈에 잘 보임, 가시성 **interior** 내부(의) **unobstructed** 가로막는 것이 없는 **virtuous** 도덕적인, 고결한 **prove** 입증[증명]하다 **install** 설치하다 **vertical** 수직의 **blind** (창문에 치는) 블라인드 **문제** **flood** 물에 잠기게 하다; *(빛 등이) …을 가득 채우다

04

148 words 2'45"

Date:

Time Taken:

TRY 수능

이어질 글의 순서

주어진 글 다음에 이어질 글의 순서로 가장 적절한 것은? [수능기출 응용]

> You have probably heard of putting a message in a bottle and ⓐ (were sent / sending) it across the sea. Unfortunately, it is impossible to tell where the bottle will wash up or how long it will take the sea to deliver it there.

(A) Because he was still more than a thousand miles away from Europe, Columbus was afraid that he would never live to share his news. So, he took a piece of paper and ⓑ (wrote down it / wrote it down).

(B) One of the earliest and most famous bottled messages was sent by Christopher Columbus. In 1493, he was returning to Spain to announce his discovery to the king and queen, and his ship became caught in a bad storm.

(C) He put it in a wooden bottle and tossed it into the ocean. It was found more than 300 years later off the coast of Morocco by the captain of an American ship.

① (A) – (C) – (B)
② (B) – (A) – (C)
③ (B) – (C) – (A)
④ (C) – (A) – (B)
⑤ (C) – (B) – (A)

유형 *Tip*

step1. **먼저 주어진 글이 어떤 내용인지 파악한 후, 이어질 글의 내용을 추측해 본다.**
첫 번째 문장을 통해 이어질 글에서 메시지를 병에 넣어 바다에 띄워 보내는 것에 관한 내용이 전개될 것임을 예측할 수 있다.

step2. **글의 순서를 정하는 데 도움이 되는 단서(지시어, 대명사, 연결사, 관사 등)에 주목한다.**
(A) 인칭대명사 he가 나오므로, (A) 앞에 he가 지칭하는 명사가 나와야 함을 추측할 수 있다.
(B) 병에 든 메시지의 시초에 대해 언급하고 있고, 크리스토퍼 콜럼버스가 처음 등장한다.
(C) 인칭대명사 He는 콜럼버스를 가리키며, 첫 번째 it은 (A)에서 언급된 소식이 적힌 종이를 가리킨다.

step3. **인과, 선후, 대조, 예시 등에 따른 글의 논리적 흐름을 파악하여 글의 순서를 정한다.**
메시지가 든 병을 바다에 띄워 보내는 것에 대해 언급하는 주어진 글 다음에는 이것의 최초 사례 중 하나인 크리스토퍼 콜럼버스의 메시지를 소개하는 (B)가 가장 먼저 오고, 그가 메시지를 병에 넣어 바다로 보낸 이유에 대해 언급하는 (A)로 이어진 후, 그가 병을 바다로 던진 후 오랜 시간이 지나서야 그것이 발견되었다는 (C)로 연결되는 것이 자연스럽다.

정답 및 해설 p.50

• 변형문제 •

1 윗글의 제목으로 가장 적절한 것은?

① A Famous Message in a Bottle
② The Search for a Long Lost Treasure
③ The Growing Problem of Ocean Waste
④ How Columbus Discovered the New World
⑤ Why You Shouldn't Send Messages in Bottles

2 윗글의 ⓐ와 ⓑ에서 어법에 맞는 것을 골라 적으시오.

ⓐ ________________ ⓑ ________________

서술형

3 윗글의 내용과 일치하도록 빈칸에 알맞은 말을 본문에서 찾아 쓰시오. (5단어)

Columbus used a message in a bottle because his ship got ________________.

share 나누다, 공유하다 **write down** …을 적다, 기록하다 **bottled** 병에 든 **announce** 알리다, 통보하다 **discovery** 발견
catch 잡다; *(예상 밖의 상황에) 처하게 하다 **toss** 던지다

Review Test

· VOCA ·

A

다음 단어의 영영풀이를 바르게 연결하시오.

1 superstition •	• ⓐ to make something popular again
2 revive •	• ⓑ a desire to eat or drink
3 remedy •	• ⓒ a treatment for an illness or injury
4 appetite •	• ⓓ having strong morals
5 virtuous •	• ⓔ a belief not rooted in reason or knowledge

B

괄호 안에서 적절한 단어를 고르시오.

1 Each room provides an (unoccupied / unobstructed) view of the scenery.

2 Brian had an (alteration / operation) on his eye after the accident.

3 The cancer cells (migrated / designated) to other organs of the body.

4 It was (pronounced / announced) that a new airport would be built in the city.

C

문맥상 다음 빈칸에 들어갈 가장 알맞은 단어를 고르시오.

1 I __________ the rotten apple into the garbage can.

① fired ② tied ③ tossed ④ grew ⑤ crossed

2 The number of __________ children is increasing due to bad eating habits.

① smart ② obese ③ abandoned ④ isolated ⑤ promising

3 Leonardo da Vinci left many __________ works of art.

① reliable ② available ③ notable ④ capable ⑤ unworthy

4 In the class, she wanted to improve her __________ for self-expression.

① role ② issue ③ capacity ④ responsibility ⑤ importance

정답 및 해설 p.51

• SENTENCE •

D

다음 문장을 밑줄 친 부분에 유의하여 우리말로 해석하시오.

1 A person standing inside can see what is going on outside.

▸ ____________________

2 Columbus was afraid that he would never live to share his news.

▸ ____________________

3 It is the first natural appetite stimulant found to be produced outside the brain.

▸ ____________________

4 Alchemy originated in ancient times, evolving independently in China, India, and Greece.

▸ ____________________

E

우리말에 맞게 주어진 단어들을 바르게 배열하여 문장을 완성하시오.

1 그것은 모든 물질이 4원소로 이루어져 있다는 믿음에 기초했다.

It was based on the belief that (is / of / matter / all / composed) four elements.

▸ It was based on the belief that ____________________ four elements.

2 어떤 사람들은 밖에 있는 사람들이 안을 들여다보기 어렵게 만드는 수직 블라인드를 설치하고 있다.

Some people are installing vertical blinds that (difficult / it / make / outsiders / for) to look in.

▸ Some people are installing vertical blinds that ____________________ to look in.

3 이것은 그들로 하여금 먹게 만들어 다시 체중이 늘어나게 한다.

This drives them to eat, (them / forcing / put / the weight / to) back on.

▸ This drives them to eat, ____________________ back on.

Talk Like an Economist

UNTACT MARKETING

04.

언택트 마케팅 (Untact Marketing) 이란?

untact는 영어에서 부정이나 반대의 뜻을 나타내는 접두사 'un-'과 '접촉(contact)'이 합쳐져 '비대면, 비접촉'을 뜻하는 단어로, 언택트 마케팅은 사람 간의 대면(對面)을 최소화하는 마케팅 기법을 뜻한다. 이 마케팅은 본래 일본에서 상점에 방문한 손님이 제품을 권장하는 점원을 불편해하지 않도록 손님을 내버려두는 판매 방식을 의미했으나, 사물인터넷, 인공지능, 빅데이터 등 IT 기술이 발전하며 그 의미가 확장되었다. 특히 언택트 마케팅은 스마트폰 세대를 겨냥하는데, 이는 이 세대가 면대면 소통보다는 기기를 통한 소통에 더 익숙하고, 소모적 인간관계에 피로를 느끼는 경향이 있기 때문이다.

언택트 마케팅은 소비자 입장에서는 편리하고 효율적이고, 기업 입장에서는 인건비를 절약할 수 있다는 장점이 있다. 반면 이로 인해 일자리가 감소하고, 디지털 기기에 익숙하지 않은 세대나 기기를 자유롭게 활용하기 어려운 장애인들은 서비스에서 배제된다는 단점도 있다.

SECTION 08

01

우리는 가족이에요

166 words 2'45"

Date:

Time Taken:

Sometimes true friendship can be found in the most unlikely circumstances. Such is the case of Owen and Mzee, a hippopotamus and a tortoise who formed a unique bond.

After a devastating tsunami, Owen, a baby hippo, was orphaned and lost in the Indian Ocean. Luckily, ① he was rescued and taken to an animal *sanctuary near Mombasa. There, ② he was placed in an enclosure with a cohabitant, a 130-year-old tortoise named Mzee.

At first, Mzee was ⓐ wary of Owen, who imitated the tortoise's behavior as if ③ he were Mzee's own child. As time passed, however, ④ he grew used to the hippo and began to teach ⑤ him what to eat and where to sleep. Soon, they became inseparable companions who did everything together, and they even developed their own system of vocal communication.

Due to ⓑ their astonishing behavior, Owen and Mzee became worldwide celebrities. They've been featured in films and are the subject of two bestselling picture books, one of which has been translated into 13 languages.

*sanctuary 보호 구역

Haller Park 오웬과 음제가 함께 살고 있는 곳은 바로 케냐에 위치한 할러 공원이다. 이곳은 케냐의 몸바사 주(州) 북쪽 해안에 위치한 아름다운 생태 보호 구역으로 특이하게도 원래 돌을 캐내는 채석장에서 생태 공원으로 탈바꿈한 곳이다. 멸종 위기에 처한 희귀 야생동물 및 희귀 나무를 포함한 방대하고 다양한 종류의 동식물이 있어, 많은 국내외 관광객들을 끌고 있는 명소이다. 방문객들은 전문 가이드들과 함께 다양한 동물들과 가까이 접촉하는 독특한 경험을 즐길 수 있다.

정답 및 해설 p.52

1

윗글의 제목으로 가장 적절한 것은?

① The Story of a Rescued Tortoise
② When Owen Met His Real Parents
③ The World's Best Animal Sanctuary
④ The World-Famous Zoo in Mombasa
⑤ The Unusual Friendship between Owen and Mzee

2

윗글의 밑줄 친 ①~⑤ 중, 가리키는 대상이 나머지 넷과 다른 것은?

VOCA

3

윗글의 밑줄 친 ⓐ wary와 바꿔 쓸 수 있는 말로 가장 적절한 것은?

① proud ② critical ③ patient
④ suspicious ⑤ sympathetic

서술형

4

다음은 윗글의 밑줄 친 ⓑ their astonishing behavior가 의미하는 바를 나타낸 것이다. 빈칸에 알맞은 말을 본문에서 찾아 쓰시오.

Owen and Mzee built up a _________ _________ doing everything _________.

unlikely …일 것 같지 않은; *예상 밖의 **circumstance** 상황 **hippopotamus** 하마(= hippo) **tortoise** 거북 **bond** 유대 **devastating** (대단히) 파괴적인, 엄청난 **tsunami** 쓰나미 **orphan** 고아로 만들다 **rescue** 구조하다 **enclosure** 울타리를 친 장소 **cohabitant** 동거인 **be wary of** …을 경계하다 **imitate** 모방하다 **inseparable** 떨어질 수 없는 **companion** 동료, 친구 **astonishing** 놀라운 **celebrity** 유명인 **feature** (배우를) 주연시키다 **translate** 번역하다 **문제** **patient** 참을성 있는 **sympathetic** 동정 어린

02

190 words 3'00"

Date:

Time Taken:

위대한 음악 신동

Itzhak Perlman is considered one of the greatest classical violinists in history. Born in Israel in 1945, Perlman decided to become a violinist when he was just three years old. He began practicing intensely every day, but before he could realize his goal, he was faced with the toughest challenge of his life. At age four, Perlman was stricken with *polio.

_____(A)_____ disabled for life, nothing could stop him from playing the violin. Over time he learned how to walk with crutches, but to this day he remains seated _____(B)_____ performing. He attended the Music Academy of Tel Aviv, where his teachers immediately recognized his talent. In 1958 he ⓐ invited to the United States to appear on the Ed Sullivan Show. This television performance made him an instant superstar. Since then, Perlman has traveled nonstop, ⓑ performed with almost every symphony orchestra as well as great musicians like Yo-Yo Ma and Placido Domingo. He also worked with composer John Williams on the *score for *Schindler's List*. His amazing onstage presence speaks eloquently on behalf of the disabled, and his commitment to their welfare is an important part of his life.

*polio 소아마비
*score (영화 등의) 배경 음악

이작 펄만 이작 펄만(Itzhak Perlman, 1945~)은 이스라엘계 미국인 바이올린 연주가로, 어린 시절 라디오에서 흘러나오는 바이올린 소리에 반해 바이올린에 대한 열정을 처음 가지게 되었다. 그는 텔아비브 콘세르바토레에 입학하여 스승 골드가르트를 만나게 되었다. 골드가르트는 그에게 연습의 중요성을 강조하며 같은 곡을 몇 시간이고 반복해서 연습하게 했다. 이런 고된 연습을 바탕으로 펄만은 탄탄한 기본기를 갖추었고, 그럼으로써 세계 최고의 기량을 갖춘 연주자가 될 수 있었다.

정답 및 해설 p.53

1 윗글의 빈칸 (A)와 (B)에 들어갈 말로 가장 적절한 것은?

(A)		(B)
① As	……	while
② As	……	after
③ Though	……	while
④ Though	……	before
⑤ Whether	……	after

서술형

2 윗글의 밑줄 친 ⓐ와 ⓑ를 어법에 맞게 고쳐 쓰시오.

ⓐ ________________ ⓑ ________________

3 윗글에서 Itzhak Perlman에 관해 언급되지 않은 것은?

① where he was born
② at what age he got polio
③ what event made him famous
④ when he had his first concert
⑤ with whom he worked on the music for *Schindler's List*

intensely 강렬하게; *열심히 **realize** 깨닫다; *실현[달성]하다 **be stricken with** (병)에 걸리다 **for life** 평생 **crutch** 목발 **instant** 즉각적인 **composer** 작곡가 **onstage** 무대 위의 **presence** 존재 **eloquently** 웅변으로; *감동적으로 **on behalf of** …을 대신해서, 대표해서 **commitment** 헌신 **welfare** 복지

03

우주에서도 맛있게!

242 words 3'45"

Date:
Time Taken:

What do astronauts eat when they're floating around in space? As it turns out, there are lots of space foods made here on Earth. However, it's very expensive to ship enough of this food into space, especially for astronauts who will be in space for many months. To solve <u>this problem</u>, scientists are developing ways by which food can be grown by the astronauts themselves once they're in space, thus ______________________.

You may think it's impossible to grow food without soil or sunlight, but in fact this is already being done here on Earth with *hydroponics. Hydroponic crops are raised in artificial environments such as greenhouses, where artificial light and substances like *charcoal and special chemical mixtures help them grow. At first, scientists worried that plants would have problems growing in space and wouldn't yield as much food as on Earth. However, not only did hydroponic plants in space grow faster than here on Earth, but some of them, such as beans, also had a higher protein content.

The nutrition of these foods is obviously very important, but scientists aren't ignoring the taste factor, either. NASA recently funded the development of 200 different recipes using hydroponically grown foods with the intention of enhancing their flavor as well as their nutrition levels. Initial taste tests have met with great success. Perhaps someday astronauts will be able to dine on hydroponic meals that are truly out of this world.

*hydroponics 수경 재배
*charcoal 숯

수경 재배 수경 재배란 식물을 키우는 데 흙을 사용하지 않고, 대신 식물 성장에 필요한 영양분과 물로 이루어진 배양액 속에서 식물을 키우는 방법을 말한다. 수경 재배의 장점은 식물의 뿌리의 상태나 성장 모습을 직접 관찰할 수 있고, 오염되지 않은 깨끗한 작물을 재배할 수 있다는 점과 집안에서 손쉽게 재배가 가능하다는 것이다. 수경 재배를 할 수 있는 식물로는 튤립, 수선화, 아이비, 토란, 고구마, 콩나물, 양파 등이 있다.

1 윗글의 주제로 가장 적절한 것은?

① how to eat space food
② hydroponic food grown in space
③ what astronauts eat while in space
④ how to grow hydroponic vegetables
⑤ the difficulty of cultivating crops in space

서술형

2 다음은 윗글의 밑줄 친 this problem이 의미하는 바를 나타낸 것이다. 빈칸에 들어갈 알맞은 말을 본문에서 찾아 쓰시오.

It is very ________ to ________ food into space.

3 윗글의 빈칸에 들어갈 말로 가장 적절한 것은?

① improving the nutrition in food
② eliminating the cost of shipping
③ reducing unnecessary manpower
④ protecting various plants on Earth
⑤ providing a better environment for astronauts

4 윗글의 내용과 일치하지 않는 것은?

① 흙이나 햇빛 없이도 식물 재배가 가능하다.
② 수경 재배는 인공조명을 사용한다.
③ 수경 재배 식물은 지구에서보다 우주에서 더 빨리 자란다.
④ 우주에서 수경 재배로 자란 식물은 영양이 부족한 것으로 드러났다.
⑤ NASA는 수경 재배 식물로 만든 식품의 맛 개선을 위해 자금을 투자했다.

astronaut 우주비행사 **float** (물 위나 공중에) 뜨다, 떠돌다 **ship** 운송[수송]하다 **artificial** 인공의 **substance** 물질 **yield** 생산하다 **content** 내용물; *함량 **nutrition** 영양 **obviously** 확실히 **fund** 자금을 대다 **enhance** 향상시키다 **initial** 처음의 **out of this world** (이 세상의 것이 아닌 것처럼) 너무도 훌륭한 **문제** **cultivate** 경작하다, 재배하다 **eliminate** 없애다, 제거하다 **manpower** 인력

04

142 words 2'45"

Date:

Time Taken:

TRY 수능

주어진 문장의 위치

글의 흐름으로 보아, 주어진 문장이 들어가기에 가장 적절한 곳은? 수능기출 응용

> In spite of this evidence of favoritism towards attractive politicians, it was demonstrated by follow-up research that voters were unaware of their bias.

According to researchers, we automatically assign favorable traits, including honesty, kindness, talent, and intelligence, to good-looking individuals. (①) Moreover, we aren't even aware (A) [of / that] physical attractiveness is playing a role when we make these judgments. (②) I believe this unconscious assumption that "good-looking equals good" can have some scary consequences. (③) For example, according to a study of the 1974 Canadian federal elections, "attractive" candidates received over two and a half times as (B) [many / much] votes as "unattractive" ones. (④) In fact, 73 percent of the surveyed voters strongly denied that physical appearance had influenced their votes; only 14 percent even acknowledged the possibility of such influence. (⑤) While voters can deny (C) [what / that] attractiveness affects electability, evidence has shown the troubling presence of this bias.

유형 *Tip*

step1. 주어진 문장이 무엇에 관한 내용인지 파악한다.
주어진 문장은 매력적인 정치인들을 향한 편애의 증거에도 불구하고, 유권자들이 자신들의 편견을 자각하지 못했다는 내용이다.

step2. 연결사나 지시어, 대명사 등의 단서로 문장 전후 관계를 따져본다.
주어진 문장의 'this evidence of favoritism towards attractive politicians'는 ④ 앞 문장의 캐나다 연방 선거 연구 결과를 의미하고, 유권자들이 자신들의 편견을 자각하지 못했다는 후속 연구 내용은 ④ 뒤의 문장에 나와 있다.

step3. 선택한 위치에 주어진 문장을 넣어 글의 흐름이 자연스러운지 확인한다.
주어진 문장은 매력적인 정치인들을 향한 편애의 증거(매력적인 후보들이 표를 더 많이 받은 것)에 해당하는 문장과 후속 연구를 설명하는 문장 사이에 들어가는 것이 적절하다.

정답 및 해설 p.57

· 변 형 문 제 ·

수능 어법

1 윗글의 (A), (B), (C)의 각 네모 안에서 어법에 맞는 표현으로 가장 적절한 것은?

	(A)		(B)		(C)
①	of	......	many	......	what
②	of	......	much	......	that
③	that	......	many	......	what
④	that	......	much	......	that
⑤	that	......	many	......	that

VOCA

2 윗글의 밑줄 친 bias와 바꿔 쓸 수 있는 말로 가장 적절한 것은?

① talent ② anxiety ③ prejudice
④ balance ⑤ satisfaction

서술형

3 윗글의 내용과 일치하도록 빈칸에 알맞은 말을 본문에서 찾아 쓰시오.

In some Canadian federal elections, __________ candidates got more votes than __________ candidates.

favoritism 편애 **attractive** 매력적인(↔ unattractive 매력 없는) ※ **attractiveness** 매력 **demonstrate** 보여주다, 입증하다 **follow-up** 뒤따르는, 후속의 **be unaware of** …을 알지 못하다 **bias** 편견 **automatically** 자동적으로, 무의식적으로 **assign** (일을) 맡기다; *(가치·기능 등을) 부여하다 **favorable** 호의적인; *유리한, 좋은 **trait** (성격상의) 특성 **unconscious** 무의식적인 **assumption** 추정, 가정 **consequence** 결과 **federal** 연방의, 연방 정부의 **candidate** 후보자 **deny** 부인[부정]하다 **acknowledge** 인정하다 **electability** 선출 가능성 **troubling** 성가신, 곤혹스러운 문제 **prejudice** 편견 **satisfaction** 만족

Review Test

· VOCA ·

A

다음 중 단어의 뜻풀이가 잘못된 것을 고르시오.

① initial: existing or occurring in the end
② bond: a close connection that holds people or things together
③ fund: to provide money or resources for a certain purpose
④ bias: an unfair tendency in favor of or against something
⑤ welfare: the health, happiness, and fortunes of an individual or group

B

괄호 안에서 적절한 단어를 고르시오.

1 Children should be (wary / primary) of strangers at all times.
2 The police were (beware / unaware) of the location of the criminal.
3 Laura put some (artificial / beneficial) flowers in the vase for the party.
4 Many writers have (imagined / imitated) Shakespeare's style and techniques.

C

문맥상 다음 빈칸에 들어갈 가장 알맞은 단어를 고르시오.

1 Fallen leaves __________ on the surface of the lake.
① hung ② shipped ③ floated ④ sank ⑤ fled

2 Firefighters arrived at the scene and __________ a man from the building.
① reserved ② rescued ③ responded ④ resolved ⑤ recorded

3 The latest model of the phone features __________ battery life.
① enhanced ② decreased ③ involved ④ installed ⑤ discounted

4 I'm honored to receive this award on __________ of our team.
① band ② behalf ③ cost ④ pursuit ⑤ presence

• SENTENCE •

D

다음 문장을 밑줄 친 부분에 유의하여 우리말로 해석하시오.

1 In 1958 he was invited to the United States to appear on the Ed Sullivan Show.

▸ ______________________________

2 Though disabled for life, nothing could stop him from playing the violin.

▸ ______________________________

3 Not only did hydroponic plants in space grow faster than here, but some of them also had a higher protein content.

▸ ______________________________

4 "Attractive" candidates received over two and a half times as many votes as "unattractive" ones.

▸ ______________________________

E

우리말에 맞게 주어진 단어들을 바르게 배열하여 문장을 완성하시오.

1 그는 그 하마에게 익숙해졌고, 그에게 무엇을 먹어야 할지 가르쳐주기 시작했다.

(grew / the hippo / he / to / used) and began to teach him what to eat.

▸ ______________________ and began to teach him what to eat.

2 과학자들은 식물들이 우주에서 자라는 데에 문제가 있을 것이라고 걱정했다.

Scientists worried that (would / plants / problems / growing / have) in space.

▸ Scientists worried that ______________________ in space.

3 그들은 두 권의 베스트셀러 책의 소재인데, 그중 하나는 13개의 언어로 번역되었다.

They are the subject of two bestselling books, (has / translated / one / which / been / of) into 13 languages.

▸ They are the subject of two bestselling books, ______________________ into 13 languages.

LIBRARIES
AROUND THE WORLD

Royal Danish Library

해가 지면 빛을 발하는 '블랙 다이아몬드', 덴마크 왕립 도서관

덴마크 왕립 도서관은 북유럽에서 가장 규모가 큰 도서관이다. 특히 이 도서관은 '블랙 다이아몬드'라 불리는 건물로 유명한데, 이 이름은 검은 대리석과 유리로 된 건물 외벽에서 비롯된 것이다.

왕립 도서관의 역사는 17세기 중반으로 거슬러올라간다. 덴마크의 왕 프레데리크 3세가 처음 설립하였고, 18세기 말 일반 대중에 개방된 후, 국내의 다른 도서관과 합병하여 지금의 규모를 자랑하게 되었다. 블랙 다이아몬드는 이 도서관의 신관으로, 1999년에 완공되었다. 엄숙한 외양과는 달리, 도서관 내부에는 열람실뿐 아니라 콘서트홀, 전시관, 카페 등 시민들을 위한 다양한 문화 공간이 조성되어 있다. 건물 중앙에서 흘러나오는 불빛과 외벽, 운하의 물이 조화를 이루는 아름다운 야경으로도 유명하다.

SECTION 09

1 암흑 속의 식사
2 원자력 산업에 대한 의견
3 노벨상 대신 필즈 메달!
4 TRY수능 무관한 문장

01

암흑 속의 식사

154 words 2'25"

Date:

Time Taken:

Eating at the Blindekuh Restaurant in Zurich is a truly once in a lifetime experience. The restaurant's name means "blind cow" in English. It also refers to a common Swiss saying, "as dark as the inside of a cow."

The theme of the restaurant is total darkness. This idea was created by the Swiss Association for Blind People, with the aim of making people aware of the reality of being sight-disabled.

Guests are greeted in the lobby, and all their belongings, including cell phones and illuminated watches, are stored in lockers. The menu is displayed in the lobby (so, order, can, that, guests, there). After ordering, each group is led through a tunnel by a waitress, who is herself blind, to a table. Eating is tricky but fun, and using your fingers to locate all the food is the best solution. Nobody will complain about your manners as ____________ ____________!

블린데쿠 식당 블린데쿠 식당은 스위스 블린트 리히트(Blind-Liecht) 재단의 후원을 받는 프로젝트이다. '어둠과 빛'을 뜻하는 이 재단은 시각 장애인들에게 취업의 기회를 제공하고자 이 식당을 열었다. 블린데쿠 식당 1호점은 1999년 9월 17일에 취리히에서 문을 열었으며, 이곳은 세계 최초로 어둠 속에서 시각 장애 체험을 할 수 있는 식당으로 알려져 있다. 현재는 블린데쿠 식당을 모방한 레스토랑들이 유럽을 비롯해 중국과 미국 등지에 많이 생겨났으며, 비장애인들이 시각 장애인들이 겪는 불편함을 어느 정도 이해하는 데 도움을 주고 있다.

정답 및 해설 p.59

1 Blindekuh Restaurant에 관한 윗글의 내용과 일치하지 않는 것은?

① 식당의 이름은 '눈먼 소'라는 의미이다.
② 시각 장애인 단체가 식당에 대한 아이디어를 냈다.
③ 모든 소지품은 사물함에 보관해야 한다.
④ 테이블에 앉으려면 터널을 지나야 한다.
⑤ 고객을 안내하는 종업원은 장애인이 아니다.

서술형

2 윗글의 괄호 안에 주어진 단어들을 다음 우리말에 맞게 배열하시오.

(메뉴는) 손님들이 그곳에서 주문할 수 있도록 (로비에 전시되어 있다)

→ The menu is displayed in the lobby ______________________________

3 윗글의 빈칸에 들어갈 말로 가장 적절한 것은?

① no one can see you
② waitresses help you
③ the food is really delicious
④ everybody has different manners
⑤ you can finish your meal very quickly

once in a lifetime 일생에 한 번뿐인 **saying** 속담 **association** 협회, 단체 **aim** 목표, 목적 **sight-disabled** 시각 장애가 있는 **greet** 맞이하다, 환영하다 **belonging** 《*pl.*》 소지품 **illuminated** 조명 장식을 한 **tricky** (하기) 힘든, 까다로운 **locate** (물건의 위치를) 찾아내다

02 원자력 산업에 대한 의견

174 words 2'35"

Date:

Time Taken:

To the Editor

After reading ⓐ your special report on the nuclear power industry published on August 14, 2018, I would like to make some comments.

I believe that further development of nuclear power, ① which you support, is not the best way to go forward and should in fact be stopped. First of all, when the costs of dealing with nuclear waste are examined, nuclear power is found to be very expensive. Secondly, nuclear waste from power plants is an environmental threat ② what will be around for a very long time. High-level nuclear waste remains ③ deadly for 250,000 years.

For these important reasons, I think the government should start ④ reducing energy consumption through investment in energy conservation measures, such as housing insulation and the development of energy-efficient appliances, cars, and machines. Investment in research and development of renewable energy from the sun, the wind, and waves would be my second policy recommendation. It's time ⑤ for the government to come up with ways to end the use of non-renewable, pollution-creating energy sources.

Michael Bowles

New York

원자력 에너지의 두 얼굴

원자력 발전이란 원자핵이 분열할 때 발생하는 열 에너지를 이용해 전기를 생산하는 방식을 말한다. 원자력 발전은 우라늄을 원료로 이용하는데, 생산 방식의 효율성이 좋아 석유·석탄을 이용할 때보다 비용이 저렴하고 이산화탄소를 거의 배출하지 않는다는 장점이 있다. 하지만 원자력 발전소에서 사고가 일어날 경우 방사능이 누출될 위험이 있고, 원자력 에너지를 만들고 난 후 생기는 찌꺼기인 핵폐기물을 처리하는 비용이 많이 든다는 문제점이 있다.

1 윗글의 내용으로 보아 밑줄 친 ⓐ your special report는 어떤 내용이었겠는가?

① 위험한 원자력 산업을 철저히 규제해야 한다.
② 원자력은 환경에 해로운 영향을 미치지 않는다.
③ 원자력 산업을 장려하고 더욱 발전시켜야 한다.
④ 원자력을 대체할 수 있는 에너지의 개발이 시급하다.
⑤ 원자력 발전소의 안전 상태를 수시로 점검해야 한다.

수능 어법

2 윗글의 밑줄 친 ①~⑤ 중, 어법상 틀린 것은?

서술형

3 〈보기〉에 주어진 단어를 바르게 배열하여 윗글의 요지를 완성하시오.

〈보기〉	for reasons and be stopped economic environmental

The development of nuclear energy should ________________________________.

nuclear power 원자력 **industry** 산업 **publish** 출판하다; *(기사 등을) 게재하다 **go forward** 진행하다, 나아가다 **examine** 조사하다, 검토하다 **power plant** 발전소 **threat** 위협 **deadly** 치명적인 **consumption** 소비 **investment** 투자 **conservation** 보존 **measure** 《*pl.*》 수단, 대책 **insulation** 단열(재) **energy-efficient** 에너지 효율적인 **appliance** 《*pl.*》 가전제품 **renewable** 재생 가능한 **recommendation** 추천 **come up with** …을 생각해내다

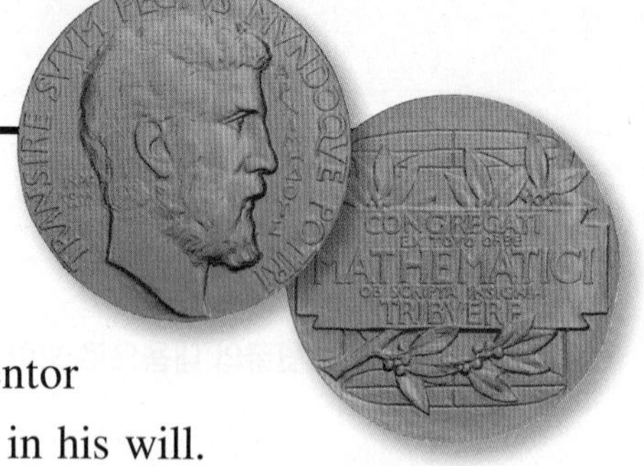

03

노벨상 대신 필즈 메달!

264 words 3'45"

Date:
Time Taken:

Swedish chemist Alfred Nobel, the inventor of dynamite, established the Nobel Prizes in his will. (A) It has been rumored that this was because Nobel and a famous mathematician once fell in love with the same woman, but the truth is that Nobel simply wasn't interested in math. (B) Although he created a prize for a number of different fields, he did not create one for mathematics. (C) Regardless of the reason, the absence of a Nobel Prize for mathematics has inspired the creation of several other awards to serve the same purpose. The most famous of these is the Fields Medal.

Named for John Charles Fields, a Canadian mathematician, the medal was first awarded in 1936. Four years earlier, Fields had died, leaving money in his will to ① establish the award. Along with $15,000, each winning mathematician has the honor of knowing that he or she has ② attained the highest honor in the field of math. The Fields Medal is awarded every four years and is restricted to mathematicians under the age of 40. This is because it is intended to serve as an ③ inspiration to do even greater work in the future. The location of the awarding ceremony varies, as it is held wherever the International Congress of the International Mathematical Union meeting is taking place that year.

Whereas many Nobel Prize winners have been quite famous, few of the people who have received the Fields Medal are well-known, as mathematicians ④ often achieve acclaim outside of their field. But by winning such a ⑤ prestigious award, they are able to enjoy their moment in the spotlight.

필즈 메달 수상을 거부한 수학자, 그리고리 페렐만

러시아의 수학자 그리고리 페렐만(Grigori Perelman, 1966~)은 '밀레니엄 7대 난제' 중 하나인 '푸앵카레의 추측'을 풀어낸 공로로 필즈 메달 수상자로 선정되었지만 시상식에 나타나지 않아 화제를 모았다. '푸앵카레의 추측'은 프랑스 수학자 앙리 푸앵카레가 처음 제시하여 100년 넘게 풀리지 않았던 문제로, 미국 클레이 수학연구소가 문제당 100만 달러의 상금을 내건 일곱 개 난제 중 하나이다. 페렐만은 10년간의 노력 끝에 이를 푸는 데 성공하고서도 유명 학술지가 아닌 인터넷 저널에만 공개하고 러시아로 돌아가 버렸다. 그는 프린스턴, 스탠퍼드 등 미국 유수 대학의 교수 초빙을 거절한 것은 물론, 클레이 수학연구소가 난제 해결에 내건 상금도 거부했다.

정답 및 해설 p.62

1 윗글의 (A) ~ (C)를 글의 흐름에 맞게 배열한 것으로 가장 적절한 것은?

① (A) – (B) – (C) ② (B) – (A) – (C) ③ (B) – (C) – (A)
④ (C) – (A) – (B) ⑤ (C) – (B) – (A)

VOCA

2 윗글의 밑줄 친 ①~⑤ 중, 문맥상 낱말의 쓰임이 적절하지 않은 것은?

3 Fields Medal에 관한 윗글의 내용과 일치하지 않는 것은?

① 캐나다인 수학자 John Charles Fields의 이름을 따서 지어졌다.
② Fields가 사망하고 4년 후에 처음으로 수여되었다.
③ 4년에 한 번 영예로운 수학자에게 수여된다.
④ 수상자들의 나이는 40세 이상으로 제한되어 있다.
⑤ 시상식은 매회 다른 장소에서 개최된다.

서술형

4 주어진 질문에 대한 답을 할 때, 빈칸에 들어갈 알맞은 말을 본문에서 찾아 쓰시오. (4단어)

What is the reason Nobel didn't create a prize for mathematics?
→ It was just because he ________________________________.

chemist 화학자 **will** 의지; *유언장 **mathematician** 수학자 **field** 들판; *분야 **regardless of** …에 상관없이 **absence** 결석; *부재 **inspire** 고무하다, 격려하다 ※ **inspiration** 영감 **attain** 이루다, 획득하다 **restrict** 제한하다, 한정하다 **vary** 다르다; *달라지다 **congress** 회의; *학술 대회 **acclaim** 찬사, 칭찬 **prestigious** 권위 있는, 명성 있는 **spotlight** 스포트라이트; *주목

04

📄107 words ⏱2'00"

Date:

Time Taken:

TRY 수능

무관한 문장

다음 글에서 전체 흐름과 관계 없는 문장은? 모의기출

Companies would like to enhance employee *contentment on the job for several reasons. Job satisfaction increases productivity because happy employees work harder, allowing them to produce more at a lower cost. ① Moreover, in many service organizations, client satisfaction often depends directly on the attitudes of employees, who are the company's face for customers. ② Because people's purchasing patterns are affected by how they feel during the buying experience, happy employees matter. ③ When workers are dissatisfied, their unhappiness makes the customer's experience worse; as a result, consumers buy less, and company performance suffers. ④ In other words, when a product costs more, but is worth it, its value becomes acceptable to the consumer. ⑤ Clearly, it is important for companies (satisfied with, their jobs, makes, to know, what, their employees).

*contentment 만족(감)

유형 *Tip*

step1. **글의 도입부에서 글의 주제를 파악한다.**
글의 도입부를 통해 회사의 입장에서 직원들의 직업 만족도가 중요한 이유에 관한 내용이 향후 전개될 것임을 알 수 있다.

step2. **연결사나 대명사 등의 쓰임에 유의하여 각 문장이 글의 주제와 연관되어 있는지 확인한다.**
①, ②, ③은 직원의 만족도가 고객 경험과 연결되어 있어 회사에 영향을 미친다는 내용이고, ⑤는 회사가 무엇이 직원을 만족시키는지 알아야 한다는 내용이므로 글의 주제와 모두 연관되어 있다.

step3. **글의 흐름과 어울리지 않는 문장을 찾는다.**
제품의 가격이 비싸도 가치가 있으면 소비자가 용인한다는 ④는 직원들의 직업 만족도의 중요성에 대해 서술하고 있는 글의 흐름에 맞지 않는다.

정답 및 해설 p.64

· 변형문제 ·

1 윗글의 제목으로 가장 적절한 것은?

① The Mystery of Consumer Behavior
② Why Employee Satisfaction Matters
③ The Keys to Increasing Job Satisfaction
④ Improving Productivity: Focus on Happy Customers
⑤ A Customer Service Rule Employees Should Stick To

서술형

2 윗글의 괄호 안에 주어진 단어들을 다음 우리말에 맞게 배열하시오.

(회사가) 무엇이 자사의 직원들이 자기 일에 만족하게 하는지를 아는 것(은 중요하다)

→ it is important for companies ______________________________

3 윗글의 내용을 다음과 같이 요약할 때, 빈칸 (A)와 (B)에 들어갈 말로 가장 적절한 것은?

> Increasing employee contentment is important because ____(A)____ employees are likely to work harder and their attitudes toward ____(B)____ affect company performance.

(A)		(B)
① independent	……	co-workers
② diligent	……	productivity
③ happy	……	the company
④ discontented	……	work
⑤ satisfied	……	customers

enhance 높이다, 향상시키다 **employee** 종업원, 고용인 **satisfaction** 만족(감) **productivity** 생산성 ※ **produce** 생산하다 **organization** 조직, 단체 **directly** 곧장, 똑바로 **attitude** 태도 **affect** 영향을 미치다 **matter** 중요하다, 문제되다 **performance** 공연; *실적, 성과 **suffer** 시달리다, 고통받다; *더 나빠지다, 악화되다 **acceptable** 용인되는, 받아들여지는 **문제** **improve** 개선하다, 향상시키다 **stick to** …을 고수하다[지키다] **independent** 독립적인 **discontented** 불만족한, 불만스러워 하는

Review Test

· VOCA ·

A

다음 단어의 영영풀이를 바르게 연결하시오.

1 deadly •	• ⓐ to limit the range of something
2 belongings •	• ⓑ using natural resources carefully not to waste them
3 restrict •	• ⓒ the things that someone owns
4 enhance •	• ⓓ able to cause death or bring fatal consequences
5 conservation •	• ⓔ to improve the quality or value of something

B

괄호 안에서 적절한 단어를 고르시오.

1 Investigators (located / localized) the fault in the plane's engine.

2 The publishing (industry / investment) is struggling to survive in the digital age.

3 Jessica is quite famous in the (plain / field) of psychology.

4 Members of the (association / appreciation) are required to pay an annual fee.

C

문맥상 다음 빈칸에 들어갈 가장 알맞은 단어를 고르시오.

1 Tim studied hard and was admitted to one of the most __________ universities in the country.

① concerned ② dedicated ③ certified ④ generous ⑤ prestigious

2 I covered my left eye so that the doctor could __________ my sight.

① examine ② greet ③ invest ④ publish ⑤ support

3 The movie drew critical __________ at the film festival.

① plan ② aim ③ acclaim ④ consumption ⑤ promise

4 Anyone can take part in the competition __________ of their age or gender.

① because ② endless ③ according ④ regardless ⑤ regarding

· SENTENCE ·

D

다음 문장을 밑줄 친 부분에 유의하여 우리말로 해석하시오.

1 Each group is led through a tunnel by a waitress, who is herself blind, to a table.

▸ ______________________________

2 Nobody will complain about your manners as no one can see you.

▸ ______________________________

3 It's time for the government to come up with ways to end the use of non-renewable energy sources.

▸ ______________________________

4 People's purchasing patterns are affected by how they feel during the buying experience.

▸ ______________________________

E

우리말에 맞게 주어진 단어들을 바르게 배열하여 문장을 완성하시오.

1 그것은 흔히 쓰이는 스위스 속담인 '소의 배 속처럼 어두운'을 나타낸다.

It refers to a common Swiss saying, "(a cow / dark / as / the inside / as / of)."

▸ It refers to a common Swiss saying, "______________________."

2 그것은 미래에 훨씬 더 위대한 일을 할 수 있는 영감으로서 작용하도록 의도된다.

(it / serve / is / to / as / intended) an inspiration to do even greater work in the future.

▸ ______________________ an inspiration to do even greater work in the future.

3 당신이 지지하는 원자력의 추가 개발은 나아가야 할 최선의 길이 아니다.

Further development of nuclear power, which you support, is (the best / go / to / not / way / forward).

▸ Further development of nuclear power, which you support, is ______________ ______________.

BLACK SWAN

05.

블랙 스완(Black Swan)이란?

‘블랙 스완’은 라틴어 표현에서 유래된 것으로, 한 로마 시인이 세상에 존재하지 않는 것을 비유하기 위해 사용한 이래 서구에서 ‘불가능’을 뜻하는 말로 쓰였다. 그러나 17세기에 서오스트레일리아에서 검은 백조(흑고니)가 발견되면서, 이 말은 ‘불가능한 줄 알았던 일이 실제로 일어나는 것’을 뜻하게 되었다.

경제 분야에서 이 말을 유행시킨 것은 나심 니콜라스 탈레브(Nassim Nicholas Taleb)라는 투자가로, 그는 2001년 출간 저서 『행운에 속지 마라(Fooled By Randomness)』에서 이 용어를 사용하였다. ‘불가능해 보였지만 실제로 발생한 경제적 위기’들의 사례로 탈레브는 블랙 먼데이(1987년 뉴욕 월 스트리트의 주가 폭락 사태), 2001년 9·11 테러, 2007년에 발생한 서브프라임 모기지 사태(미국 부동산 거품이 꺼지면서 금융 기관들이 주택담보 대출금을 회수하지 못해 잇따라 파산하여, 국제 금융 시장에 위기를 가져왔던 사태) 등을 들었다. 따라서 예기치 못한 위기에 대처할 수 있도록 준비해야 한다는 것이 그의 주장이다.

SECTION 10

01

224 words 3'20"

Date:

Time Taken:

알프스의 노스페이스

The 1,800-meter tall north face of the Eiger, a mountain in the Swiss Alps, is known as one of the most difficult in the world to climb; more than 50 people have lost their lives attempting to do so since 1935. Despite the extreme dangers, it is considered ⓐ one of the greatest challenges for alpine mountaineers.

In 1935, the first pair of climbers to attempt to reach its peak froze to death at an altitude of 3,000 meters. The next year, four more climbers died after bad weather forced them to turn back. Year after year, similar tragedies continued to take the lives of unfortunate climbers. Nevertheless, there were always more brave climbers willing to test themselves by attempting to ⓑ scale the north face.

There are several reasons that the Eiger is so difficult for climbers to conquer. It is extremely steep and full of loose stones that can easily break off and fall on climbers. At higher altitudes, *avalanches present a similar danger. The weather can also be a serious problem; the Eiger is known for its storms, which are both terrible and unpredictable. Climbers who are able to somehow overcome all of these obstacles and reach the top all make the same vow: they will never try to do it again. Defeating the Eiger is truly a once in a lifetime experience.

*avalanche 눈사태, (산)사태

정답 및 해설 p.66

1 윗글의 내용과 일치하지 않는 것은?

① Eiger의 북쪽 면은 높이가 1,800미터이다.
② 1935년 이래로 50명 이상이 Eiger 등반 중에 사망했다.
③ 최초로 Eiger 정상 등반을 시도했던 등반가 두 명은 동사했다.
④ Eiger는 경사가 심하게 가파르고 낙석의 위험이 있다.
⑤ Eiger는 폭풍이 심하지만 예측 가능하다.

서술형

2 다음은 윗글의 밑줄 친 ⓐ one of the greatest challenges가 의미하는 바를 나타낸 것이다. 빈칸에 들어갈 알맞은 말을 본문에서 찾아 쓰시오.

to __________ the north face of the __________

VOCA

3 윗글의 밑줄 친 ⓑ scale의 의미로 가장 적절한 것은?

① to move around aimlessly
② to develop in a positive way
③ to measure the weight of something
④ to reach the highest point of something
⑤ to keep or maintain in unaltered condition

아이거 산 알프스 산맥에 자리 잡은 아이거 산에는 수많은 등반 루트가 개척되어 있으나, 아이거의 북벽을 등반하는 것은 여전히 많은 등반가들 사이에서 거의 불가능하다고 여겨진다. 아이거의 북벽은 마터호른 산, 그랑드조라스 산의 북벽과 함께 알프스의 3대 북벽으로 불리며, 등반 역사상 사망 사고가 가장 많이 발생한 곳 중 하나로 악명이 높기도 하다.

attempt 시도하다 **alpine** 알프스의 **mountaineer** 등산가 **peak** 절정; *봉우리, 정상 **freeze to death** 얼어 죽다 **altitude** (해발) 고도 **tragedy** 비극(적인 사건) **scale** (높고 가파른 곳을) 오르다 **conquer** 정복하다 **steep** 가파른, 경사가 급한 **loose** (떨어질 것처럼) 헐거운 **unpredictable** 예측할 수 없는 **obstacle** 장애(물) **vow** 맹세, 서약 **defeat** 패배시키다, 이기다 **once in a lifetime** 평생 단 한 번뿐인
문제 **aimlessly** 목적 없이 **unaltered** 변하지 않은

02

세 번째 선택사항의 비밀!

192 words 2'50"

Date:

Time Taken:

Imagine you're making dinner plans with a friend. There's a restaurant with delicious food that you want to go to. But it takes 15 minutes to walk there, and you're quite hungry. Your friend suggests another restaurant. Its food is average, but it's right across the street. You might have a very hard time deciding between these two options. Both have a good point and a bad point. But then your friend suggests a third place. It also has great food, but it's a 20-minute subway ride away. Suddenly, your decision is clear. A 15-minute walk doesn't sound so bad! So you decide to go to the first place.

(happened, what, is called, the "decoy effect", just) in marketing. When consumers need to decide between two products, marketers will sometimes introduce an undesirable third option. The purpose of this third option is simply to make one of the two original choices ____________ ____________. For example, if a company's product's weak point is its high price, it might introduce a third "decoy" product with an even higher price. This will make the first product seem like a smarter choice to consumers.

닻 내림 효과 Anchoring Effect 미끼 효과와 함께 가격 정책과 관련해 마케팅에서 자주 사용되는 기법이다. 배가 닻을 내리면 움직이지 않듯이, 최초에 제시된 숫자가 기준점 역할을 하여 그 이후의 판단에 영향을 미치는 현상을 가리킨다. 예를 들어, 소비자는 마트에서 파는 할인 상품에 혹하기 쉬운데, 할인 전 가격이 기준점이 되어 상대적으로 더 싸 보이기 때문이다. 비즈니스 협상 시에도 협상 초반에 본인이 원하는 것보다 높은 조건을 제시하는 것이 유리한데, 그 이유는 처음에 제시한 조건이 기준점이 되어 협상 시 본인이 원하는 조건으로 타협을 이룰 가능성이 높기 때문이다.

정답 및 해설 p.67

서술형

1

윗글의 괄호 안에 주어진 단어들을 다음 우리말에 맞게 배열하시오.

방금 일어난 일은 (마케팅에서) '미끼 효과'라고 불린다.

→ ________________________________ in marketing.

2

윗글의 빈칸에 들어갈 말로 가장 적절한 것은?

① seem to be popular
② become part of a set
③ act as a decoy product
④ improve its minor flaws
⑤ look better in comparison

3

윗글의 내용을 한 문장으로 요약하고자 한다. 빈칸 (A)와 (B)에 들어갈 말로 가장 적절한 것은?

> The decoy effect occurs when the ___(A)___ of a third option makes one of the previous options ___(B)___.

	(A)		(B)
①	reduction	……	less popular
②	elimination	……	more expensive
③	introduction	……	more desirable
④	adoption	……	less common
⑤	promotion	……	more affordable

average 보통의 **option** 선택사항 **decoy** 유인하는 장치, 미끼 **undesirable** 바람직하지 않은, 달갑지 않은(↔ desirable 바람직한, 호감 가는) **weak point** 약점 **문제** **minor** 작은, 가벼운 **flaw** 결함 **in comparison** 비교해 보면 **previous** 이전의 **reduction** 감소 **elimination** 제거 **adoption** 채택 **affordable** (가격이) 알맞은

03

245 words 3'35"

Date:

Time Taken:

May 24, 2018

(A)

It's been more than 40 years since the Beatles, one of the most popular rock bands ever, broke up. But this amazing band continues to have an effect on younger generations. Yesterday, the John Lennon Educational Tour Bus made a stop at Eastview High School.

John Lennon, of course, was one of the greatest rock musicians of all time. Tragically, he was killed in 1980. Eighteen years later, the John Lennon Educational Tour Bus was established to continue working towards the musician's dream of teaching youngsters to express themselves through music.

A handful of lucky Eastview High School students were selected to attend a special lesson given on the bus, which is really a mobile recording studio. The topic of the lesson was how to mix vocals with drums and horns. The students met with a team of producers and engineers who showed them not only how to compose an original song but also how to record and produce one.

Since its founding, the Lennon Bus has taught similar lessons to millions of young students, targeting schools with music programs that are struggling due to budget cuts. The head of the Lennon Bus program stressed that even though many of the students were born after John Lennon's death, they still love his legendary music.

Eastview High School senior Ryan Castleton summed up his experience this way: "It gave me a lot of confidence in my musical ability. And it was a lot of fun, too!"

1 윗글의 빈칸 (A)에 들어갈 기사 제목으로 알맞은 것은?

① John Lennon's Beloved Bus
② The Lennon Bus Comes to Town
③ Stars Come Together on the Lennon Bus
④ John Lennon and His High School Memories
⑤ The Reality of High School Music Education

2 윗글의 내용과 일치하지 않는 것은?

① Beatles가 해체한 지 40년이 넘었다.
② The Lennon Bus는 John Lennon의 사망 이후 설립되었다.
③ The Lennon Bus는 전문적인 음악인을 대상으로 한다.
④ The Lennon Bus 안에서는 다양한 음악 관련 체험을 할 수 있다.
⑤ John Lennon이 사망한 후에 태어난 학생들도 그의 음악을 잘 알고 있다.

서술형

3 윗글의 내용과 일치하도록 빈칸에 알맞은 말을 본문에서 찾아 쓰시오.

The students who attended a lesson on the __________ learned about how to __________, __________, and produce music.

존 레논 공항 영국에서 존 레논의 영향력은 가히 어마어마하다. 2002년에 영국의 리버풀 공항은 비틀즈의 전 멤버이자 영국의 상징으로 칭송받는 존 레논의 이름을 따서 공항의 이름을 바꿨는데, 이는 존 레논이 리버풀 태생인 까닭이다. 공항 내에는 존 레논의 동상이 세워져 있고, 그의 곡 'Imagine'의 가사 중 일부인 'above us only sky'를 로고로 사용하고 있다.

break up 헤어지다; *(단체가) 해체하다 **have an effect on** …에 영향을 미치다 **generation** 세대 **establish** 설립하다, 개설하다 **youngster** 청소년 **a handful of** 한줌의; *소수의 **mobile** 이동하는, 이동식의 **mix** 믹싱 녹음하다 **vocal** 《*pl.*》 (음악에서의) 보컬, 노래 부분 **compose** 구성하다; *작곡하다 **original** 본래의; *독창적인 **target** 목표로 삼다; *대상으로 삼다 **struggle** 분투[고투]하다; *힘겹게 나아가다 **budget cut** 예산 삭감

04

140 words 2'30"

Date:

Time Taken:

TRY 수능

빈칸 추론

다음 빈칸에 들어갈 말로 가장 적절한 것을 고르시오. 모의기출

It's (A) [hard enough / enough hard] to stick with goals you want to accomplish, but sometimes we make goals we're not even thrilled about in the first place. (①) We set resolutions based on what we're supposed to do, or what others think we're supposed to do, rather than what really matters to us. (②) For example, reading more is a good habit, but if you're only doing it because you feel like that's (B) [which / what] you're supposed to do, not because you actually want to learn more, you're going to have a hard time reaching the goal. (③) Instead, make goals based on ______________________. (④) Now, this isn't to say you should read less. (⑤) The idea is to first consider what matters to you, then figure out what you need to do (C) [to get / getting] there.

① your moral duty
② a strict deadline
③ your own values
④ parental guidance
⑤ job market trends

유형 *Tip*

step1. 빈칸에 들어갈 내용은 주로 글의 주제 및 요지에 관련되므로, 전체 글의 주제 및 요지를 파악한다.
자신에게 중요한 것을 고려해 목표를 세워야 한다고 주장하는 글이다.

step2. 빈칸 주변의 어구들이 정답을 찾는 데 단서가 되는 경우가 많다.
'if you're only doing it because you feel like ... reaching the goal'을 통해, 의무감 때문에 무언가를 하는 것보다는 자신이 정말 하고 싶어서 하는 것이 목표 달성에 있어 중요하다는 요지가 드러난다.

step3. 선택한 정답을 빈칸에 넣어 글의 흐름이 자연스러운지 확인한다.
빈칸 앞뒤의 내용을 통해, 자신만의 가치에 기초해 목표를 세워야 한다는 내용이 되어야 함을 유추할 수 있다.

· 변형문제 ·

1 윗글의 요지로 가장 적절한 것은?

① 스스로에게 중요한 것을 목표로 삼아라.
② 목표는 최대한 구체적으로 세워야 한다.
③ 실현 가능한 목표를 세우는 것이 바람직하다.
④ 항상 다른 사람의 기대에 부응할 필요는 없다.
⑤ 올바른 독서 습관을 기르려면 많이 읽어야 한다.

2 윗글의 흐름으로 보아, 주어진 문장이 들어가기에 가장 적절한 곳은?

This makes it nearly impossible to stick to the goal.

수능어법

3 윗글의 (A), (B), (C)의 각 네모 안에서 어법에 맞는 표현으로 가장 적절한 것은?

	(A)		(B)		(C)
①	hard enough	……	which	……	to get
②	hard enough	……	what	……	getting
③	hard enough	……	what	……	to get
④	enough hard	……	which	……	to get
⑤	enough hard	……	what	……	getting

stick with …을 계속하다 **accomplish** 완수하다, 성취하다 **thrilled** 황홀해 하는, 아주 신이 난 **in the first place** 우선, 먼저 **resolution** 다짐[결심] **rather than** … 보다는[대신에] **matter** 중요하다, 문제되다 **consider** 고려하다 **figure out** 이해하다, 알아내다 **문제** **deadline** 기한, 마감 시간 **guidance** 지도, 안내

Review Test

• VOCA •

A

다음 단어의 영영풀이를 바르게 연결하시오.

1 attempt •	• ⓐ the top of a mountain
2 tragedy •	• ⓑ to try to do something
3 obstacle •	• ⓒ something that stands in the way of progress
4 mobile •	• ⓓ an event that causes great sadness
5 peak •	• ⓔ able to move from one place to another

B

괄호 안에서 적절한 단어를 고르시오.

1 Some doctors are concerned about the (unaltered / undesirable) effects that the overuse of electronic devices has on our health.

2 The magazine (includes / targets) single women in their twenties and early thirties.

3 He made a firm (resolution / reflection) to save half of his salary.

4 This story encouraged people to overcome their difficulties and (accompany / accomplish) their goals.

C

문맥상 다음 빈칸에 들어갈 가장 알맞은 단어를 고르시오.

1 Korea __________ Japan in the soccer game last Wednesday.

① struggled ② revealed ③ defeated ④ overlooked ⑤ compared

2 The __________ American teenager sends 5,000 text messages a month.

① previous ② average ③ steep ④ original ⑤ affordable

3 To legally __________ our company, we need to get permits from the city.

① require ② affect ③ avoid ④ promise ⑤ establish

4 The customer returned the suit because it had a(n) __________ in it.

① flaw ② decoy ③ option ④ guidance ⑤ scale

정답 및 해설 p.72

· SENTENCE ·

D

다음 문장을 밑줄 친 부분에 유의하여 우리말로 해석하시오.

1 There are several reasons that the Eiger is <u>so difficult for climbers to conquer</u>.

▸ ____________________

2 You might <u>have a very hard time deciding</u> between these two options.

▸ ____________________

3 The topic of the lesson was <u>how to mix vocals with drums and horns</u>.

▸ ____________________

4 The idea is to consider <u>what matters to you</u>, then figure out <u>what you need to do</u> to get there.

▸ ____________________

E

우리말에 맞게 주어진 단어들을 바르게 배열하여 문장을 완성하시오.

1 아이거 산은 그곳의 폭풍으로 유명한데, 그것은 끔찍하면서도 예측 불가능하다.

(is / The Eiger / known / its storms / for), which are both terrible and unpredictable.

▸ ____________________, which are both terrible and unpredictable.

2 그들은 버스에서 진행되는 특별 수업에 참여했는데, 그 버스는 이동식 녹음실이다.

They (on the bus / a special lesson / attended / given), which is a mobile recording studio.

▸ They ____________________, which is a mobile recording studio.

3 여러분은 단지 그것이 여러분이 해야 하는 것이라고 느끼기 때문에 그것을 하고 있다.

You're only doing it because you feel like that's (to / you're / what / do / supposed).

▸ You're only doing it because you feel like that's ____________________.

LIBRARIES AROUND THE WORLD

Abbey Library of Saint Gall

긴 역사와 경건한 아름다움을 자랑하는, 장크트갈렌 수도원 도서관

스위스 북동부의 도시 장크트갈렌에는 스위스에서 가장 오래된 도서관이자, 중세학과 관련해 세계적으로 중요한 도서관이 있다. 바로 7세기경에 설립된 장크트갈렌 수도원 부속 도서관이다.

중세 시대에 장크트갈렌 수도원은 청빈, 정결, 복종을 계율로 삼는 베네딕트 파(派)에 속해 있었다. 매일 일정 시간 책을 읽어야 하는 수도사의 엄격한 계율 때문에 수도원 도서관은 책을 점점 더 많이 모으게 되었고, 수도사들은 필사본을 점점 더 많이 만들게 되었다. 이러한 역사로 인해 이 도서관은 오늘날 중세를 연구하는 역사학자들에게 소중한 자료를 제공하고 있다. 중세 수도사들이 직접 제작한 8~15세기의 필사본을 가장 많이 보유한 것으로 알려져 있고, 그 수는 무려 2,100여권에 달한다. 또한 16만 권의 장서, 1500년 이전에 인쇄된 책의 초기 간행본 1,600여 점을 소장하고 있다.

이 도서관은 역사적으로 중요한 도서 자료뿐 아니라, 내부 건축 양식으로도 그 가치를 인정받고 있다. 도서관 내부는 가장 뛰어난 바로크 양식 공간으로 꼽힌다. 긴 역사와 경건한 아름다움을 자랑하는 장크트갈렌 수도원 부속 도서관은 장크트갈렌 수도원과 함께 1983년에 유네스코 세계문화유산으로 지정되었다.

SECTION 11

01 손가락과 유리잔 사이

203 words 3'10"

Date:

Time Taken:

Glass is a slippery material, so why doesn't it slip right through our fingers when we hold it? It is partly due to the friction between molecules in the glass and molecules in our skin. (the glass, of, touching, the area, skin, the greater), the stronger the friction. Researchers recently discovered that our fingers actually adapt to slippery materials by increasing the contact area. Surprisingly, they do this by using sweat.

The adaptation involves small changes on the outer layer of our skin, where our fingerprints are located. The *ridges of our fingerprints help us hold onto rough materials, but they can't help with smooth materials like glass. So when our body senses a smooth material, it releases a little bit of sweat onto the skin. The sweat causes the ridges to flatten, which allows more skin to touch the glass and increases the amount of friction. As a result, we can easily keep a firm grip on the glass.

Scientists researching this unusual process have found that it doesn't happen immediately. Sometimes it takes only a few seconds to start and other times it can take as long as 20 seconds, depending on the individual being tested and the weight of the object.

*ridge 길쭉하게 솟은[돋은] 부분

땀의 기능 땀의 대표적인 기능은 바로 체온조절이다. 더운 여름 인체는 땀을 흘림으로써 체온을 일정하게 유지하고 신체 기관들이 정상적인 기능을 유지토록 한다. 땀의 또 다른 흥미로운 기능은 감정을 반영한다는 점이다. 특히 손바닥과 발바닥에 있는 땀샘들은 불안이나 초조, 흥분과 같은 감정에 반응해 땀을 만들어낸다. 중요한 시험을 앞두고 있거나, 좋아하는 이에게 고백하려는 순간 손에 땀이 나는 경험을 해본 적이 있을 것이다. 이렇게 감정으로 인해 나는 땀의 특성을 이용해 거짓말 탐지기를 만들기도 하는데, 용의자가 심리적 불안을 느껴 손과 발에서 땀이 나면 전기 전도성이 높아지는 점을 이용하는 것이다.

정답 및 해설 p.73

1 윗글의 주제로 가장 적절한 것은?

① the sensory cells of our fingers
② the definition of friction and its role
③ why sweat is important for our bodies
④ different molecules in various materials
⑤ how our fingers hold on to slippery things

서술형

2 윗글의 괄호 안에 주어진 단어들을 다음 우리말에 맞게 배열하시오.

유리잔에 닿는 피부의 면적이 더 커질수록, (마찰도 더 강해진다).

→ ______________________________, the stronger the friction.

3 윗글의 내용과 일치하면 T에, 일치하지 않으면 F에 표시하시오.

	T	F
(1) The friction between the molecules of glass and those of our fingers helps us to hold the glass.	□	□
(2) The ridges of our fingerprints flatten due to sweat when we're holding glass.	□	□
(3) Our body immediately produces sweat on our fingers when it feels a slippery material.	□	□

slippery 미끄러운 ※ **slip** 미끄러지다 **material** 물질, 재료 **friction** 마찰 **molecule** 분자 **adapt** 맞추다; *적응하다 ※ **adaptation** 적응 **contact** 접촉 **sweat** 땀 **involve** 수반하다 **outer** 외부의, 바깥의 **fingerprint** 지문 **locate** 두다, 설치하다 **rough** 거친 **release** 방출하다 **flatten** 납작[반반]해지다; 납작하게[반반하게] 만들다 **firm** 단단한, 견고한 **grip** 꽉 붙잡음 **unusual** 특이한 **process** 과정 **immediately** 즉시, 즉각 **individual** 개인 **문제** **sensory cell** 감각 세포 **definition** 정의

02

왜 하필 녹색일까?

165 words 2'45"

Date:

Time Taken:

Why do doctors wear green gowns instead of white coats during surgery? There is actually a scientific reason.

Our eyes' retina is made up of two types of receptor cells — *rods and *cones. Rods are sensitive to weak light and can sense low levels of light. Cones are sensitive to stronger light and can interpret color. But cones get fatigued from looking at strong colors for a long time. When fatigued cones see a white surface, they are left with an afterimage. An afterimage refers to the complementary color that you sometimes see after you look away from a strong color.

Medical surgeries are normally accompanied by bleeding. (A) When doctors look at red blood for a long time, their cones become fatigued. (B) This afterimage confuses the doctors' vision and lowers their concentration. (C) So if they look at other doctors wearing white coats, they see a green afterimage, as green is the complementary color of red. Thus, to prevent this, doctors wear green gowns during surgery.

*rods 간상체
*cones 추상체

1 윗글의 제목으로 가장 적절한 것은?

① What Is an Afterimage?
② Symbolic Use of Colors
③ How Our Eyes See Colors
④ How to Prevent Tired Eyes
⑤ The Science behind Doctor's Gowns

2 윗글의 (A)~(C)를 글의 흐름에 맞게 배열한 것으로 가장 적절한 것은?

① (A) – (B) – (C)　② (A) – (C) – (B)　③ (B) – (C) – (A)
④ (C) – (A) – (B)　⑤ (C) – (B) – (A)

서술형
3 윗글의 내용과 일치하도록 빈칸에 알맞은 말을 본문에서 찾아 쓰시오.

If doctors wear white coats during surgery, their fatigued cones can be left with an afterimage that is __________, the complementary color of __________.

의사들의 가운에 숨겨진 과학

의사들의 가운은 왜 하얀색일까? 그것은 최고의 위생 상태를 유지하기 위해서이다. 흰색은 얼룩이나 때가 묻으면 눈에 잘 띄는 색이므로, 청결 유지가 필수인 의사의 옷에 사용된다. 그런데 최근에는 소매가 긴 가운이 병원균을 옮겨 질병을 전염시킬 위험이 있다고 여겨져서 사라지고 있는 추세이다. 영국에서는 정부가 아예 의사의 가운 착용을 금지했고, 우리나라에서도 환자와 접촉 빈도가 상대적으로 높은 대형 병원을 중심으로 의사들이 소매와 밑단이 짧은 형태의 새로운 가운을 착용하기 시작했다. 새로운 의사 복장은 의사가 환자를 진료할 때 환자의 상처 부위에 잘 닿지 않기 때문에 질병을 전염시킬 위험이 낮다.

surgery 수술　**retina** 망막　**receptor** 수용체　**sensitive** 민감한　**sense** 감지하다　**interpret** 해석하다, 이해하다　**fatigued** 지친, 피곤한　**afterimage** 잔상　**complementary color** 보색　**accompany** …을 수반하다, 동반하다　**bleeding** 출혈　**vision** 시력; *시야　**concentration** 집중(력)　**prevent** 예방하다, 방지하다　**문제**　**symbolic** 상징적인

03

똑똑해지는 사람들

264 words 3'45"

Date:

Time Taken:

Did you know that you're probably smarter than your parents? That's because intelligence levels have been increasing from one generation to the next. New Zealand political scientist James R. Flynn discovered this surprising fact through an analysis of data on IQ scores. It showed that they go up on average by three points per decade. Known as the "Flynn effect," this interesting phenomenon has left many wondering what its causes might be.

A longer period of schooling is one important reason put forward, and improved nutrition is another. ______(A)______, neither reason has compelling support. (①) For instance, Flynn actually discovered that the IQ scores of American children rose even when time spent in school stayed constant. (②) Moreover, studies show that intellectual impairment is only caused by significant malnutrition. (③) A more general explanation may be the increased complexity of society. (④) The increased use of computers also probably helps to boost their logical thinking and intellectual creativity. (⑤) ______(B)______, new gadgets they're using — such as smartphones — demand more abstract reasoning, which their parents often lack. It seems that the increasing sophistication of modern life may stimulate a more complex mind.

There is, at the moment, no clear understanding of what exactly is boosting intelligence. Although it is still uncertain, it is likely that all of these factors combine and interact to make each generation smarter than the last. Perhaps we will need to wait a few generations to find individuals who are smart enough to work out this puzzle precisely!

서술형

1 다음은 윗글의 밑줄 친 this surprising fact가 의미하는 바를 나타낸 것이다. 빈칸에 들어갈 알맞은 말을 본문에서 찾아 쓰시오.

__________ __________ have been __________ in each generation.

2 윗글의 빈칸 (A)와 (B)에 들어갈 말로 가장 적절한 것은?

(A)		(B)	(A)		(B)
① As a result	……	Moreover	② However	……	In the end
③ However	……	What's more	④ For instance	……	In the end
⑤ For instance	……	Moreover			

3 윗글의 흐름으로 보아, 주어진 문장이 들어가기에 가장 적절한 곳은?

> These days, children are provided with a huge amount of information and are facing more complex problems.

4 윗글에서 플린 효과의 원인으로 언급되지 않은 것은?

① extended schooling
② enhanced nutrition
③ complex education
④ increased computer use
⑤ using new gadgets

디지털 치매 Digital Dementia 디지털 치매란 스마트폰이나 컴퓨터 등의 디지털 기기에 과도한 의존이 인간의 두뇌 기능 중 인식, 계산, 암기력 등의 능력을 저하시키는 현상을 말한다. 예를 들어, 휴대전화에 저장된 주소록이 없으면 전화번호를 외우지 못해 전화를 걸지 못한다거나, 네비게이션이 없으면 전에 갔던 곳도 찾아가지 못하는 현상 등을 들 수 있다.

political scientist 정치학자 **analysis** 분석 **phenomenon** 현상 **put forward** (의견을) 내다, 제기하다 **nutrition** 영양(↔ malnutrition 영양 실조(증)) **compelling** 흥미를 돋우는; *설득력 있는 **constant** 끊임없는; *변함없는 **impairment** 장애 **significant** 상당한, 현저한 **boost** 신장시키다, 북돋우다 **gadget** 장치, 기계 **abstract** 추상적인, 관념적인 **sophistication** 세련; *복잡화, 정교화 **stimulate** 자극[격려]하다, 활발하게 하다 **work out** …을 해결하다[(답을) 알아내다] **문제** **extended** 길어진, 늘어난 **enhanced** 증대한, 향상된

04

148 words 2'30"

Date:

Time Taken:

TRY 수능

도표

다음 도표의 내용과 일치하지 않는 것은? [모의기출]

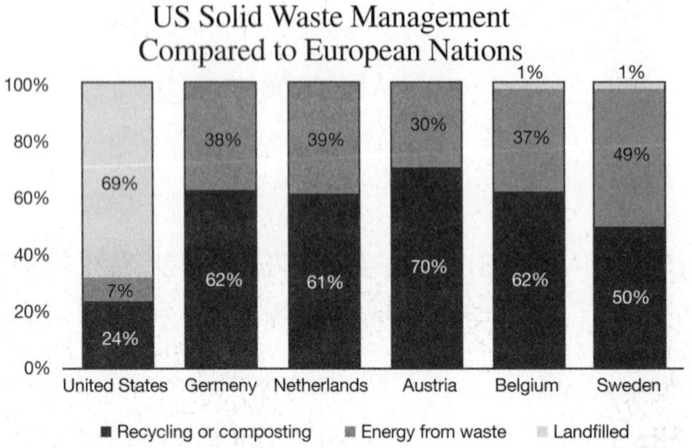

The above graph shows how the United States (A) [managed / managing] solid waste compared to five European nations in 2011. ① The United States had lower percentages of "Recycling or *composting" and "Energy from waste," and a higher percentage of "Landfilled" than the five European nations. ② Burying solid waste in landfills was the most (B) [common / commonly] used solid waste management technique in the United States, accounting for 69 percent of total solid waste disposal. ③ On the other hand, "Landfilled" took up zero (or statistically insignificant) percent in Germany, the Netherlands and Austria, and just 1 percent in Belgium and Sweden respectively. ④ Among the five European nations, Austria recorded the lowest percentage of "Energy from waste," which was more than five times (C) [that / those] of the United States. ⑤ The United States recycled or composted about a quarter of its total solid waste, but Sweden recycled or composted half of its total solid waste.

*composting 퇴비화

유형 *Tip*

step1. **도표의 제목을 보고 무엇에 관한 내용인지 파악한다.**
미국과 유럽 5개국의 고형 폐기물 처리 방식에 관한 것임을 알 수 있다.

step2. **도표에 나타난 특징적인 수치, 증감 추이 등에 주목한다.**
미국은 유럽 5개국 대비 매립 방식 비중이 가장 높고, 폐기물 에너지화 비중은 가장 낮으며, 전체 고형 폐기물의 약 4분의 1을 재활용하거나 퇴비화했다.

step3. **선택지의 순서대로 도표의 내용과 대조하며 내용 일치 여부를 판단한다.**
오스트리아의 폐기물 에너지화 비중은 30%이고, 미국은 7%이다.

정답 및 해설 p.77

· 변형문제 ·

수능어법

1 윗글의 (A), (B), (C)의 각 네모 안에서 어법에 맞는 표현으로 가장 적절한 것은?

	(A)		(B)		(C)
①	managed	......	common	......	that
②	managed	......	commonly	......	that
③	managed	......	common	......	those
④	managing	......	commonly	......	that
⑤	managing	......	commonly	......	those

VOCA

2 윗글의 밑줄 친 accounting for의 의미로 가장 적절한 것은?

① thinking of as
② saying where people are
③ giving an explanation
④ being the cause of something
⑤ representing a certain amount

서술형

3 윗글의 내용과 일치하도록 빈칸에 알맞은 말을 본문에서 찾아 쓰시오.

In 2011, the European countries in the chart had the highest percentage of "__________ __________ __________" in their waste management, while the U.S. used the solid waste management technique of burying it in __________ the most.

manage 처리하다 ※ **management** 처리 **solid** 고체의 **waste** 폐기물 **recycling** 재활용 ※ **recycle** 재활용하다 **bury** (땅 속에) 묻다 **landfill** 쓰레기 매립지 **commonly** 흔히, 보통 **technique** 기법, 기술 **disposal** 처리 **take up** …을 차지하다 **respectively** 각각 **문제** **think of A as B** A를 B로 생각하다[여기다] **explanation** 해명, 설명

Review Test

· VOCA ·

A

다음 단어의 영영풀이를 바르게 연결하시오.

1 grip · · ⓐ the act of focusing one's thoughts

2 adaptation · · ⓑ a state where a person's abilities are reduced or weakened

3 concentration · · ⓒ not physical or concrete

4 abstract · · ⓓ the act of changing your behavior to make it suitable for a new situation

5 impairment · · ⓔ a strong, firm hold on something

B

괄호 안에서 적절한 단어를 고르시오.

1 This plant is (sensitive / sensory) to temperature change.

2 The restaurant has (extended / expected) hours during the New Year holidays.

3 Children under seven must be (accomplished / accompanied) by an adult.

4 Economic growth tends to (accumulate / stimulate) energy consumption.

C

문맥상 다음 빈칸에 들어갈 가장 알맞은 단어를 고르시오.

1 The launch of a new product line helped the company __________ sales.

① decline ② reach ③ invest ④ imitate ⑤ boost

2 It can be difficult to __________ the meaning of your pet's behavior.

① criticize ② utilize ③ interpret ④ deny ⑤ release

3 After a night shift, he was so __________ that he couldn't concentrate on the movie.

① constant ② enhanced ③ located ④ fatigued ⑤ satisfied

4 Using a straightening iron, she was able to __________ her curly hair.

① sense ② cure ③ recycle ④ prevent ⑤ flatten

정답 및 해설 p.78

· SENTENCE ·

D

다음 문장을 밑줄 친 부분에 유의하여 우리말로 해석하시오.

1 The greater the area of skin touching the glass, the stronger the friction.

▸ ______________________________

2 It is likely that all of these factors interact to make each generation smarter than the last.

▸ ______________________________

3 Burying solid waste in landfills was the most commonly used solid waste management technique in the United States.

▸ ______________________________

4 That's because intelligence levels have been increasing from one generation to the next.

▸ ______________________________

E

우리말에 맞게 주어진 단어들을 바르게 배열하여 문장을 완성하시오.

1 우리는 이 수수께끼를 정확하게 풀어낼 만큼 충분히 똑똑한 사람들을 찾을 것이다.

We will find individuals (are / who / work out / enough / smart / to) this puzzle precisely.

▸ We will find individuals ______________________ this puzzle precisely.

2 '플린 효과'로 알려진 이 흥미로운 현상은 많은 이들에게 그것의 원인들이 무엇인지를 궁금하게 했다.

Known as the "Flynn effect," this interesting phenomenon has left many (be / what / causes / its / wondering / might).

▸ Known as the "Flynn effect," this interesting phenomenon has left many ______________________.

3 정확히 무엇이 지능을 향상시키는지에 관한 확실한 이해는 없다.

(no / there / clear / is / understanding) of what exactly is boosting intelligence.

▸ ______________________ of what exactly is boosting intelligence.

Talk Like an Economist

LONG TAIL THEORY

06.

롱테일 법칙 (Long Tail Theory) 이란?

'롱테일 법칙(long tail theory)'이란 80%의 사소한 다수가 20%의 핵심 소수보다 뛰어난 가치를 창출한다는 이론이다. 도표의 가로축에 상품을 많이 팔리는 순서대로 두고, 각 제품의 판매량을 세로축에 표시하면, 적게 팔리는 상품들의 판매량을 나타내는 선은 마치 공룡의 긴 꼬리(long tail)처럼 도표의 오른쪽 아래에 낮고 길게 이어진다. 롱테일 법칙이라는 용어는 이 긴 꼬리에 해당하는 상품들의 총 판매량이 많이 팔리는 상품의 판매량을 압도한다는 뜻에서 지어졌다. 한 예로 온라인 서점 아마존닷컴의 총 판매량 중 절반 이상은 오프라인 서점에서는 진열하지도 않는, 이른바 '팔리지 않는 책'들이 차지한다. 롱테일 법칙은 인터넷의 발달과 관련이 있는 것으로 분석된다. 인터넷상에서는 전시 공간의 제약이 없기 때문에 비주류 상품들까지도 소비자에게 소개될 수 있다. 따라서 예전에는 소비자의 눈에 띄지 않았던 다수의 제품들이 소수의 인기 제품들보다 잘 팔리는 현상이 나타나게 된 것이다.

SECTION 12

01

같은 사람이 아니라고?

162 words 2'35"

Date:

Time Taken:

While walking down the street, a woman is approached by a stranger. He asks for directions, and they start to have a conversation. Suddenly, two men carrying a large piece of wood walk between them. During the interruption, the stranger walks away and is replaced by a different man. After the wood is gone, he continues the conversation. What just happened? Well, the two men were conducting a scientific experiment. And here's the amazing part — the woman didn't even notice that the person she was talking to had changed! (①) This phenomenon is known as "change blindness." (②) In certain situations, people don't notice changes however large they are. (③) The reason is that it is impossible for the brain to process every single piece of information it detects. (④) Therefore, it must choose what to focus on. (⑤) In other words, when changes occur in things we aren't focusing on, we tend not to notice them!

선택맹 선택맹은 자신이 선택한 것의 결과가 바뀌더라도 이를 인식하지 못하는 상태를 말한다. 한 연구에서 연구원들은 남성 실험 참가자들에게 두 여성의 사진을 보여주고, 어떤 여성이 더 매력적인지 선택하게 했다. 참가자들이 사진을 선택한 후, 연구원들은 선택된 사진을 다른 사진과 몰래 교체한 뒤 참가자들에게 그들이 선택한 여성이 더 매력적인 이유를 설명해 줄 것을 요청했다. 이 과정에서 사진이 바뀌었다는 사실을 알아챈 사람은 30% 미만에 불과했다고 한다.

정답 및 해설 p.79

1 윗글의 제목으로 가장 적절한 것은?

① How the Brain Decides What to Focus on
② New Ways to Look at Things around You
③ Changes: Why We Don't Always See Them
④ Paying Attention Is Easier Than You Think
⑤ The Unexpected Results of Helping a Stranger

2 윗글의 흐름으로 보아, 주어진 문장이 들어가기에 가장 적절한 곳은?

As a result, a lot of information gets passed by.

서술형

3 윗글의 내용을 다음과 같이 요약할 때, 빈칸에 알맞은 말을 본문에서 찾아 쓰시오.

People can't notice every __________ because the brain can't __________ all the __________ it detects.

approach 다가가다 **interruption** 중단, 방해 **replace** 대체하다 **conduct** (특정한 활동을) 하다 **phenomenon** 현상 **blindness** 맹목, 무지 **process** 처리하다 **detect** 감지하다 문제 **pass by** …을 스쳐 지나가다

02

당신의 소중한 코를 위해

195 words 3'10"

Date:

Time Taken:

Do you suffer from nasal congestion or respiratory illnesses? These problems are more common than ever in our modern world, as the air we breathe is polluted with many kinds of chemicals, dust, and pollen. But now there's a new method of protection that will let you breathe easily again: Neti.

Neti is a device that uses *saline solution to safely and effectively clean out your nasal passageways. Doctors have found that it is (the body, the majority of diseases, that, through these passageways, enter), so keeping them clean is especially important. Ordinarily, the *sinuses are protected by a filtering system of hair and *mucus membranes, but increased levels of pollutants can <u>clog up</u> this natural defense. When you use Neti, you'll be sending a gentle stream of saltwater through your nasal passages, and this liquid will wash away bacteria, viruses, or other harmful materials.

It sounds simple, but Neti has proven to be highly effective in fighting off illness. So if you're looking for relief from a bad case of allergies or an uncomfortable respiratory tract infection, Neti is just the product for you. Stop by your local pharmacy and pick one up today.

*saline solution 식염수
*sinus 공동(空洞) (코 안쪽과 연결된 머리뼈의 빈 공간)
*mucus membrane 점막

미세먼지와 호흡기질환

세계보건기구(WHO)가 1군 발암물질로 분류한 미세먼지는 오늘날 전 세계적으로 주요한 환경 문제로 인식되고 있다. 일반적인 먼지와 달리 미세먼지는 입자의 지름이 사람 머리카락 굵기의 1/7 정도로 매우 작아 코, 기관지에서 걸러지지 않고 우리 몸속으로 바로 들어온다. 기관지에 미세먼지가 쌓이면, 기관지 점막이 건조해져 세균이 쉽게 침투할 수 있다. 따라서, 폐렴과 같은 질환에 더 취약해진다. 이를 예방하기 위해서는, 미세먼지에 장시간 노출되는 것을 피하는 것이 최상의 방법이다. 미세먼지에 노출된 후 기침, 가래, 호흡곤란, 발열 등의 호흡기 증상이 심해질 경우에는 병원에 가는 것이 좋다.

정답 및 해설 p.81

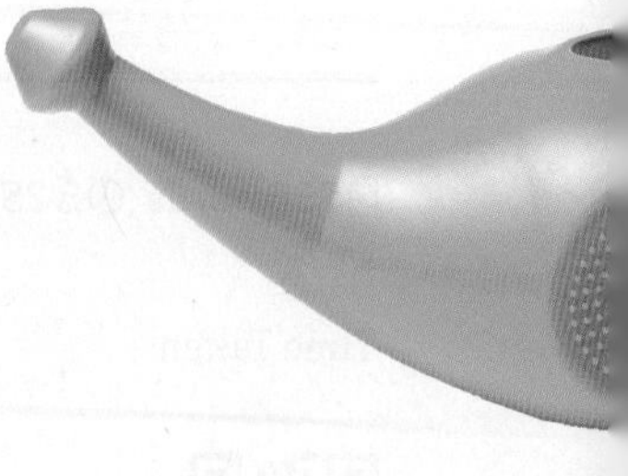

1 윗글의 목적으로 가장 적절한 것은?

① 코 질환의 종류에 대해 설명하려고
② 코 막힘을 완화하는 제품을 홍보하려고
③ 코 막힘의 완화 과정에 대해 설명하려고
④ 공기 청정기 설치의 필요성을 강조하려고
⑤ 코 막힘을 완화하는 약의 사용법을 안내하려고

서술형

2 윗글의 괄호 안에 주어진 단어들을 다음 우리말에 맞게 배열하시오.

대부분의 질병이 몸속으로 들어오는 것은 바로 이 통로를 통해서(이다)

→ it is ______________________________

VOCA

3 윗글의 밑줄 친 clog up과 바꿔 쓸 수 있는 말로 가장 적절한 것은?

① defeat
② block
③ reinforce
④ bring
⑤ develop

4 Neti에 관한 윗글의 내용과 일치하지 않는 것은?

① It helps people to breathe easily.
② It uses a type of liquid.
③ It cleans out bacteria and viruses from nasal passages.
④ Allergies and respiratory infections are its side effects.
⑤ It is sold in pharmacies.

suffer from …로 고통받다 **nasal** 코의 **congestion** 혼잡; *막힘 **respiratory** 호흡의, 호흡 기관의 **chemical** 화학물질 **pollen** 꽃가루 **device** 장치 **passageway** 통로 **filter** 여과하다, 거르다 **pollutant** 오염 물질 **clog** 막다 **saltwater** 소금물 **relief** 안도; *경감[완화] **tract** 관(管) **infection** 감염 **stop by** …에 들르다 **pharmacy** 약국 **문제** **reinforce** 강화하다 **side effect** 부작용

03

대나무 자전거를 타본 적이 있나요?

250 words ⏱3'25"

Date:

Time Taken:

What is your bicycle made of? Most likely, it's constructed of some kind of metal. But ① not all bikes are made of metal. These days, some of the best bikes in the world are being made of bamboo!

So why bamboo? It's because of the way its fibers are arranged. In wood, the strongest fibers are packed tightly together at the center of the tree. But the center of a bamboo stalk is full of empty spaces, with the strongest fibers on the outer surface. This is ② why bamboo is so light. This fiber structure also makes bamboo both stronger and more difficult to bend than wood. And most importantly, bamboo easily absorbs vibrations and impacts.

When a bicycle designer learned about the advantages of bamboo, he realized that making bamboo bicycle frames would be a great way for poor people ③ to earn a living. Since bamboo grows quickly, it is a cheap and available resource in many places. He started an organization ④ called Bamboosero, which travels around the world teaching people in developing nations how to make bamboo bicycle frames. The frames are sold for about $700 each, and part of the profit is used to ⑤ training more people in the art of making bamboo bikes.

It's amazing what can happen when people "think outside the box." Cyclists benefit from the smooth ride and classic beauty of these unique bicycles, while the people who make them are able to support themselves in a way that doesn't harm the environment.

서술형

1 주어진 질문에 대한 답을 할 때, 빈칸에 들어갈 알맞은 말을 본문에서 찾아 쓰시오.

What makes bamboo so light and difficult to bend?

→ It's because the __________ of a bamboo stalk is __________ and the strongest fibers are on its __________ __________.

수능어법

2 윗글의 밑줄 친 ①~⑤ 중, 어법상 틀린 것은?

VOCA

3 윗글의 밑줄 친 "think outside the box"가 의미하는 바로 가장 적절한 것은?

① think innovatively
② accept things easily
③ consider things logically
④ go to another place to think
⑤ appreciate everything's value

대나무 혁명 대나무가 활용도 높은 원자재로 새롭게 주목받고 있다. 이른바, '대나무 혁명'이다. 건축·디자인 전문가들은 대나무가 지닌 친환경적 요소에 주목한다. 대나무는 하루에 1m 이상 자랄 정도로 생장 속도가 빠를 뿐만 아니라 이산화탄소를 흡수하고 산소를 배출하는 기능이 일반 나무들보다 뛰어나며 땅의 부식을 더 효과적으로 막아준다. 또한 잡아당기는 힘에 견디는 능력이 강철보다 우수하고, 압착에 저항하는 힘은 콘크리트보다 세서 건축 소재로 매우 우수하다고 볼 수 있다.

construct 건설하다; *구성하다 **fiber** 섬유질 **arrange** (일을) 처리하다; *배열하다 **pack** (짐을) 싸다; *(물건으로) 빽빽이 채우다 **stalk** (식물의) 줄기 **surface** 표면[표층] **absorb** 흡수하다 **vibration** 진동 **impact** 충격 **available** 이용할 수 있는 **resource** 자원; *재료 **profit** 이익, 수익 **benefit from** …로부터 이득을 보다 **smooth** 매끈한, 부드러운 **문제** **appreciate** 진가를 알아보다

04

121 words 2'20"

Date:

Time Taken:

TRY 수능

내용 일치

Lydecker 형제에 관한 다음 글의 내용과 일치하지 않는 것은? [모의기출 응용]

From the 1930s to the 1950s, ⓐ the amazing special effects in the movies making by Republic Pictures were created by the brothers Howard and Theodore Lydecker. ① They specialized in producing extremely realistic effects on very low budgets. They used carefully constructed models and insisted that ② their effects be created "in camera." This means that ③ they were created during the original filming, which made their effects believable. Since the effects were shot on the same *film stock as the movie itself, the quality of the image was very high. ④ The Lydeckers also developed a method of flying model aircraft that made them look like real planes. This technique gave ⑤ them total control over the aircraft's movement, and it is still used today.

*film stock (사용하지 않은) 영화 촬영용 필름

① Republic Pictures가 만든 영화의 특수 효과를 담당했다.
② 적은 예산으로 매우 사실적인 효과를 만들어냈다.
③ 세심하게 제작된 모형들을 촬영에 사용했다.
④ 영화 촬영 후 특수 효과를 별도로 추가했다.
⑤ 모형 비행기를 사용하는 기법을 개발했다.

유형 *Tip*

step1. 본문을 읽기 전에 선택지의 내용을 살펴보고, 어떤 내용에 주목하며 읽어야 할지 파악한다.
선택지에 제시된 내용을 통해 라이데커 형제가 한 일, 특수 효과 분야에 기여한 점, 촬영에 사용된 모형의 특징, 특수 효과 사용 시점, 모형 비행기 사용 기법이 언급된 부분에 주목하며 읽어야 함을 알 수 있다.

step2. 보통 선택지의 순서대로 본문이 진행되므로, 차례대로 내용을 대조하며 읽는다.
'This means that they were created during the original filming, which made their effects believable.'을 통해, 특수 효과가 영화 촬영 시에 함께 만들어졌음을 알 수 있다.

step3. 본문에 언급된 정보만을 토대로 내용 일치 여부를 판단한다.
자신의 생각이나 상식에 근거하여 판단하지 않도록 유의한다.

정답 및 해설 p.84

· 변형문제 ·

1 윗글의 제목으로 가장 적절한 것은?

① The Developments of Movie Making
② The First Movie in History to Use Special Effects
③ Why Movies with Computer Graphics Are Avoided
④ Brothers Who Achieved Progress in Special Effects
⑤ The Increasing Importance of Special Effects in Movies

서술형

2 윗글의 밑줄 친 ⓐ에서 어법상 틀린 부분을 찾아 바르게 고쳐 쓰시오.

3 밑줄 친 ①~⑤ 중, 가리키는 대상이 나머지 넷과 다른 것은?

special effect 특수 효과 **specialize in** …을 전문으로 하다 **realistic** 사실적인 **budget** 예산 **insist** 고집하다, 주장하다 **original** 원래의; *(복사본이 아닌) 원본의 **filming** (영화의) 촬영 **believable** 그럴듯한 **shoot** 쏘다; *촬영하다(shot-shot) **aircraft** 비행기

Review Test

· VOCA ·

A

다음 중 단어의 뜻풀이가 잘못된 것을 고르시오.

① filter: to remove unwanted material from something as it passes through

② interruption: something that causes an action to stop

③ original: personally created by a particular artist; not a copy

④ pollutant: anything that makes the air, water, or soil clean

⑤ budget: an estimate of expenses for a given period

B

괄호 안에서 적절한 단어를 고르시오.

1 Put baking soda in your refrigerator to (absorb / emit) odors.

2 You can find many great teaching (resources / resolutions) for children online.

3 Both employers and employees can (benefit / reinforce) from flexible work hours.

4 It is important to (construct / constitute) grammatically correct sentences when you write an English essay.

C

문맥상 다음 빈칸에 들어갈 가장 알맞은 단어를 고르시오.

1 Please select a new profile picture to __________ your current one.

① add ② attach ③ replace ④ upload ⑤ confirm

2 We __________ the chairs in a circle around the table.

① arranged ② removed ③ developed ④ produced ⑤ compared

3 Fans always __________ the star on the street and ask for his autograph or a picture.

① conduct ② avoid ③ organize ④ approach ⑤ infect

4 The restaurant __________ in traditional Mexican dishes.

① sells ② processes ③ launches ④ operates ⑤ specializes

정답 및 해설 p.85

· SENTENCE ·

D

다음 문장을 밑줄 친 부분에 유의하여 우리말로 해석하시오.

1 The woman didn't notice that the person she was talking to had changed.

▸ ______________________________

2 It is through these passageways that the majority of diseases enter the body.

▸ ______________________________

3 It's amazing what can happen when people "think outside the box."

▸ ______________________________

4 They insisted that their effects be created "in camera."

▸ ______________________________

E

우리말에 맞게 주어진 단어들을 바르게 배열하여 문장을 완성하시오.

1 우리가 집중하지 않고 있는 것들에 변화가 생길 때, 우리는 그것들을 알아채지 못하는 경향이 있다.

When changes occur in things we aren't focusing on, we (them / not / tend / notice / to).

▸ When changes occur in things we aren't focusing on, we ______________________________.

2 이제 당신이 다시 수월하게 숨 쉬게 해줄 새로운 보호 수단이 있다.

Now there's a new method of protection that (let / breathe / you / easily / will) again.

▸ Now there's a new method of protection that ______________________________ again.

3 그들은 그것들이 실제 비행기처럼 보이게 하는 모형 비행기 조종 기법을 개발했다.

They developed a method of flying model aircraft that (look / real planes / made / like / them).

▸ They developed a method of flying model aircraft that ______________________________.

지은이

NE능률 영어교육연구소

NE능률 영어교육연구소는 혁신적이며 효율적인 영어 교재를 개발하고
영어 학습의 질을 한 단계 높이고자 노력하는 NE능률의 연구조직입니다.

리딩튜터 〈수능PLUS〉

펴 낸 이 주민홍
펴 낸 곳 서울특별시 마포구 월드컵북로 396(상암동) 누리꿈스퀘어 비즈니스타워 10층
㈜NE능률 (우편번호 03925)
펴 낸 날 2018년 8월 5일 개정판 제1쇄 발행
2022년 7월 15일 제11쇄
전 화 02 2014 7114
팩 스 02 3142 0356
홈페이지 www.neungyule.com
등록번호 제1-68호
I S B N 979-11-253-2389-1 53740
정 가 13,000원

고객센터

교재 내용 문의 : contact.nebooks.co.kr (별도의 가입 절차 없이 작성 가능)
제품 구매, 교환, 불량, 반품 문의 : 02-2014-7114
☎ 전화문의는 본사 업무시간 중에만 가능합니다.

NE능률 교재 MAP

독해

아래 교재 MAP을 참고하여 본인의 현재 혹은 목표 수준에 따라 교재를 선택하세요.
NE능률 교재들과 함께 영어실력을 쑥쑥~ 올려보세요!
MP3 등 교재 부가 학습 서비스 및 자세한 교재 정보는 www.nebooks.co.kr 에서 확인하세요.

초1-2
- 초등영어 리딩이 된다 Start 1
- 초등영어 리딩이 된다 Start 2
- 초등영어 리딩이 된다 Start 3
- 초등영어 리딩이 된다 Start 4

초3
- 리딩버디 1

초3-4
- 리딩버디 2
- 초등영어 리딩이 된다 Basic 1
- 초등영어 리딩이 된다 Basic 2
- 초등영어 리딩이 된다 Basic 3
- 초등영어 리딩이 된다 Basic 4

초4-5
- 리딩버디 3
- 주니어 리딩튜터 스타터 1

초5-6
- 초등영어 리딩이 된다 Jump 1
- 초등영어 리딩이 된다 Jump 2
- 초등영어 리딩이 된다 Jump 3
- 초등영어 리딩이 된다 Jump 4
- 주니어 리딩튜터 스타터 2

초6-예비중
- 1316팬클럽 독해 1
- 주니어 리딩튜터 1
- Junior Reading Expert 1
- Reading Forward Basic 1

중1
- 주니어 리딩튜터 2
- Junior Reading Expert 2
- Reading Forward Basic 2
- 열중 16강 독해+문법 1
- Reading Inside Starter

중1-2
- 1316팬클럽 독해 2
- 주니어 리딩튜터 3
- 정말 기특한 구문독해 입문
- Junior Reading Expert 3
- Reading Forward Intermediate 1
- 열중 16강 독해+문법 2
- Reading Inside 1

중2-3
- 1316팬클럽 독해 3
- 주니어 리딩튜터 4
- 정말 기특한 구문독해 기본
- Junior Reading Expert 4
- Reading Forward Intermediate 2
- Reading Inside 2

중3
- 리딩튜터 입문
- 정말 기특한 구문독해 완성
- Reading Forward Advanced 1
- 열중 16강 독해+문법 3
- Reading Inside 3

중3-예비고
- Reading Expert 1
- 리딩튜터 기본
- Reading Forward Advanced 2

고1
- 빠바 기초세우기
- 리딩튜터 실력
- Reading Expert 2
- TEPS BY STEP G+R Basic

고1-2
- 빠바 구문독해
- 리딩튜터 수능 PLUS
- Reading Expert 3

고2-3, 수능 실전
- 빠바 유형독해
- 빠바 종합실전편
- Reading Expert 4
- TEPS BY STEP G+R 1

고3 이상, 수능 고난도
- Reading Expert 5
- 능률 고급영문독해

수능 이상/ 토플 80-89 · 텝스 600-699점
- ADVANCED Reading Expert 1
- TEPS BY STEP G+R 2
- RADIX TOEFL Blue Label Reading 1,2

수능 이상/ 토플 90-99 · 텝스 700-799점
- ADVANCED Reading Expert 2
- RADIX TOEFL Black Label Reading 1

수능 이상/ 토플 100 · 텝스 800점 이상
- RADIX TOEFL Black Label Reading 2
- TEPS BY STEP G+R 3

READING TUTOR

고등 독해의
절대 자신감

리딩튜터 수능 PLUS

정답 및 해설

NE 능률

READING TUTOR

고등 독해의
절대 자신감

리딩튜터 수능 PLUS

정답 및 해설

SECTION 01

01 1 ③ 2 ⓐ was renovated ⓑ were spent 3 ①
02 1 After waiting ten minutes for someone to help you 2 ④ 3 ② 4 ①
03 1 ① 2 ③ 3 (1) T (2) T (3) F
04 ⑤ 변형문제 1 ① 2 ① 3 how you deliver information, how you receive it

01 감옥에서 하룻밤을 P. 10

정답 1 ③ 2 ⓐ was renovated ⓑ were spent 3 ①

문제해설 1 ③ 1851년은 감옥이 지어진 해이므로, 이때 호텔로 개조된 것은 아니다.

2 ⓐ 문장의 주어인 it은 리버티 호텔을 가리키고, 문맥상 이 건물이 '개조되었다'는 내용이 되어야 하므로 수동태인 was renovated가 적절하다.
ⓑ 수백만 달러가 '쓰였다'는 내용이 되어야 하므로 수동태인 were spent로 쓰는 것이 알맞다.

3 (A) 문맥상 역사적 건축물과 현대적 호텔의 호화로운 특징을 '결합하다'라는 내용이 자연스러우므로 combines가 되어야 한다. confine은 '국한시키다'라는 의미이다.
(B) 간수들이 죄수들을 경찰 운송 수단으로부터 감방으로 '이송했다'라는 내용이 자연스러우므로 transfer가 적절하다. transmit은 '전송하다'라는 의미이다.
(C) 문맥상 모든 것이 '진짜인' 것처럼 여겨진다는 내용이 적절하므로 authentic이 되어야 한다. awkward는 '어색한'이라는 의미이다.

본문

① If you're looking for / a unique lodging experience / during your tour of New England, / head to the Liberty Hotel in Boston. ② You're sure to find / the history of the building / quite interesting. ③ Before it was renovated, / it was the notorious Charles Street Jail. ④ Millions of dollars were spent / to convert the former jail / into a unique structure / that combines historic architecture / with the luxury features of a modern hotel.
⑤ The original granite structure, / built in 1851, / was a National Historical Landmark. ⑥ Today, / careful planning has made / the Liberty Hotel / an interesting mix of / public spaces, historical features, and guestrooms. ⑦ The area / where the guards used to transfer prisoners / from the police carriages / to their cells / was transformed into the entrance / of a restaurant called Scampo, / which means "escape" in Italian. ⑧ Another restaurant in the hotel / features original bars / from the old cell doors and windows, / and the waiters and waitresses / wear shirts with prison numbers on them. ⑨ Everything feels very authentic, / but don't worry / — you'll be able to leave / whenever you want!

해석 ① 만약 당신이 뉴잉글랜드 관광 중에 독특한 숙박 경험을 하고 싶다면, 보스턴에 있는 리버티 호텔로 가보아라. ② 당신은 틀림없이 그 건물의 역사가 상당히 흥미롭다고 생각하게 될 것이다. ③ 그것은 개조되기 전에는 악명 높은 찰스 스트리트 감옥이었다. ④ 수백만 달러가 예전의 감옥을 역사적인 건축물과 현대적인 호텔의 호화로운 특징을 결합하는 독특한 건물로 개조하기 위해 쓰였다.

⑤ 1851년에 지어진 본래의 화강암 건물은 국립 역사 유적지였다. ⑥ 오늘날, 세심한 계획이 리버티 호텔을 공공장소와 역사적으로 중요한 특징, 그리고 객실을 흥미롭게 조합한 것으로 만들어냈다. ⑦ 간수들이 죄수들을 경찰 운송수단으로부터 감방으로 이송하곤 했던 곳은 스캄포라는 식당의 입구로 탈바꿈했는데, 스캄포는 이탈리아어로 '탈출'을 의미한다. ⑧ 그 호텔의 또 다른 식당은 옛 감방 문과 창문 본래의 창살을 특징으로 하며, 남녀 종업원들은 죄수 번호가 적혀 있는 셔츠를 입는다. ⑨ 모든 것이 진짜인 것처럼 여겨지지만, 걱정하지 마라. 원하는 때 언제든지 떠날 수 있으니까!

구문해설

④ Millions of dollars were spent **to convert** the former jail into a unique structure [that combines ...].
→ to convert는 〈목적〉을 나타내는 부사적 용법의 to부정사
→ [ ]는 선행사 a unique structure를 수식하는 주격 관계대명사절

⑤ The original granite structure, [built in 1851], was a National Historical Landmark.
→ [ ]는 삽입어구로 쓰인 과거분사구로 The original granite structure를 부연 설명함.

⑥ Today, careful planning has **made** the Liberty Hotel **an interesting mix** ....
→ make+목적어+목적격보어(명사): …을 ~으로 만들다

⑦ The area [where the guards **used to transfer** prisoners ...] was transformed into the entrance of a restaurant *called Scampo*, [which means "escape" in Italian].
(S: The area / V: was transformed)
→ 첫 번째 [ ]는 선행사 The area를 수식하는 관계부사절
→ used to+동사원형: (과거에) …하곤 했다
→ called Scampo는 a restaurant를 뒤에서 수식하는 과거분사구
→ 두 번째 [ ]는 선행사 Scampo를 부연 설명하는 계속적 용법의 주격 관계대명사절

02 당신은 가짜 손님 P. 12

정답

1 After waiting ten minutes for someone to help you **2** ④ **3** ② **4** ①

문제해설

1 '10분간 기다린 후에'라는 뜻은 After waiting ten minutes로 쓰고, to부정사의 의미상의 주어 for someone을 to help you 앞에 쓴다.

2 help는 목적격보어로 to부정사 또는 동사원형을 취하므로 ④ understanding은 (to) understand가 되어야 한다.

3 시장 조사원들이 종업원의 서비스 질을 평가할 목적으로 미스터리 쇼퍼들을 고용한다는 내용에 이어, 미스터리 쇼퍼들은 종업원들에게 특정 행동 및 질문을 하도록 지시를 받는다는 내용의 (A)가 오고, 그들이 종업원들로부터 받은 서비스를 기록하고 평가한다는 내용의 (C)가 이어진 후, 이렇게 모은 정보는 시장 조사원들에 의해 분석된다는 (B)로 이어지는 것이 자연스럽다.

4 미스터리 쇼퍼는 종업원의 서비스 질을 평가하기 위해 고용된다고 했으므로, ① '고객 서비스를 개선하기' 위한 유용한 도구가 될 수 있다는 내용이 문맥상 적절하다.

② 목표 고객들을 조사하기

③ 제품에 대한 유용한 정보를 얻기

④ 윤리적 문제에 대해 사람들을 인터뷰하기

⑤ 제품을 판매하는 최상의 방법을 제안하기

본문

① You've decided to buy a new laptop / at a big electronics store. ② After waiting ten minutes / for someone to help you, / you finally approach a sales clerk. ③ He sighs / and reluctantly agrees to help you. ④ After he makes a quick recommendation, / he walks away / and leaves you alone. ⑤ Normally, / when customers experience this kind of bad service, / they stop going to that store. ⑥ However, / the store's owners have no way of knowing / why these customers have stopped coming. ⑦ That's why some stores use "mystery shoppers."

⑧ Market researchers employ mystery shoppers / to measure the quality of employee service / at retail stores. ⑨ (A) Mystery shoppers are instructed / to behave in a certain way / and ask the sales clerks / specific questions. ⑩ (C) They record the responses / they receive / and rate the quality of the customer service. ⑪ (B) The data / they collect / is then analyzed / by the market researchers. ⑫ Information provided by mystery shoppers / can help companies to understand the strengths and weaknesses / of their employees. ⑬ Some criticism has been raised / about the ethical aspects of this system / because of concerns about deceiving the sales clerks, / but it can be a useful tool / for improving customer service.

해석

① 당신은 한 대형 전자제품 매장에서 새 노트북 컴퓨터를 구입하기로 했다. ② 누군가가 당신을 도와주기를 10분간 기다린 후에, 당신은 마침내 한 점원에게 다가간다. ③ 그는 한숨을 쉬더니, 당신을 도와줄 것에 마지못해 동의한다. ④ 그는 순식간에 추천을 해준 후에 가버리고 당신을 혼자 남겨둔다. ⑤ 보통, 고객들이 이런 유형의 형편없는 서비스를 경험하면, 그들은 그 가게에 가지 않는다. ⑥ 하지만 가게 주인들은 이 고객들이 왜 오지 않게 되었는지를 알 길이 없다. ⑦ 그것이 일부 상점들이 '미스터리 쇼퍼들'을 이용하는 이유이다.

⑧ 시장 조사원들은 소매점에서의 종업원의 서비스 질을 평가하기 위해 미스터리 쇼퍼들을 고용한다. ⑨ (A) 미스터리 쇼퍼들은 특정 방식으로 행동하고 종업원들에게 특정 질문을 하도록 지시를 받는다. ⑩ (C) 그들은 자신들이 얻은 대답을 기록하고 고객 서비스의 질을 평가한다. ⑪ (B) 그들이 모은 정보는 그런 다음 시장 조사원들에 의해 분석된다. ⑫ 미스터리 쇼퍼들에 의해 제공되는 정보는 기업들이 자사 직원들의 강점과 약점을 아는 데 도움이 될 수 있다. ⑬ 판매원들을 속이는 것에 대한 우려 때문에 이 제도의 윤리적 측면에 대한 일부 비판이 제기되어 왔지만, 그것은 고객 서비스를 개선하기 위한 유용한 도구가 될 수 있다.

구문해설

⑥ However, the store's owners have no way of knowing [why these customers **have stopped coming**].

→ [ ]는 knowing의 목적어로 쓰인 간접의문문으로 「의문사+주어+동사」의 어순으로 씀.

→ stop+v-ing: …하는 것을 멈추다 *cf.* stop+to-v: …하기 위해 멈추다

⑩ They **record** (V_1) the responses [(that[which]) they receive] and **rate** (V_2) the quality ....

→ [ ]는 선행사 the responses를 수식하는 목적격 관계대명사절로, 관계대명사 that[which]이 생략됨.

→ 동사 record와 rate는 and로 연결된 병렬구조

⑫ Information [provided by mystery shoppers] can **help** companies **to understand** ....

→ [ ]는 Information을 뒤에서 수식하는 과거분사구

→ 「help+목적어+to-v[동사원형]」은 '…가 ~하는 것을 돕다'라는 뜻이며, help는 목적격보어로 to부정사와 동사원형 둘 다 취할 수 있음.

03 이런 아이스크림 보셨나요? P. 14

정답 **1** ① **2** ③ **3** (1) T (2) T (3) F

문제해설 **1** (A) 아이스크림이 녹는 것은 '결함'이므로 flaw가 적절하다. flow는 '흐름'이라는 의미이다.

(B) 폴리페놀이라는 물질로 디저트를 만들던 중 녹지 않는 아이스크림을 만드는 법을 발견한 것이므로 '우연한'을 의미하는 accidental이 적절하다. intentional은 '의도적인'이라는 의미이다.

(C) 일본 연구원들이 녹지 않는 아이스크림을 만들었다고 하는 것이므로 '주장'을 의미하는 claims가 적절하다. excuse는 '변명'이라는 의미이다.

2 폴리페놀의 특성을 이용해 녹지 않는 아이스크림을 만들었다고 했다.
일본 연구원들은 폴리페놀을 이용해서 오랜 시간 동안 아이스크림을 굳게 유지하는 방법을 발견했다.

3 (1) 녹지 않는 아이스크림은 과일에서 얻은 성분으로 만들어진다.
(2) 폴리페놀은 물과 기름이 분리되지 않게 한다.
(3) 녹지 않는 아이스크림은 20도 이하의 온도에서만 굳은 상태로 있다. → 28도 실온에서 녹지 않았다는 연구 결과가 있다.

본문

① Ice cream is the perfect summertime snack, / except for one big flaw — / it melts. ② Thanks to science, / however, / this problem may soon be a thing of the past.
③ There is already some ice cream / that melts at a slower rate, / but Japanese researchers have now created a type of ice cream / that doesn't seem to melt at all. ④ Interestingly, / this discovery was accidental — / they had been using a liquid / taken from strawberries, called polyphenol, / to make a dessert. ⑤ However, / when the polyphenol was added to the dessert's cream, / the cream instantly became solid. ⑥ This occurred / because polyphenol prevents water and oil from separating, / allowing the cream to stay firm / and keep its shape.
⑦ Realizing that polyphenol would have the same effect on other substances, / the researchers began using it / to make ice cream products / that don't melt.
⑧ In order to test their claims, / a reporter purchased some of the ice cream / and left it outside in 28 °C weather. ⑨ After five minutes, / it was still cold / and had not begun to melt.
⑩ There are even some reports / that it can last for more than three hours / without melting.
⑪ Currently, / it is not being sold outside of Japan, / so you'll have to go there / if you want to find out for yourself.

해석 ① 아이스크림은 녹는다는 한 가지 큰 결점만 빼고는 완벽한 여름 간식이다. ② 그러나, 과학 덕분에, 이 문제는 곧 과거의 일이 될지도 모른다.
③ 이미 더 천천히 녹는 아이스크림이 있지만, 일본 연구원들은 이제 전혀 녹지 않는 것처럼 보이는 아이스크림 종류

를 만들어 냈다. ④ 흥미롭게도, 이러한 발견은 우연이었다. 그들은 디저트를 만들기 위해 폴리페놀이라고 하는, 딸기에서 추출된 액체를 사용해 왔다. ⑤ 그러나, 폴리페놀이 디저트의 크림에 첨가되었을 때, 크림은 즉시 딱딱해졌다. ⑥ 이것은 폴리페놀이 물과 기름이 분리되는 것을 막아 크림이 단단한 상태로 있게 해서 그 모양을 유지하게 해주기 때문에 일어났다. ⑦ 폴리페놀이 다른 물질에도 같은 효과를 가질 수 있다는 것을 알고서, 연구원들은 그것을 사용해서 녹지 않는 아이스크림 제품을 만들기 시작했다.
⑧ 그들의 주장을 실험해 보기 위해, 한 리포터가 아이스크림을 사서 그것을 28도의 날씨에 야외에 두었다. ⑨ 5분 후에, 그것은 여전히 차가웠고 녹기 시작하지 않았다. ⑩ 심지어 그것이 녹지 않고 3시간 이상이나 지속될 수 있다는 몇몇 보고도 있었다. ⑪ 현재, 그것은 일본 밖에서는 판매되고 있지 않아서, 여러분이 직접 알아보고 싶다면 그곳에 가야만 할 것이다.

구문해설 ⑥ This occurred because polyphenol **prevents** water and oil **from separating**, *allowing* the cream to stay firm and (to) keep its shape.

→ prevent+목적어+from v-ing: (목적어)가 …하는 것을 막다
→ allowing 이하는 〈연속동작〉을 나타내는 분사구문 (=and it allows ....)
→ allow+목적어+to-v: (목적어)가 …하게 해주다
→ to stay와 (to) keep이 and로 연결된 병렬구조

⑦ **Realizing** [that polyphenol would have the same effect on other substances], the researchers began using *it* to make ice cream products [that don't melt].

→ Realizing ... other substances는 〈시간〉을 나타내는 분사구문(=When they realized ...,)
→ 첫 번째 [ ]는 Realizing의 목적어로 쓰인 명사절
→ it은 앞에 나온 polyphenol을 가리킴.
→ 두 번째 [ ]는 선행사 ice cream products를 수식하는 주격 관계대명사절

⑩ There are even some reports [that it can last for more than three hours **without melting**].

→ some reports와 [ ]는 동격 관계
→ without v-ing: …하지 않고

04 주제 · 제목 · 요지 P. 16

정답 ⑤ 변형문제 **1** ① **2** ① **3** how you deliver information, how you receive it

문제해설 구성원들 사이에서 서로 협력하여 일을 하려면 자신이 정보를 받는 방식에만이 아니라 다른 사람들에게 정보를 전달하는 방식에도 똑같이 능숙해야 한다는 내용이므로 ⑤가 요지로 가장 적절하다.

변형문제

1 '특정한'을 의미하는 particular는 '일반적인'을 의미하는 ① general과 반의어 관계이다.
② 구체적인, 명확한; 특정한 ③ 상세한

④ 동일한, 똑같은　　　　　　　　⑤ 훌륭한

2 (A) 주어가 단수인 the maximum number이므로 수 일치에 의해 단수 동사 is가 와야 한다.
(B) 문장의 주어 역할을 하는 명사절을 이끌고 선행사를 포함하는 관계대명사가 와야 하므로 What이 적절하다.
(C) 조건을 나타내는 부사절에서는 현재시제가 미래시제를 대신하므로 are가 적절하다.

3 both는 앞 문장에서 언급된 how you deliver information과 how you receive it을 가리킨다.

본문

① One exercise in teamwork / I do at a company retreat / is to put the group in a circle. ② At one particular retreat, / there were eight people in the circle, / and I slowly handed tennis balls to one person / to start throwing around the circle. ③ If N equals the number of people in the circle, / then the maximum number of balls / you can have in motion / is N minus 1. ④ Why? ⑤ Because it's almost impossible / to throw and catch / at the same time. ⑥ The purpose of the exercise is / to demonstrate the importance of an individual's action. ⑦ People are much more concerned about catching the ball / than throwing it. ⑧ What this demonstrates is / that it's equally important to the success of the exercise / that the person you're throwing to / catches the ball / as that you are able to catch the ball. ⑨ If you are less concerned about / how you deliver information / than with how you receive it, / you'll ultimately fail at delegation. ⑩ You have to be equally skilled / at both.

해석

① 회사 야유회에서 내가 하는 협업 훈련 한 가지는 그 집단을 원형으로 둘러 세우는 일이다. ② 어느 특정 야유회에서는, 여덟 명이 원을 그리고 둘러섰는데, 나는 천천히 한 사람에게 테니스공을 건네주어 원을 따라 던지기 시작하게 했다. ③ N이 원을 그리고 둘러선 사람들의 수와 같다고 하면, 여러분이 움직이게 할 수 있는 공의 최대 수는 N-1이다. ④ 왜 그럴까? ⑤ (공을) 던져 주면서 동시에 받는 것은 거의 불가능하기 때문이다. ⑥ 그 훈련의 목적은 개인의 행동의 중요성을 보여 주는 것이다. ⑦ 사람들은 공을 던져 주는 것보다는 잡는 데 더 관심이 있다. ⑧ 이것이 보여 주는 것은, 여러분이 공을 던져 주는 대상인 사람이 공을 잡는 것이, 여러분이 공을 잡을 수 있는 것만큼이나 그 훈련의 성공에 똑같이 중요하다는 것이다. ⑨ 만약 여러분이, 자신이 정보를 어떻게 받는가보다 자신이 정보를 어떻게 전달하는가에 관심을 더 적게 가진다면, 여러분은 결국 (임무의) 위임에 실패할 것이다. ⑩ 두 가지 모두에 똑같이 능숙해야 한다.

구문해설

① One exercise (S) in teamwork [(that[which]) I do at a company retreat] is (V) **to put** the group in a circle.
→ [ ]는 선행사 One exercise를 수식하는 목적격 관계대명사절로, 관계대명사 that[which]이 생략됨.
→ to put은 문장의 보어 역할을 하는 명사적 용법의 to부정사

③ ..., then **the** maximum **number of** (S) balls [(that[which]) you can have in motion] is (V) N minus 1.
→ the number of+복수명사: …의 수 (*cf.* a number of+복수명사: 많은 …)
→ [ ]는 선행사 balls를 수식하는 목적격 관계대명사절로, 관계대명사 that[which]이 생략됨.

⑦ People **are** *much* more **concerned about** catching the ball than throwing it.
→ be concerned about: …에 관심을 가지다
→ much는 '훨씬'이라는 의미로 비교급을 수식하는 부사로 쓰임.

→ 전치사 about의 목적어로 쓰인 동명사 catching과 throwing이 접속사 than으로 병렬 연결됨.

⑧ [What this demonstrates] is [**that** *it*'s equally important to the success of the exercise {*that* the person (whom) you're throwing to catches the ball} as (it's important to the success of the exercise) that you are able to catch the ball].
→ 첫 번째 [ ]는 관계대명사 What이 이끄는 명사절로 문장의 주어
→ 두 번째 [ ]는 접속사 that이 이끄는 명사절로 문장의 보어
→ it은 가주어이고 { }가 접속사 that이 이끄는 진주어
→ the person과 you 사이에 목적격 관계대명사 whom이 생략됨.
→ as는 '…만큼'을 나타내는 접속사로 쓰임.

Review Test P. 18

A **1** ⓒ **2** ⓐ **3** ⓔ **4** ⓑ **5** ⓓ B **1** concerned **2** substance **3** deceived **4** transmit C **1** ② **2** ⑤ **3** ④ **4** ④ D **1** 수백만 달러가 예전의 감옥을 독특한 건물로 개조하기 위해 쓰였다. **2** 그것은 기업들이 자사 직원들의 강점과 약점을 이해하도록 도와준다. **3** 폴리페놀은 물과 기름이 분리되는 것을 막아 크림이 단단한 상태로 있게 해준다. **4** 회사 야유회에서 내가 하는 협업 훈련 한 가지는 그 집단을 원형으로 둘러 세우는 일이다. E **1** You're sure to find the history **2** have no way of knowing **3** it can last for more than

해석

A

1 악명 높은: ⓒ 나쁘거나 사악한 것으로 유명한
2 지시하다: ⓐ 누군가에게 어떤 일을 해달라고 공식적으로 말하다
3 분석하다: ⓔ 무언가를 세부적으로 조사하다
4 감옥: ⓑ 죄수들이 수용되는 장소
5 주요 지형지물: ⓓ 알아보기 쉬운 것

B

1 최근에 많은 사람들이 기후 변화에 대해 염려하고 있다.
2 나는 이런 종류의 물질이 너무 끈적거려서 좋아하지 않는다.
3 광고와 마케팅 기법에 속지 마세요.
4 휴대전화 사용은 정보를 전달하는 빠르고 쉬운 방법이다.

C

1 의사는 상처를 볼 수 있도록 가만히 있어달라고 환자에게 부탁했다.
① 놀라고 ② 있어달라고 ③ 운전해달라고 ④ 느껴달라고 ⑤ 가져가라고

2 연구팀은 이 민간 요법이 실제로 효과가 있음을 입증했다.
① 창조했다 ② 적용했다 ③ 요구했다 ④ 배달했다 ⑤ 입증했다

3 메리는 아무것도 하고 싶지 않아서, 마지못해 엄마를 돕기로 했다.
① 운 좋게도 ② 빨리 ③ 기꺼이 ④ 마지못해 ⑤ 놀랍게도

4 그 금은 진짜라서 많은 돈의 가치가 있는 것으로 밝혀졌다.
① 가짜의 ② 이상한 ③ 현실 같지 않은 ④ 진짜의 ⑤ 비정상적인

SECTION 02

01 **1** ② **2** proteins, dropping **3** ④ **4** (1) F (2) T
02 **1** ① **2** ④ **3** ⑤ **4** where chefs needed to cook a lot of food in a short time
03 **1** ③ **2** ⓐ were ⓑ causing **3** ⑤ **4** (A) ⓐ (B) ⓒ (C) ⓑ
04 ⑤ 변형문제 **1** ④ **2** has received orders which make this date impossible **3** ④

01 우리 식량에 무슨 일이? P. 22

정답 **1** ② **2** proteins, dropping **3** ④ **4** (1) F (2) T

문제해설

1 이산화탄소 증가가 식용 작물에 부정적인 영향을 끼친다는 내용이므로 ② '증가된 이산화탄소가 식량에 끼치는 영향'이 주제로 가장 적절한다.
① 급속한 기후 변화의 이유
③ 영양분이 적은 식용 작물의 종
④ 현대인들을 위한 일일 필수 영양소
⑤ 식물을 키우기 위한 완벽한 환경

2 식용 작물의 미네랄, 비타민, 그리고 단백질 같은 영양분의 수준이 과거 수십 년 동안 하락해 오고 있다.

3 이산화탄소 증가가 식용 작물에 미치는 부정적 영향을 입증하는 실험이므로, 문맥상 이산화탄소 수치가 높은(high) 실내 공간이라고 해야 한다.

4 (1) 이산화탄소는 식물이 제대로 자라는 데 필요하지 않다. → 이산화탄소는 식물이 자라는 데 필요하다고 했다.
(2) 너무 많은 이산화탄소는 식물에서 주요 미네랄의 감소를 초래할지도 모른다.

본문

① Can climate change make the food / you eat / less healthy? ② As strange as it may sound, / it could be possible.
③ Studies have shown / that the levels of minerals, vitamins, and proteins in food crops / have been dropping / over the past 50 to 70 years. ④ Some scientists believe / this is related to the use of crops / that produce more food / but contain fewer nutrients. ⑤ However, / others suggest / it has been caused / by the increase of carbon dioxide (CO_2) / in the air over the same period. ⑥ Although plants require CO_2 to grow, / a large increase in CO_2 / seems to have a negative effect on them.
⑦ This has been demonstrated in experiments / in which plants were grown in an indoor space

/ with high CO_2 levels. ⑧ The results of the experiments showed / that important changes took place / in a wide category of plants / that includes wheat, rice, potatoes, and other food crops / we depend on. ⑨ In each case, / important minerals / such as calcium, potassium, zinc and iron / were reduced.

⑩ Although more studies need to be done, / this could potentially lead to an environmental disaster, / as many people around the world / already struggle to get enough nutrition / in their daily diets.

해석

① 기후 변화는 여러분이 먹는 음식을 건강에 덜 좋게 만들 수 있는가? ② 이상하게 들릴지 모르지만, 그것은 가능할지도 모른다.

③ 연구 결과에 따르면 식용 작물의 미네랄, 비타민, 그리고 단백질 수준이 과거 50년에서 70년에 걸쳐 계속 하락해 오고 있다. ④ 일부 과학자들은 이것이 더 많은 식량을 생산하지만 더 적은 영양분을 포함하는 식용 작물의 사용과 관련 있다고 믿는다. ⑤ 그러나, 다른 과학자들은 그것이 같은 기간 동안 대기 중 이산화탄소 증가에 의해 야기되었다고 시사한다. ⑥ 식물이 자라는 데 이산화탄소가 필요하지만, 이산화탄소의 대폭 증가는 식물에 부정적인 영향을 미치는 것처럼 보인다.

⑦ 이것은 이산화탄소 수치가 높은 실내 공간에서 작물이 재배된 실험들에서 입증되었다. ⑧ 실험 결과는 밀, 쌀, 감자와 우리가 의존하는 기타 식용 작물을 포함하는 폭넓은 작물 범주에서 중요한 변화가 발생했다는 것을 보여주었다. ⑨ 각각의 경우에, 칼슘, 칼륨, 아연과 철과 같은 중요한 미네랄이 감소되었다.

⑩ 더 많은 연구가 행해져야 하지만, 이것은 잠재적으로 환경 재난으로 이어질 수 있는데, 왜냐하면 전 세계의 많은 사람들이 이미 매일의 식사에서 충분한 영양을 얻기 위해 고군분투하고 있기 때문이다.

구문해설

① Can climate change **make** the food [(that[which]) you eat] **less healthy**?

→ make+목적어+목적격보어(형용사): (목적어)가 …하게 하다

→ [ ]는 선행사 the food를 수식하는 목적격 관계대명사절로, 관계대명사 that[which]이 생략됨.

⑦ This has been demonstrated in experiments [**in which** plants were grown in an indoor space with high CO_2 levels].

→ [ ]는 선행사 experiments를 수식하는 관계대명사절로, in which는 장소를 나타내는 관계부사 where로 바꿔 쓸 수 있음.

⑧ The results of the experiments showed [that important changes took place in a wide category of plants [that includes wheat, rice, potatoes, and other food crops {(that[which]) we depend on}]].

→ 첫 번째 [ ]는 showed의 목적어로 쓰인 명사절

→ 두 번째 [ ]는 선행사 a wide category of plants를 수식하는 주격 관계대명사절

→ { }는 선행사 other food crops를 수식하는 목적격 관계대명사절로, 관계대명사 that[which]이 생략됨.

02 초콜릿이 녹아서… P. 24

정답 1 ① 2 ④ 3 ⑤ 4 where chefs needed to cook a lot of food in a short time

문제해설 1 퍼시 스펜서가 우연히 마그네트론 앞에서 초콜릿 바가 녹는 것을 발견했고 그것을 계기로 전자레인지를 발명했다는 내용이므로, 제목으로는 ① '우연한 발명'이 가장 적절하다.

② 퍼시 스펜서: 최고의 요리사 ③ 무엇이 팝콘을 튀기는가?
④ 전자레인지의 위험성 ⑤ 레이더: 세상을 바꾸기

2 선행사가 the point이고, 뒤에 문장 성분을 모두 갖춘 완전한 절이 왔으므로, ④ which는 관계부사 where 또는 「전치사+관계대명사」인 at which로 고쳐야 알맞다. 관계부사 where는 추상적 의미의 장소를 나타내는 말을 선행사로 취할 수 있다.

3 전자레인지가 가정에서 처음 쓰인 시기에 대한 구체적인 언급은 없으므로, ⑤ '언제 가정에서 처음 쓰였는가?'가 정답이다.

① 누가 발명했는가? ② 처음에는 얼마나 컸나?
③ 처음에 왜 식당에서만 사용되었나? ④ 최초의 전자레인지는 어떤 문제점이 있었나?

4 장소를 나타내는 선행사 restaurants 다음에 where가 이끄는 관계부사절을 쓰는 것이 적절하므로, where chefs needed to cook a lot of food in a short time이 알맞다.

본문

① Percy Spencer was a natural inventor / who knew how to apply his curiosity. ② Shortly after World War II, / he was walking through his laboratory / when he paused in front of a magnetron, / a device used to power radar systems. ③ Suddenly, / he realized / that a chocolate bar in his pocket / was melting. ④ But Spencer didn't panic. ⑤ Instead, / he put some unpopped popcorn in a bag / and held it in front of the magnetron. ⑥ As Spencer had suspected, / the small hard popcorn soon exploded, / becoming fluffy and white. ⑦ This simple experiment eventually led to / the invention of the microwave oven. ⑧ The first of these devices was enormous — / it was 167 centimeters tall / and weighed 340 kilograms. ⑨ Because of this, / it was only used in restaurants / where chefs needed to cook a lot of food / in a short time. ⑩ There were also other problems. ⑪ Meat didn't turn brown, / and French fries turned white. ⑫ But, / over decades, / improvements were made, / and eventually the microwave oven reached the point / where it was the perfect addition / to the average family's kitchen. ⑬ Today, / people around the world use these ovens / to melt their chocolate / and pop their popcorn.

해석 ① 퍼시 스펜서는 자신의 호기심을 응용하는 방법을 아는 타고난 발명가였다. ② 제2차 세계대전 직후, 그는 자신의 실험실에서 걸어 다니다가 레이더 시스템에 전력을 공급하는 데 사용되는 장치인 마그네트론 앞에 잠시 멈춰 섰다. ③ 갑자기, 그는 자신의 주머니 속에 있던 초콜릿 바가 녹고 있다는 것을 깨달았다. ④ 하지만 스펜서는 당황하지 않았다. ⑤ 대신에, 그는 봉지 안에 튀기지 않은 팝콘을 넣고 그것을 마그네트론 앞에서 들고 있었다. ⑥ 스펜서가 짐작했던 것처럼, 작고 딱딱한 팝콘은 곧 터져서 솜털 같고 하얗게 되었다. ⑦ 이 간단한 실험은 마침내 전자레인지의 발명으로 이어졌다. ⑧ 최초의 이 기기는 거대했는데, 167센티미터 높이에 무게가 340킬로그램이었다. ⑨ 이 때문에, 그것은 요리사들이 짧은 시간에 많은 음식을 요리해야 하는 식당에서만 사용되었다. ⑩ 다른 문제점들도 있었다. ⑪

고기는 갈색으로 변하지 않았고, 프렌치 프라이는 하얗게 변했다. ⑫ 그러나 수십 년에 걸쳐 개선이 이루어졌고, 마침내 전자레인지는 일반 가정 주방의 완벽한 추가 구성물이 되는 지점에 이르렀다. ⑬ 오늘날, 전 세계의 사람들이 이 전자레인지를 초콜릿을 녹이고 팝콘을 튀기는 데 사용한다.

구문해설

① Percy Spencer was a natural inventor [who knew **how to apply** his curiosity].

→ [ ]는 선행사 a natural inventor를 수식하는 주격 관계대명사절

→ how+to-v: …하는 방법

② ... when he paused in front of a magnetron, a device [used to power radar systems].

→ a magnetron과 a device는 동격 관계

→ [ ]는 a device를 뒤에서 수식하는 과거분사구

⑥ As Spencer **had suspected**, the small hard popcorn soon exploded, [becoming fluffy and white].

→ had suspected는 주절의 과거 시점(exploded)보다 더 이전에 일어난 일을 나타내는 대과거

→ [ ]는 〈연속동작〉을 나타내는 분사구문(= and it became ....)

⑬ Today, people around the world use these ovens **to melt** their chocolate and (**to**) **pop** their popcorn.

→ to melt 이하는 〈목적〉을 나타내는 부사적 용법의 to부정사구

→ to melt와 (to) pop이 and로 연결된 병렬구조

03 '왜?'라고 다섯 번 묻기 P. 26

정답

1 ③ **2** ⓐ were ⓑ causing **3** ⑤ **4** (A) ⓐ (B) ⓒ (C) ⓑ

문제해설

1 문제에 대한 효과적인 해결책을 도출하기 위해 사용할 수 있는 '5 Whys' 기법을 설명하는 글이므로 ③ '효과적인 문제 해결 기법'이 주제로 가장 적절하다.

① 질문에 답하는 실용적인 기술 ② 조명 시간의 영향

④ 5 Whys 기법의 단점들 ⑤ 제퍼슨 기념비의 보수 관리 문제

2 ⓐ 가정법 과거의 if절은 「if+주어+동사의 과거형」으로 나타내며, be동사는 인칭과 수에 관계없이 were를 쓰므로 were를 쓰는 것이 알맞다.

ⓑ 〈부대상황〉을 나타내는 분사구문이 오는 것이 적절한데, 분사의 의미상의 주어 The lights가 동작을 유발하는 주체이므로 능동의 의미를 나타내는 현재분사 causing이 되어야 한다.

3 제퍼슨 기념비의 표면이 '훼손되고' 있다는 의미이므로, deteriorating은 '부식하다, 썩다'를 의미하는 ⑤ decaying과 바꿔 쓸 수 있다.

① 개선하다 ② 흔들리다 ③ 움직이다 ④ 강화하다

4 5 Whys 기법은 거꾸로 거슬러가며 문제의 근원에 접근하는 방식이라고 했다. 따라서, 두 번째 '왜'로는 청소 세제를 바꾸게 된 원인은 비둘기 배설물이 증가했기 때문이라는 내용인 ⓐ가 오는 것이 적절하다. 비둘기 배설물 증가의 원인이 되는 세 번째 '왜'의 답으로는 많아진 거미를 먹기 위해 더 많은 비둘기가 오고 있었다는 내용인

ⓒ를 들 수 있다. 거미들이 증가한 원인이 되는 네 번째 '왜'의 답으로는 거미들의 먹이인 곤충이 늘었다는 내용인 ⓑ가 적절하다.

본문

① What would you do / if you were given a problem / that seemed too complex to solve? ② Guess? ③ Give up? ④ A better trick to try / is the 5 Whys technique. ⑤ To use this approach, / you start with the end result / and work backwards. ⑥ This simply involves asking "why?" / at each stage.

⑦ Recently, / a team of workers / responsible for maintaining the Jefferson Memorial in Washington, D.C., / applied the 5 Whys / to come up with a solution to a problem / they were facing.

⑧ Problem: / The surface of the Jefferson Memorial / was deteriorating rapidly.

⑨ 1. Why?: / They had recently switched / to stronger cleaners / for the Memorial's exterior surface.

⑩ 2. Why?: / ⓐ <u>There was an increase / in the amount of pigeon droppings / on the memorial.</u>

⑪ 3. Why?: / ⓒ <u>More pigeons were coming to the memorial / to feed on the growing number of spiders there.</u>

⑫ 4. Why?: / ⓑ <u>Spiders had moved there / to prey on the increasing number of insects / in the area.</u>

⑬ 5. Why?: / The lights / surrounding the memorial / had been adjusted / to turn on at dusk / a few months ago, / causing a swell in the population of insects / which are most active at dusk.

⑭ Solution: / Readjust the timing of the lights / so that they come on later in the evening.

⑮ This story shows the importance of / getting to the root of a problem / in a thorough and organized manner, / rather than simply rushing to judgment. ⑯ If you fail to ask enough questions, / you may misunderstand the real reason / for the problem / and never formulate an effective solution.

해석

① 만약 너무 복잡해서 풀 수 없어 보이는 문제가 당신에게 주어진다면 어떻게 하겠는가? ② 추측하겠는가? ③ 포기하겠는가? ④ 시도해볼 만한 더 나은 방법은 5 Whys 기법이다. ⑤ 이 접근법을 사용하려면 최종 결과에서 시작해서 거꾸로 거슬러가라. ⑥ 이것은 단순히 각 단계에서 '왜?'라고 묻는 것을 필요로 한다.

⑦ 최근에, 워싱턴 D.C.에 있는 제퍼슨 기념비 유지를 맡고 있던 한 근로자 팀이 그들이 직면하고 있던 문제에 대한 해결책을 찾기 위해 5 Whys를 적용했다.

⑧ 문제: 제퍼슨 기념비의 표면이 급격히 훼손되고 있었다.

⑨ 1. 왜?: 그들은 최근에 기념비의 외부 표면을 닦기 위해 더 독한 세제로 바꿨다.

⑩ 2. 왜?: ⓐ <u>기념비 위의 비둘기 배설물의 양이 증가했다.</u>

⑪ 3. 왜?: ⓒ <u>더 많은 비둘기들이 그곳에서 증가하는 수의 거미들을 잡아먹기 위해 이 기념비로 오고 있었다.</u>

⑫ 4. 왜?: ⓑ <u>거미들이 그 구역에서 증가하는 수의 곤충들을 잡아먹기 위해 그곳으로 이동했다.</u>

⑬ 5. 왜?: 기념비를 둘러싸고 있는 조명이 몇 달 전에 해 질 무렵에 켜지도록 조정되어, 해 질 무렵에 가장 활동적인 곤충 개체 수의 증가를 유발했다.

⑭ 해결책: 조명이 저녁에 더 늦게 켜지도록 조명 시간을 다시 조정하라.

⑮ 이 이야기는 그저 서둘러 판단하기보다는, 철저하고 조직적인 방법으로 문제점의 근원에 접근하는 것의 중요성을

보여준다. ⑯ 만약 당신이 충분한 질문을 하지 못한다면, 당신은 문제점에 대한 진짜 이유를 잘못 이해할 수 있고, 결코 효과적인 해결책을 만들어내지 못할 수도 있다.

구문해설 ① What **would** you **do if** you **were given** a problem [that seemed *too* complex *to solve*]?

→「if+주어+동사의 과거형, 주어+조동사의 과거형+동사원형」은 가정법 과거구문으로, 현재 사실의 반대를 가정

→ [ ]는 선행사 a problem을 수식하는 주격 관계대명사절

→ too+형용사+to-v: 너무 …해서 ~할 수 없다

⑦ Recently, a team of workers (S) [responsible for maintaining ...], applied (V) the 5 Whys (O) **to come up with** a solution to a problem [(that[which]) they were facing].

→ 첫 번째 [ ]는 a team of workers를 뒤에서 수식하는 형용사구

→ to come up with 이하는 〈목적〉을 나타내는 부사적 용법의 to부정사구

→ 두 번째 [ ]는 선행사 a problem을 수식하는 목적격 관계대명사절이며, 관계대명사 that[which]가 생략됨.

⑬ ...: The lights [surrounding the memorial] had been adjusted to turn on ..., [causing a swell in the population of insects {which are most active at dusk}].

→ 첫 번째 [ ]는 The lights를 수식하는 현재분사구

→ 두 번째 [ ]는 〈부대상황〉을 나타내는 분사구문

→ { }는 선행사 insects를 수식하는 주격 관계대명사절

04 글의 목적 P. 28

정답 ⑤ 변형문제 **1** ④ **2** has received orders which make this date impossible **3** ④

문제해설 결혼식 날짜가 변경되어 연주자에게 연주 날짜를 앞당겨 줄 수 있는지 문의하는 글이므로, 글의 목적으로는 ⑤가 적절하다.

변형문제

1 ④ 날짜 변경 외에 다른 모든 사항은 그대로라고 했다.

2 주격 관계대명사 which와 「make+목적어+목적격보어(형용사)」 구문을 활용하여 주어진 단어들을 배열한다.

3 밑줄 친 accommodate는 '(요구 등에) 부응하다'라는 의미로 ④ '누군가의 요구에 부응하다'가 가장 적절하다.

① 단체에 가입하다

② …을 위한 공간을 마련하다

③ 새로운 상황에 익숙해지다

⑤ 누군가에게 머물 장소를 제공하다

본문

① Dear Lauren Baker,

② We thank you for agreeing to play the music / for my daughter's wedding / on September 17. ③ Unfortunately, / her fiancé, / who is in the military, / has received orders / which make this date impossible, / so we are moving the wedding date / forward two weeks to September 3. ④ Would it be possible for you to accommodate us / on this date instead? ⑤ All the other aspects of our agreement / will remain the same. ⑥ We would be most grateful / if you could make this change / and I really hope to see the extra touch of elegance / added to my daughter's wedding. ⑦ Will you be gracing us with your presence? ⑧ If you are unable to, / please let us know / as soon as possible / so that we can make other arrangements.

⑨ Sincerely,
Bill Gibson

해석

① 로렌 베이커 씨께,

② 9월 17일에 열리는 제 딸의 결혼식에서 음악을 연주해 주시는 것에 동의해 주셔서 감사합니다. ③ 안타깝게도, 군대에 있는 딸의 약혼자가 이 날짜를 불가능하게 하는 명령을 받아서, 결혼식 날짜를 2주 앞당긴 9월 3일로 바꾸려 합니다. ④ 대신 이날로 저희에게 맞추어주시는 게 가능할까요? ⑤ 우리가 합의한 모든 다른 사항들은 그대로 유지될 것입니다. ⑥ 만약 이렇게 바꿔 주실 수 있다면 대단히 감사드리겠고 제 딸의 결혼식에 우아함이 더해지는 것을 정말로 보고 싶습니다. ⑦ 당신이 참석해 주셔서 자리를 빛내 주시겠습니까? ⑧ 만약 불가능하다면 다른 조치를 취할 수 있도록 가능한 한 빨리 알려 주시기 바랍니다.

⑨ 마음을 담아, 빌 깁슨

구문해설

⑥ We **would be** most grateful **if** you **could** make this change and I really hope to see(V') the extra touch of elegance(O') added(OC') to my daughter's wedding.

→ if+주어+동사의 과거형, 주어+조동사의 과거형+동사원형: 만약 …하면[라면], ~할 텐데 〈가정법 과거〉

→「지각동사(see)+목적어(the ... elegance)+목적격보어(added)」 구문으로, 목적어와 목적격보어가 의미상 수동 관계이므로, 목적격보어로 과거분사가 쓰였다.

⑧ If you are unable to, please **let us know** *as soon as possible* so that we can make other arrangements.

→ let(사역동사)+목적어+목적격보어(동사원형): (목적어)가 …하게 하다

→ as soon as possible: 가능한 한 빨리

→ so that+주어+조동사+동사원형: …하도록 〈목적〉

Review Test

P. 30

A ② B **1** suspected **2** thorough **3** Improvement **4** demonstrated C **1** ③ **2** ② **3** ③ **4** ④
D **1** 기후 변화는 여러분이 먹는 음식을 건강에 덜 좋게 만들 수 있는가? **2** 기념비를 둘러싸고 있는 조명이 해 질 무렵에 켜지도록 조정되었다. **3** 다른 조치를 취할 수 있도록 가능한 한 빨리 알려 주시기 바랍니다. **4** 만약 너무 복잡해서 풀 수 없어 보이는 문제가 당신에게 주어진다면 어떻게 하겠는가? E **1** who knew how to apply his curiosity **2** produce more food but contain fewer nutrients **3** fail to ask enough questions

해석

A

① 폭발하다: 격렬하게 터지거나 깨지다
② 거대한: 크기나 양이 매우 작은
③ 잠재적으로: 가능하겠지만 아직 실제가 아닌
④ 호기심: 무언가에 대해 알고자 하는 강한 욕망
⑤ 강화하다: 어떤 것을 더 힘세고 더 강력하게 만들다

B

1 수는 자기 아들이 그녀에게 거짓말을 하고 있을지도 모른다고 의심했다.
2 모든 차량은 철저하고 세심한 검사를 거친다.
3 그 자동차 설계의 개선은 연료 효율의 증가로 이어졌다.
4 그 실험은 물이 섭씨 0도에서 언다는 것을 입증했다.

C

1 한류 덕분에 서울을 방문하는 사람의 수에 증가가 있었다.
① 범주 ② 멈춤 ③ 증가 ④ 정도, 수준 ⑤ 접근법

2 순한 맛을 좋아하면, 고춧가루 양을 줄이세요.
① 더하세요 ② 줄이세요 ③ 조리하세요 ④ 포함시키세요 ⑤ 준비하세요

3 그녀는 항상 상황의 긍정적인 면을 찾으려고 노력한다.
① 계획 ② 장치 ③ 측면 ④ 부족 ⑤ 우아(함)

4 많은 아프리카의 저개발 국가들은 지속적인 전기 공급을 제공하기 위해 고군분투한다.
① 초래한다 ② 돕는다 ③ 조정한다 ④ 고군분투한다 ⑤ 남아 있다

SECTION 03

01 **1** ① **2** ③ **3** ③ **4** random, dice
02 **1** ② **2** ⑤ **3** some of them taking almost a year to complete
03 **1** ③ **2** ② **3** ③ **4** shop for food
04 ⑤ 변형문제 **1** ① **2** ⑤ **3** a good pair of shoes

01 주사위로 작곡한 곡 P. 34

정답 1 ① 2 ③ 3 ③ 4 random, dice

문제해설

1 세부적인 부분이 무작위적인 확률에 의해 결정되는 우연성 음악에 대해 설명하는 글이므로, 제목으로는 ① '우연성 음악: 그것은 무엇인가?'가 적절하다.
② 세계 최초의 우연성 음악 ③ 시를 쓰기 위해 주사위를 던지는 방법
④ 음악을 작곡하는 다양한 방법 ⑤ 모차르트, 우연성 음악의 창시자

2 ③ 곡의 세부적인 부분들은 우연히 정해지도록 남겨둔다고 했다.

3 (A) 문맥상 우연성 음악은 하나의 음악 작곡 방식을 '가리킨다'는 의미가 되어야 하므로, refers to가 와야 한다. prefer to는 '…하는 것을 선호하다'라는 의미이고 뒤에 동사가 온다.
(B) 문맥상 우연성 음악 작곡법이 존 케이지가 그의 음악에 무작위적인 세부사항을 '더하도록' 도왔다는 내용이 되어야 하므로 add가 적절하다. remove는 '제거하다'라는 의미이다.
(C) 우연성 방식을 사용하는 '창의적인' 방법을 찾을 수 있다는 내용이 문맥상 적절하므로, creative가 알맞다. critical은 '비판적인'이라는 의미이다.

4 몇몇 유명한 음악가들은 주사위를 던진 무작위적인 결과를 이용하여 그들의 작품을 작곡했다.

본문

① It is hard to believe / that some great composers, / possibly including Mozart, / wrote music / by throwing dice. ② But it's true! ③ We call this aleatoric music.
④ Aleatoric music refers to / a style of musical composition, / popularized in the early 1950s, / that uses some form of random chance. ⑤ It has a fixed structure / but leaves the details to be decided / by chance. ⑥ For example, / musical measures can each be assigned / a different number. ⑦ The sequence of each measure / is then determined / by throwing dice.
⑧ An example of aleatoric music / is the work of John Cage. ⑨ Cage composed experimental music / in the 1950s / using the I Ching. ⑩ This method helped him / add random details / to his music. ⑪ Cage also used coin tossing and other methods / to compose his songs.
⑫ The aleatoric method has also been used / in other forms of art, / such as story writing and poetry. ⑬ Maybe you can find a creative way / to use it yourself.

해석

① 아마도 모차르트를 포함하여 일부 위대한 작곡가들이 주사위를 던져서 음악을 작곡했다는 것은 믿기 힘들다. ② 하지만 그것은 사실이다! ③ 우리는 이것을 우연성 음악이라고 부른다.
④ 우연성 음악은 1950년대 초반에 대중화된, 무작위적인 확률의 일종을 사용하는 음악 작곡 방식을 가리킨다. ⑤ 그것은 고정된 체계가 있지만, 세부적인 부분은 우연히 정해지도록 남겨둔다. ⑥ 예를 들어, 소절들에는 각각 서로 다른 번호가 배정될 수 있다. ⑦ 그러고 나서 각 소절의 순서는 주사위를 던짐으로써 결정된다.
⑧ 우연성 음악의 한 사례로 존 케이지의 작품이 있다. ⑨ 케이지는 1950년대에 팔괘(八卦)를 사용하여 실험적인 음악을 작곡했다. ⑩ 이 방식은 그가 자신의 음악에 무작위적인 세부 사항을 더하도록 도왔다. ⑪ 케이지는 곡을 작곡하기 위해 동전 던지기와 다른 방법들도 사용했다.
⑫ 이 우연성 방식은 글쓰기나 시와 같은 다른 유형의 예술에서도 사용되어 왔다. ⑬ 아마도 당신은 우연성 방식을 사용하는 창의적인 방법을 직접 찾을 수 있을 것이다.

구문해설 ① **It** is hard **to believe** [that some great composers, {possibly including Mozart}, wrote music *by throwing* dice].
S′ 삽입어구 V′

→ It은 가주어, to believe 이하가 진주어이며, [ ]는 believe의 목적어 역할을 하는 명사절임.

→ { }는 문장 중간에 삽입된 어구

→ by+v-ing: …함으로써

④ Aleatoric music refers to a style of musical composition, [popularized in the early 1950s], [that uses some form of random chance].

→ 첫 번째 [ ]는 문장 중간에 삽입된 어구로, a style of musical composition을 부연 설명함.

→ 두 번째 [ ]는 선행사 a style of musical composition을 수식하는 주격 관계대명사절

⑪ Cage also used coin tossing and other methods **to compose** his songs.

→ to compose는 〈목적〉을 나타내는 부사적 용법의 to부정사

02 불꽃의 향연, 라스파야스 P. 36

정답 **1** ② **2** ⑤ **3** some of them taking almost a year to complete

문제해설 **1** ② *라스파야스*는 성(聖) 요셉을 위한 축일로 시작되었다고 했으며, 그가 화재로 사망했다는 언급은 없다.

2 관계대명사 that은 계속적 용법으로 쓸 수 없으므로 ⑤ that을 관계대명사 which로 고쳐야 알맞다.

3 주절의 주어 They와 분사구문의 의미상의 주어 some of them이 다르므로, 분사의 의미상의 주어를 나타내어 some of them taking almost a year to complete으로 쓰는 것이 알맞다.

본문

① Perhaps / the most extraordinary part of my trip to Spain / was / when the city of Valencia seemed to catch fire / during a loud, smoky, and exciting party! ② This was during a spectacular festival / known as *Las Fallas*, or "the fires."

③ *Las Fallas* is one of the most unique festivals / in Spain. ④ Though it started / as a feast day for St. Joseph, / it has become a wonderful five-day celebration / that is very popular. ⑤ Valencia is normally home to 1 million people, / but during *Las Fallas* / the population grows to 3 million!

⑥ The festival involved creating and destroying *ninots*, / which are like puppets or dolls. ⑦ Made out of cardboard, wood, plaster or papier-mache, / the *ninots* depicted current events, / featuring corrupt politicians / and other Spanish celebrities. ⑧ I was impressed at / how lifelike they were. ⑨ They had been made by local organizations, / some of them taking almost a year / to complete. ⑩ Many *ninots* were very tall / and thus needed cranes for transportation / on the day of *la planta* (the rising).

⑪ The *ninots* were put in place / until *la crema* (the burning), / when young men chopped holes in the *ninots* / and stuffed them full of fireworks. ⑫ At midnight, / I joined a crowd of people outside. ⑬ The streetlights were turned off. ⑭ Then / the *ninots* were set on fire, / and

a spectacular fireworks display began! ⑮ Only one *ninot*, / which was saved by popular vote, / was not burned. ⑯ It was taken to the local Museum of the Ninot / to sit alongside *ninot indultats* (the pardoned puppets) / of previous years.
⑰ It was an incredible experience / I'll never forget. ⑱ Any tourist who wants a wild, exciting experience / should try to attend!

해석

① 아마도 나의 스페인 여행에서 가장 놀라운 부분은 시끄럽고 연기가 자욱하며 신나는 파티 동안 발렌시아 시가 불붙은 것처럼 보인 때였을 것이다! ② 이것은 *라스파야스*, 즉 '불'이라고 알려진 화려한 축제 동안에 있었던 일이었다. ③ *라스파야스*는 스페인에서 가장 독특한 축제 중 하나이다. ④ 성(聖) 요셉을 위한 축일로 시작되었지만, 그것은 매우 인기 있는 5일간의 멋진 축하 행사가 되었다. ⑤ 발렌시아는 평소에는 백만 명의 사람이 사는 곳인데, *라스파야스* 동안에는 인구가 3백만 명까지 증가한다!
⑥ 축제는 *니노트*들을 만드는 것과 파괴하는 것을 포함하는데, *니노트*들은 꼭두각시나 인형 같은 것들이다. ⑦ 판지, 나무, 회반죽, 또는 종이 반죽으로 만들어진 *니노트*는 부패한 정치인들과 그 외 스페인 유명인사들을 특징적으로 나타내며 시사 문제를 묘사했다. ⑧ 나는 그것들이 얼마나 실물 같은지에 감명받았다. ⑨ 그것들은 지역 단체들에 의해 만들어졌는데, 그것들 중 일부는 완성하는 데 거의 1년이 걸렸다. ⑩ 많은 *니노트*들은 키가 매우 컸으며, 따라서 *라플란타*(승천)의 날에 수송하기 위해 기중기가 필요했다.
⑪ *니노트*들은 *라크레마*(화형) 때까지 세워져 있었고, 이날 젊은 남자들이 *니노트*에 구멍을 만들고 폭죽으로 가득 채웠다. ⑫ 자정에, 나는 바깥에 있는 사람들 무리에 합류했다. ⑬ 가로등들이 꺼졌다. ⑭ 그러고 나서 *니노트*들에 불이 지펴졌고, 화려한 불꽃놀이가 시작되었다! ⑮ 대중의 투표에 의해 구제된 단 하나의 *니노트*만이 불태워지지 않았다. ⑯ 그것은 그 지역의 니노트 박물관으로 보내져 이전 연도들의 *니노트 인둘타트*들(사면된 꼭두각시들)과 함께 자리 잡았다.
⑰ 그것은 결코 잊지 못할 굉장한 경험이었다. ⑱ 멋지고 신나는 경험을 원하는 관광객이라면 꼭 참석해야 한다!

구문해설

① Perhaps the most extraordinary part of my trip to Spain (S) was (V) (the time) [when the city of Valencia seemed ...]!
→ [ ]는 선행사 the time이 생략된 관계부사절

⑥ The festival **involved creating** and **destroying** *ninots*, [which are like puppets or dolls].
→ 동사 involved의 목적어로 동명사 creating과 destroying이 and로 연결된 병렬구조
→ [ ]는 선행사 *ninots*를 부연 설명하는 계속적 용법의 주격 관계대명사절

⑦ [Made out of cardboard, ...], the *ninots* depicted current events, [featuring corrupt politicians ...].
→ 첫 번째 [ ]는 the *ninots*를 부연 설명하는 수동형 분사구문
→ 두 번째 [ ]는 〈부대상황〉을 나타내는 분사구문

⑪ ... until *la crema* (the burning), [when young men chopped holes ...].
→ [ ]는 선행사 *la crema* (the burning)을 부연 설명하는 계속적 용법의 관계부사절

⑯ It was taken to the local Museum of the Ninot **to sit** alongside ....
→ to sit은 〈결과〉를 나타내는 부사적 용법의 to부정사

03 이런 사막도 있다! P. 38

정답 1 ③ 2 ② 3 ③ 4 shop for food

문제해설 1 식품을 구하기 힘든 지역인 식품 사막 문제를 해결하기 위한 방법들에 대한 글이므로 ③ '식품을 이용 가능하게 하는 방법 찾기'가 제목으로 가장 적절하다.

① 정원으로 식품 사막에 맞서 싸워라 ② 건강에 좋은 식품을 고르는 법을 배워라

④ 대규모 농업 프로젝트가 진행되는 소도시 ⑤ 사막에서 식품 재배하기: 그것이 가능한가?

2 (A) 뒤에 셀 수 있는 명사 place의 복수형인 places가 왔으므로 few가 알맞다. little은 셀 수 없는 명사와 쓰인다.

(B) 문맥상 전국 식품의 '대부분'이라는 뜻이고, 전치사 앞에서 쓰일 수 있어야 하므로 대명사인 most가 적절하다. almost는 '거의'라는 뜻의 부사로 동사나 형용사, 부사 등을 수식할 때 쓰인다.

(C) 페어 앤드 스퀘어가 처음 생긴 과거 시점(was created)을 기준으로 그 이전에 10년 넘게 식료품점이 없었다는 내용이므로, 과거완료 hadn't had가 적절하다.

3 주어진 문장은 식품 사막을 퇴치하려는 투쟁이 다른 도시에서도 일어나고 있다는 내용이므로, 식품 사막 퇴치의 또 다른 예시인 원 시드 시카고 프로젝트가 언급되는 문장 앞 ③에 들어가야 알맞다.

4 밑줄 친 this situation은 앞에서 언급한 문제 상황인 '식품 사막'을 의미하며, 이를 설명하는 문장인 'This is an area where there are few affordable places for people to shop for food.'에서 정답에 대한 단서를 얻을 수 있다.

사람들이 식품을 살 알맞은 장소를 쉽게 찾을 수 없다.

본문

① A desert is an area / where there is little rain / and almost nothing grows. ② But there is also another kind of desert — / a food desert. ③ This is an area / where there are few affordable places / for people to shop for food. ④ Ironically, / in America, / these food deserts are often found / in the places / where most of the nation's food is grown. ⑤ To deal with this situation, / a government-supported nonprofit supermarket / was created. ⑥ Called Fare & Square, / it is located in Chester, / a small city in Pennsylvania / that hadn't had a grocery store / for more than 10 years. ⑦ Before Fare & Square opened, / it was estimated / that more than half of the city's families / had to travel long distances / to purchase food. ⑧ Now, / however, / all of the city's residents have easy access to the food / they need. ⑨ The fight against food deserts / is also taking place / in another city. ⑩ The One Seed Chicago Project helps people / living in the city / by giving them seeds / so they can start their own small vegetable gardens. ⑪ These seeds can be planted / in yards, local community gardens / or even windowsills. ⑫ By growing their own vegetables, / people can eat fresh, healthy food / without driving long distances to supermarkets. ⑬ Although these two projects won't solve the problem of food deserts, / they are the first step to assuring / that all people can get healthy food, / no matter where they live.

해석 ① 사막은 비가 거의 오지 않고 거의 아무것도 자라지 않는 곳이다. ② 그런데 또 다른 종류의 사막이 있는데, 바로 식

품 사막이다. ③ 이곳은 사람들이 식품을 살 알맞은 장소가 거의 없는 지역이다. ④ 역설적이게도, 미국에서 이 식품 사막은 전국 식품의 대부분이 재배되는 곳에서 종종 발견된다. ⑤ 이 상황을 해결하기 위해, 정부 지원의 비영리 슈퍼마켓이 만들어졌다. ⑥ 페어 앤드 스퀘어(Fare & Square)라고 불리는 이것은 10년 이상 식료품점이 없었던 펜실베이니아의 작은 도시인 체스터에 위치하고 있다. ⑦ 페어 앤드 스퀘어가 문을 열기 전에는, 그 도시 가정의 절반 이상이 식품을 사기 위해 먼 거리를 이동해야만 했다고 추산되었다. ⑧ 그러나, 이제는 그 도시 주민 모두가 그들이 필요로 하는 식품을 쉽게 얻을 수 있다. ⑨ 식품 사막에 대한 투쟁은 또 다른 도시에서도 일어나고 있다. ⑩ 원 시드 시카고 프로젝트는 그 도시에 살고 있는 사람들에게 그들만의 작은 채소밭을 시작할 수 있도록 씨앗을 나눠줌으로써 그들을 돕는다. ⑪ 이 씨앗은 뜰이나 지역 사회 정원과 창턱에도 심을 수 있다. ⑫ 그들만의 채소를 재배함으로써, 사람들은 슈퍼마켓으로 먼 거리를 운전해 가지 않고도 신선하고 건강에 좋은 식품을 먹을 수 있다. ⑬ 비록 이 두 프로젝트가 식품 사막 문제를 해결하지는 못하겠지만, 그것들은 그들이 어디에 살든지 모든 사람이 건강에 좋은 식품을 구할 수 있도록 하는 첫걸음이다.

구문해설 ③ This is an area [where there are few affordable places **for people** *to shop* for food].

→ [ ]는 선행사 an area를 수식하는 관계부사절

→ for people은 to shop의 의미상의 주어

→ to shop 이하는 few affordable places를 수식하는 형용사적 용법의 to부정사구

⑩ The One Seed Chicago Project helps people [living in the city] **by giving** them seeds *so* (*that*) they *can start* their own small vegetable gardens.

→ [ ]는 people을 뒤에서 수식하는 현재분사구

→ by+v-ing: …함으로써

→ so (that)+주어+can+동사원형: …가 ~할 수 있도록

⑬ ..., they are the first step **to assuring** [that all people can get healthy food, *no matter where* they live].

→ 전치사 to의 목적어로 동명사 assuring이 옴.

→ [ ]는 assuring의 목적어 역할을 하는 명사절

→ no matter where: 어디서 …하더라도

04 지칭 추론 P. 40

정답 ⑤ 변형문제 **1** ① **2** ⑤ **3** a good pair of shoes

문제해설 ⑤는 소년의 아버지를 가리키고, 나머지는 모두 소년을 가리킨다.

변형문제

1 소년의 아버지의 마음을 상하지 않게 하면서 소년에게 새 신발을 사준 지혜로운 스미스 선생님의 선행에 대한 내용이므로, 제목으로는 ① '현명한 남자의 선행'이 가장 적절하다.

② 아들에 대한 아버지의 사랑 ③ 자부심의 부정적인 영향

④ 세상에서 가장 친절한 구두 제조인 ⑤ 학교에서 영어를 제일 잘하는 사람

2 스미스 선생님이 소년에게 새 신발을 주려고 생각해낸 계획에 해당하는 내용이다. 소년을 불러 영어 시험을 봐야 한다고 말하는 내용인 (C)가 오고, 소년이 알 만한 쉬운 질문을 했다는 내용인 (B) 다음에, 시험을 잘 본 것에 대해 칭찬하며 두 개의 메시지를 주었다는 내용인 (A)로 이어지는 것이 적절하다.

3 시험을 잘 본 것에 대한 상으로 신발이 주어지는 상황을 만든 것이므로, 밑줄 친 the "prize"는 앞 문장에서 언급한 a good pair of shoes를 가리킨다.

본문

① One day, / Mr. Smith saw a young boy walking to school / in old, worn-out shoes. ② He was clearly in need of new ones, / but Mr. Smith knew / the boy's father was a proud man / who would be offended and humiliated / if his son were treated like a charity case. ③ So Mr. Smith came up with a plan / to provide the boy with shoes / without upsetting his father. ④ (C) During the morning recess, / he called the boy into his office, / saying he had to test him / on his English proficiency. ⑤ (B) He then asked the boy / several easy questions / that were very much within the youth's grasp. ⑥ (A) When the boy answered them correctly, / Mr. Smith said "Wonderful!" / and gave the youngster two written messages. ⑦ The first was for a local shoemaker, / instructing him to give a good pair of shoes / to the boy, / for which Mr. Smith would pay. ⑧ The second was for the boy's father, / telling him about the "prize" / won by hisson.

해석

① 어느 날, 스미스 선생님은 한 소년이 낡고 해진 신발을 신고 학교로 걸어오고 있는 것을 보았다. ② 그는 분명히 새 신발이 필요했지만, 스미스 선생님은 그 소년의 아버지가 자기 아들이 자선 대상자처럼 취급을 받는다면 불쾌해하고 수치스러워할 자존심이 강한 사람이라는 것을 알고 있었다. ③ 그래서 스미스 선생님은 소년의 아버지를 기분 상하지 않게 하면서 소년에게 신발을 주는 하나의 계획을 생각해냈다. ④ (C) 아침 휴식 시간에, 그는 소년을 자신의 사무실로 불러서 영어 능력 시험을 봐야 한다고 말했다. ⑤ (B) 그런 다음 그는 소년에게 소년이 확실히 이해할 수 있는 몇 가지 쉬운 질문을 했다. ⑥ (A) 소년이 정답을 말했을 때, 스미스 선생님은 "훌륭해!"라고 말하고 소년에게 글로 쓴 두 개의 메시지를 주었다. ⑦ 첫 번째 것은 지역 구두 제조인을 위한 것이었는데, 스미스 선생님이 지불할 테니 소년에게 좋은 신발 한 켤레를 주라고 지시하는 것이었다. ⑧ 두 번째 것은 소년의 아버지를 위한 것으로, 아들이 받은 상에 관해 알려주는 것이었다.

구문해설

② He was clearly in need of new **ones**, but Mr. Smith knew the boy's father was a proud man [who *would be offended* and *humiliated if* his son *were treated* like a charity case].

→ ones는 앞의 문장에 나온 명사 shoes의 반복 사용을 피하기 위해 쓴 부정대명사

→ [ ]는 선행사 a proud man을 수식하는 주격 관계대명사절

→「if+주어+동사의 과거형, 주어+조동사의 과거형+동사원형」은 '만약 …라면 ~할 텐데'라는 뜻으로 현재 사실의 반대를 가정하는 가정법 과거임. if절에 be동사가 쓰일 경우 수 · 인칭에 관계없이 were를 쓰는 것이 일반적임.

⑤ He then asked the boy (IO) several easy questions (DO) [that were very much within the youth's grasp].

→ [ ]는 선행사 several easy questions를 수식하는 주격 관계대명사절

⑦ The first was for a local shoemaker, [instructing him to give a good pair of shoes to the boy, {for which Mr. Smith would pay}].

→ [ ]는 〈부대상황〉을 나타내는 분사구문

→ { }는 선행사 a good pair of shoes를 부연 설명하는 계속적 용법의 목적격 관계대명사절

Review Test

P. 42

A **1** ⓐ **2** ⓓ **3** ⓔ **4** ⓑ **5** ⓒ **B** **1** assigned **2** spectacular **3** estimated **4** stuffed **C** **1** ③ **2** ⑤ **3** ③ **4** ② **D** **1** 케이지는 곡을 작곡하기 위해 동전 던지기와 다른 방법들을 사용했다. **2** 대중의 투표에 의해 구제된 단 하나의 *니노트*만이 불태워지지 않았다. **3** 그 도시 가정의 절반 이상이 식품을 사기 위해 먼 거리를 이동해야만 했다. **4** 스미스 선생님은 소년의 아버지를 기분 상하지 않게 하면서 소년에게 신발을 주는 하나의 계획을 생각해냈다. **E** **1** which are like puppets or dolls **2** an area where there is little rain **3** telling him about the "prize" won

해석

A

1 작곡가: ⓐ 곡을 쓰는 사람

2 대중화하다: ⓓ 어떤 것이 잘 알려지게 하다

3 부패한: ⓔ 부정직하고 부도덕하게 행동하는

4 숙달: ⓑ 높은 수준의 능력 또는 기술

5 묘사하다: ⓒ 그림, 이야기 등에서 무언가를 나타내다

B

1 각 학생은 기숙사의 방을 배정받았다.

2 성으로 가는 길의 풍경은 장관이었다.

3 2050년이 되면 세계 인구가 90억 명에 도달할 것이라고 추정된다.

4 잭은 배낭에 선글라스와 손전등 그리고 약간의 음식을 채워 넣었다.

C

1 그 의사는 그의 환자에게 그 수술이 안전하다고 보장했다.
① 경고했다 ② 사면했다 ③ 보장했다 ④ 지시했다 ⑤ 불평했다

2 이 베스트셀러 소설은 스토리텔링에 대한 작가의 놀라운 재능을 보여준다.
① 평균적인 ② 이상한 ③ 열등한 ④ 즐거운 ⑤ 놀라운

3 많은 사람들이 그의 무례한 행동에 기분이 상했다.
① 침착했다 ② 들떴다 ③ 기분이 상했다 ④ 고무되었다 ⑤ 영감을 받았다

4 단 몇 명의 직원만이 그 기밀 서류에 접근할 수 있다.
① 휴식 ② 접근 ③ 순서, 연속 ④ 지식 ⑤ 가능성

SECTION 04

01 1⑤ 2③ 3④ 4 sweet stimuli
02 1⑤ 2③ 3 sliding, downforce
03 1⑤ 2③ 3⑤ 4 225
04 ① 변형문제 1⑤ 2⑤ 3①

01 고양이 혀의 비밀 P. 46

정답 1⑤ 2③ 3④ 4 sweet stimuli

문제해설

1 고양이가 단맛을 느끼지 못하는 이유를 유전학적으로 설명하는 글이므로, 주제로는 ⑤ '고양이가 단 음식의 맛을 느끼지 못하는 유전적 이유'가 가장 적절하다.
① 뇌가 맛을 감지하는 방법
② 고양이가 다른 동물들보다 오래 사는 이유
③ 서로 다른 미각 수용기 유전자의 역할
④ 고양이의 유전자는 인간의 유전자와 어떻게 다른가

2 문맥상 포유류의 뇌가 혀의 수용기 세포를 통해 미각 신호를 '받는다'는 내용이 적절하므로 ③ give를 receive 등으로 바꿔야 한다.

3 빈칸 다음 문장의 these meat-eating cats는 단맛 미뢰가 없는 고대의 고양이를 가리키는데, 다른 고양이들은 멸종된 반면 이 고양이들은 살아남았다고 했으므로, 빈칸에는 ④ '더 높은 생존율'이 들어가는 것이 가장 적절하다.
① 더 큰 뇌 ② 더 낮은 지능 ③ 더 작은 신체 골격 ⑤ 더 형편없는 영양 상태

4 고양이는 단맛 자극을 감지하는 미각 수용기 유전자가 없기 때문에 육식을 선호한다.

본문

① It has long been suspected / that domestic cats, / along with lions, tigers, and leopards, / prefer eating meat / because they cannot taste sweet foods. ② Now there's proof! ③ According to a study, / cats lack a key taste receptor gene / that is needed to detect sweet stimuli. ④ This missing gene is likely responsible for / the evolution of cats' carnivorous behavior.
⑤ In the process of evolution, / genetic influences on taste / might have played an important role / in food selection and nutrition / in both humans and animals. ⑥ The brains of all mammals / receive taste signals / from the tongue's receptor cells. ⑦ These cells are joined together / to form taste buds. ⑧ In humans, / each taste bud is made up of / 50 to 100 receptor cells / representing the five major tastes: / salty, sour, sweet, bitter and umami. ⑨ Scientists believe / that, for some reason, / ancient cats / that lacked the sweetness taste buds / had a higher survival rate / than other cats. ⑩ Over time, / these meat-eating cats remained / while others died out.

해석 ① 사자, 호랑이, 표범과 마찬가지로, 집 고양이는 단 음식의 맛을 느끼지 못하기 때문에 육식을 더 좋아하는 것이라

고 오랫동안 여겨져 왔다. ② 이제 증거가 있다! ③ 한 연구에 의하면, 고양이에게는 단맛의 자극을 감지하는 데 필요한 핵심적인 미각 수용기 유전자가 없다고 한다. ④ 이 빠진 유전자가 고양이의 육식 습성의 진화의 원인인 듯하다. ⑤ 진화의 과정에서, 미각에 미치는 유전적인 영향은 인간과 동물 모두에게 먹이 선택과 영양에 있어 중요한 역할을 했을지도 모른다. ⑥ 모든 포유류의 뇌는 혀에 있는 수용기 세포로부터 미각 신호를 받는다. ⑦ 이 세포들이 함께 모여서 미뢰를 구성한다. ⑧ 인간의 경우, 각각의 미뢰는 짠맛, 신맛, 단맛, 쓴맛 그리고 감칠맛의 다섯 가지 주요한 맛을 대표하는 50개에서 100개의 수용기 세포로 구성되어 있다. ⑨ 과학자들은 어떤 이유에서인지 단맛 미뢰가 없는 고대의 고양이들이 다른 고양이들보다 더 높은 생존율을 보였다고 믿는다. ⑩ 시간이 지나면서, 다른 고양이들은 멸종된 반면에, 이 육식 고양이들은 살아남았다.

구문해설 ① **It** *has* long *been suspected* [that domestic cats, ..., prefer eating meat ...].

→ It은 가주어, 접속사 that이 이끄는 명사절인 [ ]가 진주어

→ has been suspected는 〈계속〉을 나타내는 현재완료 수동태

③ ..., cats lack a key taste receptor gene [that is needed **to detect** sweet stimuli].

→ [ ]는 선행사 a key taste receptor gene을 수식하는 주격 관계대명사절

→ to detect는 〈목적〉을 나타내는 부사적 용법의 to부정사

⑤ ..., genetic influences on taste **might have played** an important role ....

→「might+have p.p」는 '…했을지도 모른다'의 의미로 과거 사실에 대한 불확실한 추측을 나타냄.

⑦ These cells are joined together **to form** taste buds.

→ to form은 〈결과〉를 나타내는 부사적 용법의 to부정사

02 차에도 날개가 필요해요 P. 48

정답 1 ⑤ 2 ③ 3 sliding, downforce

문제해설 **1** ⑤ 다운포스는 사동차의 속도보다 더 빠른 비율로 증가하며, 자동차의 속도가 두 배가 되면 다운포스는 네 배가 된다고 했다.

2 (A) 문맥상 '…하기 위해 사용되다'를 의미하는 「be used+to-v」가 적절하므로 make가 쓰이는 것이 알맞다. 「be used to+v-ing」는 '…하는 데 익숙하다'의 의미이다.

(B) this force를 부연 설명하는 삽입어구로, this force는 '알려지는' 대상이므로 수동의 의미를 나타내는 과거분사 known이 알맞다.

(C) 선행사 the friction between the car's tires and the track에 대해 부연 설명하는 계속적 용법의 주격 관계대명사 which가 와야 알맞다. 관계대명사 that은 계속적 용법으로 사용할 수 없다.

3 스포일러는 다운포스를 만들어내는데, 이 다운포스가 자동차와 도로 사이의 마찰을 증가시켜 자동차가 미끄러지는 것을 방지한다고 했다.

스포일러는 다운포스를 만들어냄으로써 자동차가 미끄러지는 것을 방지하는데, 다운포스는 마찰력을 증가시킨다.

본문

① Fans of motorsports are probably aware / that race cars usually have a kind of wing, / called a spoiler, / on both the front and the rear of the vehicle. ② It might seem like / they are only used / to make the car look cool, / but they actually serve a practical purpose.

③ These spoilers are set / at a precise angle / in order to force passing air up / and through them. ④ One of the basic laws of physics / is that for every force / there is an equal and opposite force; / therefore spoilers, / by forcing air upward, / create a force / that pushes the car downward. ⑤ In effect, / this force, / known as downforce, / increases the automobile's weight / without increasing its mass. ⑥ This is important / when racing at high speeds, / as downforce increases the friction / between the car's tires and the track, / which prevents the car from sliding.

⑦ As a race car's speed increases, / so does the downforce / created by its spoilers. ⑧ Downforce, / however, / increases at a faster rate. ⑨ If the car's speed doubles, / its downforce will become four times stronger. ⑩ This is important information / for race car drivers. ⑪ In a Formula One race car / going through a turn / at 300 kilometers per hour, / correctly calculating the downforce / can mean the difference / between winning the race and crashing into a wall.

해석

① 모터스포츠 팬들은 아마 경주용 차들이 일반적으로 차량의 전방과 후방에 스포일러라고 불리는 일종의 날개를 가지고 있다는 것을 알고 있을 것이다. ② 그것들이 그저 차를 멋지게 보이게 하려고 사용되는 것 같겠지만, 사실 그것들은 실용적인 목적으로 쓸모가 있다.

③ 이 스포일러들은 지나가는 공기가 위쪽으로, 그리고 그것들(=스포일러들)을 통과하게 하도록 정확한 각도로 놓인다. ④ 물리학의 기본 법칙 중 하나는, 모든 힘에 대해서는 동등하고 반대로 작용하는 힘이 있다는 것이다. 따라서 스포일러는 공기를 위로 밀어 올림으로써 차량을 아래로 누르는 힘을 만들어낸다. ⑤ 다운포스라고 알려진 이 힘은, 사실상 자동차의 질량을 증가시키지 않고도 그것의 무게를 증가시킨다. ⑥ 이것은 빠른 속도로 경주할 때 중요한데, 다운포스가 자동차 타이어와 도로 사이의 마찰을 증가시켜서, 자동차가 미끄러지는 것을 방지하기 때문이다.

⑦ 경주용 자동차의 속도가 증가함에 따라, 자동차의 스포일러에 의해 만들어지는 다운포스 또한 증가한다. ⑧ 그러나 다운포스는 더 빠른 비율로 증가한다. ⑨ 만약 자동차의 속도가 두 배가 되면, 그것의 다운포스는 네 배 더 강해질 것이다. ⑩ 이것은 경주용 자동차 운전자들에게 중요한 정보이다. ⑪ 시속 300km로 회전을 하는 포뮬러원 경주용 자동차에서, 다운포스를 정확히 계산하는 것은 경주에서 이기는 것과 벽에 부딪히는 것 사이의 차이를 의미할 수 있다.

구문해설

① ... that race cars usually have a kind of wing, [called a spoiler], on both the front and the rear of the vehicle.

→ [ ]는 that절에 삽입된 어구로, a kind of wing을 부연 설명함.

④ One of the basic laws of physics is [that for every force there is an equal and opposite force]; therefore spoilers(S), **by forcing air upward**, create(V) a force(O) [that pushes the car downward].

→ 첫 번째 [ ]는 주격보어로 쓰인 명사절

→ by forcing air upward는 문장의 주어와 동사 사이에 삽입된 전치사구

→ 두 번째 [ ]는 선행사 a force를 수식하는 주격 관계대명사절

⑦ As a race car's speed increases, **so does the downforce** [created by its spoilers].

→ 앞 문장 또는 앞 절의 내용을 받는 so가 문두에 오면「so+do[does/did]+주어」의 어순을 이루어 '…도 마찬가지이다'라는 의미가 됨.

→ [ ]는 the downforce를 수식하는 과거분사구

⑪ In a Formula One race car [going through a turn ...], [correctly calculating the downforce] can mean the difference **between** *winning* the race **and** *crashing* into a wall.

→ 첫 번째 [ ]는 a Formula One race car를 수식하는 현재분사구

→ 두 번째 [ ]는 주어로 쓰인 동명사구

→「between A and B」에서 A와 B 자리에 동명사 winning과 crashing이 병렬구조를 이룸.

03 태양으로부터 피부를 보호하세요! P. 50

정답 **1** ⑤ **2** ③ **3** ⑤ **4** 225

문제해설

1 SPF는 MED에 기반하는데 MED는 햇볕에 타기 전까지 걸리는 시간을 재서 계산한다고 했으므로, SPF는 ⑤ '햇볕 아래에서 타지 않고 얼마나 오래 있을 수 있는지'를 측정하는 척도임을 알 수 있다.

① 태양 광선이 얼마나 강한지
② 당신의 피부가 얼마나 밝은지 또는 어두운지
③ 어떤 종류의 광선이 차단돼야 하는지
④ 자외선 차단제를 한 번에 얼마나 발라야 하는지

2 피부가 흰 사람의 MED는 10분 정도이고, 피부가 어두운 사람의 MED는 15분 정도라고 했으므로, 글을 바르게 이해한 사람은 인혜다.
햇볕으로부터 피부가 보호되는 시간은 MED와 SPF를 곱한 값이므로, 글을 바르게 이해한 사람은 나연이다.

3 사역동사 let은 목적어와 목적격보어가 능동 관계이면 목적격보어로 동사원형을 취하므로 ⑤ to begin을 begin으로 고쳐야 한다.

4 만약 당신이 SPF 15인 자외선 차단제를 바르고 있고 당신의 MED가 15분이라면, 당신은 225분 동안 보호된다.

본문

① Have you ever wondered / what "sun protection factor (SPF)" really means? ② And how is it calculated?
③ To begin with, / the SPF of a sunscreen is a measure / of how long you can stay in the sun / without burning. ④ This time period is also based on something / called your minimal erythemal dose (MED). ⑤ How can you calculate / your personal MED? ⑥ You can stay out in the sun / and time how long it takes / before your skin begins to tingle and burn. ⑦ You can also estimate this time / based on statistics. ⑧ Light-skinned people tend to have an MED / of approximately 10 minutes. ⑨ People with medium to dark skin / tend to have an MED / of

about 15 minutes. ⑩ Multiplying your MED / by your sunscreen's SPF, / you can calculate / how long you'll be protected / before burning. ⑪ So, / if you're wearing a sunscreen / with an SPF of 15 / and your MED is 10 minutes, / you are protected / for 150 minutes (15 times 10).
⑫ Remember the two golden rules of SPF: / If you feel yourself burning, / run for cover. ⑬ And / if you take a dip in the pool or ocean, / reapply your sunscreen / and let the countdown begin again!

해석 ① 당신은 '자외선 차단 지수(SPF)'가 실제로 무엇을 의미하는지 궁금하게 여겨 본 적이 있는가? ② 그리고 그것은 어떻게 계산되는지를?
③ 우선, 자외선 차단제의 SPF는 당신이 햇볕 아래에서 타지 않고 얼마나 오래 있을 수 있는지에 대한 척도이다. ④ 이 시간은 또한 당신의 최소 홍반량(MED)이라고 불리는 것에 기초한다. ⑤ 자신의 MED를 어떻게 계산할 수 있을까? ⑥ 햇볕 아래에 서서 피부가 따가워지고 타기 시작하기 전까지 얼마나 걸리는지 시간을 재면 된다. ⑦ 당신은 또한 통계를 바탕으로 이 시간을 추정할 수도 있다. ⑧ 피부가 흰 사람들은 대략 10분 정도의 MED를 가지는 경향이 있다. ⑨ 중간 피부에서 어두운 피부를 가진 사람들은 15분 정도의 MED를 가지는 경향이 있다. ⑩ 당신의 MED와 당신의 자외선 차단제의 SPF를 곱하면, 당신은 (피부가) 타기 전에 얼마나 오랫동안 보호될 것인지를 계산할 수 있다. ⑪ 따라서, 만약 당신이 SPF 15의 자외선 차단제를 바르고 있고 당신의 MED가 10분이라면, 당신은 150분(15 곱하기 10) 동안 보호된다.
⑫ SPF의 두 가지 황금률을 기억하라. 만약 당신이 (햇볕에) 타고 있는 것이 느껴진다면, 가릴 수 있는 것을 찾아 뛰어라. ⑬ 그리고 만약 당신이 수영장이나 바다에서 잠깐 수영한다면, 자외선 차단제를 다시 바르고 시간을 다시 재기 시작하라!

구문해설 ① **Have** you ever **wondered** [what "sun protection factor (SPF)" really means]?
→ Have wondered는 〈경험〉을 나타내는 현재완료
→ [ ]는 Have wondered의 목적어 역할을 하는 간접의문문

⑩ [Multiplying your MED by your sunscreen's SPF], you can calculate [how long you'll be protected before burning].
→ 첫 번째 [ ]는 〈조건〉을 나타내는 분사구문
→ 두 번째 [ ]는 calculate의 목적어로 쓰인 간접의문문

⑫ ...: If you **feel** yourself **burning**, run for cover.
→ 지각동사 feel의 목적격보어로 진행의 의미를 나타내는 현재분사 burning이 쓰임.

04 심경 P. 52

정답 ① 변형문제 **1** ⑤ **2** ⑤ **3** ①

문제해설 브라이언이 곰을 만나서 겁에 질려 곰이 사라진 후에도 계속 무서워하는 상황이므로 브라이언의 심경은 ① '무섭고 겁이 난'이 적절하다.
② 차분하고 여유 있는 ③ 지루하고 무관심한 ④ 자랑스럽고 만족한 ⑤ 부끄럽고 우울한

변형문제

1 곰과 갑자기 마주쳐 느끼게 된 공포와 위험에 관한 내용이므로 글의 제목으로는 ⑤ '예기치 않은 위험과의 조우'가 가장 적절하다.

① 필수적인 인명 구조 팁

② 흑곰: 열렬한 산딸기 애호가

③ 시골에서의 근사한 경험

④ 나이 든 곰보다 더 영리한 어린 소년

2 ⑤는 브라이언이 낸 소리를 가리키고 나머지는 모두 곰을 가리킨다.

3 (A) 접속사와 주어가 생략된 분사구문으로, 분사구문의 의미상 주어인 it(곰)과 분사가 능동 관계이므로 현재분사 Shining이 적절하다.

(B) his disbelief와 동격 관계인 명사절을 이끄는 접속사가 와야 하므로 that이 적절하다.

(C) 문맥상 '떠는 것을 멈출 수 없었다'의 의미이므로 동명사 shivering이 적절하다. (*cf.* stop+to-v: …하기 위해 멈추다)

본문

① The sun caught the ends of the hairs / along the bear's back. ② Shining black and silky, / it stood on its hind legs, half up, / and studied Brian, just studied him. ③ Then it lowered itself / and moved slowly to the left, / eating berries / as it rolled along, / delicately using its mouth to lift each berry from the stem. ④ In seconds it was gone. ⑤ Gone, / and Brian still had not moved. ⑥ His tongue was stuck to the top of his mouth, the tip half out, / and his eyes were wide. ⑦ Then Brian made a low sound, / "Nnnnnnnggg." ⑧ It made no sense. ⑨ It was just a sound of fear, / of his disbelief / that something that large could have come / so close to him / without his knowing. ⑩ Brian couldn't stop shivering, / thinking that the bear could return / and attack him anytime.

해석

① 태양이 곰의 등을 따라 나 있는 털의 끝부분을 비추었다. ② 검게 비단처럼 빛나면서, 그것은 뒷다리로 서서, 몸을 절반 정도 일으킨 채, 브라이언을 살펴보았는데 단지 그를 살펴볼 뿐이었다. ③ 그러고 나서 곰은 몸을 낮추었고 왼쪽으로 천천히 움직였는데, 나아가면서 입을 섬세하게 사용하여 줄기에서 산딸기를 하나씩 들어 따 먹었다. ④ 곧 곰은 가 버렸다. ⑤ (곰이) 사라졌지만, 브라이언은 여전히 움직이지 못했다. ⑥ 그의 혀는 끝이 반쯤 나온 채 입천장에 달라붙어 있었고 그의 눈은 커져 있었다. ⑦ 그러고 나서 브라이언은 "Nnnnnnnggg"라고 낮은 소리를 냈다. ⑧ 그것은 아무 뜻이 없었다. ⑨ 그것은 단지 공포의 소리, 그렇게나 커다란 것이 그도 모르는 새에 그에게 그토록 가까이 다가올 수도 있었다는 것이 믿기지 않는다는 소리였다. ⑩ 브라이언은 언제든 그 곰이 되돌아와 그를 공격할 수도 있다고 생각하며 몸을 떠는 것을 멈출 수 없었다.

구문해설

③ Then it lowered **itself** and moved slowly to the left, *eating* berries as it rolled along, delicately using its mouth to lift each berry from the stem.

→ itself는 재귀대명사로, 주어와 목적어가 동일한 대상인 it(=the bear)을 가리킴.

→ eating ... along은 〈연속동작〉을 나타내는 분사구문(=and it ate ...,)

→ to lift는 〈결과〉를 나타내는 부사적 용법의 to부정사

⑨ It was just a sound of fear, of his disbelief [that something **that** large could have come

so close to him without his knowing].
→ his disbelief와 [ ]는 동격 관계
→ that은 '그렇게, 그만큼'을 의미하는 부사로 쓰임.

Review Test

P. 54

A 1 ⓐ 2 ⓓ 3 ⓒ 4 ⓑ 5 ⓔ B 1 nutrition 2 delicately 3 vehicles 4 calculate C 1 ② 2 ④ 3 ② 4 ③ D 1 당신은 타기 전에 얼마나 오랫동안 보호될 것인지를 계산할 수 있다. 2 그것은 몸을 낮추었고 왼쪽으로 천천히 움직였는데, 나아가면서 산딸기를 따 먹었다. 3 미각에 미치는 유전적인 영향은 먹이 선택에 있어 중요한 역할을 했을지도 모른다. 4 다운포스라고 알려진 이 힘은, 자동차의 질량을 증가시키지 않고도 그것의 무게를 증가시킨다. E 1 so does the downforce created by 2 You can time how long it takes 3 something that large could have come

해석 A

1 (동물이) 길든: ⓐ 애완동물로 길들여져 키워진
2 감지하다: ⓓ 어떤 것의 존재를 발견하다
3 진화: ⓒ 어떤 것의 시간에 걸친 발달
4 실용적인: ⓑ 실제 사용에 적합한
5 (몸을) 떨다: ⓔ 추위나 공포로 몸을 살짝 떨다

B

1 건강을 유지하고 싶다면 적절한 영양이 중요하다.
2 그것은 깨지기 쉬우니까, 그것을 섬세하게 다뤄야 한다.
3 전기 차량이 점점 인기를 얻고 있다.
4 이 애플리케이션은 당신이 환율을 쉽고 빠르게 계산할 수 있게 해준다.

C

1 나는 정말 피곤할 때, 밤에 별이 빛나는 것을 보기 좋아한다.
① 제공하는 것을 ② 빛나는 것을 ③ 없는 것을 ④ 창조하는 것을 ⑤ 사라지는 것을

2 그 도자기는 5,000년 이상 된 것으로 추정된다.
① 고안된다 ② 구성된다 ③ 지정된다 ④ 추정된다 ⑤ 나타나진다

3 BMI(신체질량지수)란 한 사람의 키와 체중에 기초한 체지방의 척도이다.
① 수용기 ② 척도 ③ 신호 ④ 마찰(력) ⑤ 자극

4 두 시간마다 얼굴에 자외선 차단제를 다시 바르는 것을 잊지 마라.
① 돕는 ② 가지고 다니는 ③ 다시 바르는 ④ 구입하는 ⑤ 교환하는

SECTION 05

01 **1** ⑤ **2** (1) T (2) F (3) T **3** poorly maintained roads
02 **1** ③ **2** ① **3** land, a public park
03 **1** ④ **2** image, another object **3** ②
04 ④ 변형문제 **1** ② **2** ⓑ **3** happiness

01 책을 가져오는 낙타 P. 58

정답 **1** ⑤ **2** (1) T (2) F (3) T **3** poorly maintained roads

문제해설 **1** 주어진 문장은 어떤 점에도 불구하고 사람들이 책을 빌린다는 내용으로, 그 앞에는 책 읽기나 대여를 어렵게 만드는 상황이 오는 것이 적절하다. 케냐인들이 사용하는 언어와 달리 책이 영어로 되어 있다는 것이 여기에 부합하므로, 주어진 문장은 ⑤에 들어가는 것이 알맞다.

2 (1) 낙타 도서관은 케냐 북부의 일부 지역을 정기적으로 지나간다.
(2) 낙타 도서관의 낙타들은 주말에 일한다. → 월요일부터 목요일까지 일한다고 했다.
(3) 낙타 도서관은 사람들이 빌릴 수 있는 수천 권의 책을 운반한다.

3 케냐에서 자동차보다 낙타가 이동 수단으로 더 적합한 이유는 무엇인가?
→ 낙타는 매우 힘이 세며 열악하게 정비된 도로에서 자동차보다 더 수월하게 이동할 수 있다.

본문

① Although it has books / that people can borrow, / just like any other library, / the "Camel Library" is one-of-a-kind. ② It brings books / to villages / on the backs of camels!
③ In the past, / distant villages in northern Kenya / had little or no access to books. ④ There were no libraries nearby, / and people could not travel / to far-off libraries in cities. ⑤ You might think / that trucks or cars would be better / than camels / for a mobile library, / but not in Kenya. ⑥ Poorly maintained roads / make transportation by vehicle very difficult, / so camels are more reliable / and better suited / to the local conditions. ⑦ Camels are very strong / and can go for a long time / without water.
⑧ Recently, / the Camel Library had 12 camels / that worked from Monday to Thursday / and carried about 7,000 books / to 12 different sites. ⑨ The library visits each village / once every two weeks, / spending an entire day there. ⑩ Villagers can borrow books to read / and return them / the next time the Camel Library arrives. ⑪ Even though the people of Kenya speak Swahili, / most of the books are in English. ⑫ Despite this, / many people borrow books / from the Camel Library. ⑬ That's because / it is their only source of new reading material.

해석 ① 그것은 여느 다른 도서관과 마찬가지로, 사람들이 빌릴 수 있는 책이 있긴 하지만, '낙타 도서관'은 아주 독특하다. ② 그것은 낙타의 등에 책을 싣고 마을들로 운반한다!
③ 과거에 케냐 북부의 멀리 떨어진 마을들은 책을 접할 기회가 거의 없거나 아예 없었다. ④ 근처에 도서관이 없었고, 사람들은 도시의 멀리 떨어진 도서관으로 갈 수도 없었다. ⑤ 당신은 낙타보다는 트럭이나 자동차가 이동도서관

으로 더 낫다고 생각할지도 모르지만, 케냐에서는 그렇지 않다. ⑥ 열악하게 정비된 도로들이 자동차로 통행하는 것을 매우 힘들게 만들어서, 낙타가 더 믿을 만하고 그 지역의 상황에 더 적합하다. ⑦ 낙타는 매우 힘이 세고 오랫동안 물 없이도 이동할 수 있다.

⑧ 최근에 낙타 도서관에는 월요일부터 목요일까지 일하며 열두 개의 다른 지역으로 약 7,000권의 책을 운반하는 낙타가 열두 마리 있었다. ⑨ 그 도서관은 각 마을을 2주에 한 번씩 방문하며, 그곳에서 온종일을 보낸다. ⑩ 마을 사람들은 읽을 책을 빌리고 다음번에 낙타 도서관이 도착하면 책을 반납하면 된다. ⑪ 케냐 사람들은 스와힐리어를 사용하지만, 대부분의 책은 영어로 되어 있다. ⑫ 이 점에도 불구하고, 많은 사람들은 낙타 도서관에서 책을 빌린다. ⑬ 이는 그것이 새로운 읽을거리의 유일한 공급원이기 때문이다.

구문해설

① Although it has books [that people can borrow], just like any other library, ...

→ [ ]은 선행사 books를 수식하는 목적격 관계대명사절

⑧ Recently, the Camel Library had 12 camels [that **worked** from Monday to Thursday and **carried** about 7,000 books ...].

→ [ ]는 선행사 12 camels를 수식하는 주격 관계대명사절

→ worked와 carried가 and로 연결된 병렬구조

⑨ The library visits each village **once every two weeks**, [spending an entire day there].

→ once every two weeks: 2주마다 한 번, 격주로 한 번

→ [ ]는 〈부대상황〉을 나타내는 분사구문

⑩ Villagers can borrow books **to read** and return them the next time the Camel Library arrives.

→ to read는 books를 수식하는 형용사적 용법의 to부정사

02 여기는 쌍둥이들의 천국! P. 60

정답

1 ③ 2 ① 3 land, a public park

문제해설

1 ③ 쌍둥이들을 위한 축제를 만들자고 제안한 적은 없다.

2 (A) the festival을 수식하는 분사이며 축제는 '개최되는' 것이므로, 수동의 의미를 나타내는 과거분사 held가 와야 한다.

(B) '너무 …해서 ~하다'는 「so + 형용사 + that + 주어 + 동사」로 나타내므로 so가 와야 한다.

(C) marry는 타동사이므로 전치사 없이 바로 목적어를 취한다. 따라서 married가 쓰여야 한다.

3 도시는 윌콕스 형제 가족들로부터 공원을 위한 땅을 받는 대가로 도시 이름을 트윈스버그로 바꾸었다.

본문

① Each year / in Twinsburg, Ohio, / the world's largest gathering of twins / takes place. ② Thousands of sets of twins / attend the festival / held in memory of Moses and Aaron Wilcox, / the pair of twin brothers / who gave Twinsburg its name.

③ Moses and Aaron were born / in Killingworth, Connecticut, / on May 18, 1772. ④ They looked so similar / that even their friends and family / couldn't differentiate between them. ⑤ Not only were their appearances identical, / but their lives followed similar courses / as well. ⑥ They married a pair of sisters / and each had nine children. ⑦ Together, / the families moved to a town in Ohio, / where they made an odd proposal / — they would donate land / for a public park / if the town would change its name / to Twinsburg. ⑧ The town agreed, / and the deal was done. ⑨ A few years later, / the twins died on the same day / and were buried together / in a single grave. ⑩ A plaque was erected in the park / to honor the Wilcox twins and / everything that they had done for the town.

해석 ① 오하이오의 트윈스버그에서는 매년 세계에서 가장 큰 쌍둥이들의 모임이 열린다. ② 수천 쌍의 쌍둥이들이 트윈스버그에 그 이름을 선사한 쌍둥이 형제인 모지스 윌콕스와 애런 윌콕스를 기리며 개최되는 이 축제에 참석한다.
③ 모지스와 애런은 1772년 5월 18일에 코네티컷의 킬링워스에서 태어났다. ④ 그들은 매우 비슷하게 생겨서 친구들과 가족조차도 그들을 구별하지 못했다. ⑤ 그들은 외모만 똑같았던 게 아니라 인생까지도 비슷한 과정을 거쳤다. ⑥ 그들은 한 자매와 결혼하여 각각 아홉 명의 자녀를 두었다. ⑦ (두 형제의) 가족들은 다 함께 오하이오에 있는 한 도시로 이사했는데, 그곳에서 그들은 만일 그 도시가 이름을 트윈스버그로 바꾼다면 공원을 위한 땅을 기증하겠다는 특이한 제안을 했다. ⑧ 그 도시는 동의했고, 거래가 성사되었다.
⑨ 몇 년 후에 쌍둥이는 같은 날에 사망했고, 하나의 무덤에 함께 묻혔다. ⑩ 윌콕스 쌍둥이와 그들이 도시를 위해 한 모든 것을 기리기 위해, 공원 안에 명판이 세워졌다.

구문해설 ② Thousands of sets of twins attend the festival [held in memory of Moses and Aaron Wilcox, the pair of twin brothers {who gave Twinsburg its name}].

→ [ ]는 the festival을 수식하는 과거분사구
→ Moses and Aaron Wilcox와 the pair of twin brothers는 동격 관계
→ { }는 선행사 the pair of twin brothers를 수식하는 주격 관계대명사절

⑤ **Not only** (부정어구) were (동사) their appearances (주어) identical, **but** (**also**) their lives followed ....
→ not only A but (also) B: A뿐만 아니라 B도
→ 부정어구 Not only가 문장 맨 앞에 와서 주어와 동사가 도치됨.

⑦ Together, the families moved to a town in Ohio, [where they made an odd proposal ...].
→ [ ]는 선행사 a town in Ohio를 부연 설명하는 계속적 용법의 관계부사절

⑩ A plaque was erected in the park **to honor** the Wilcox twins and everything [that they *had done* for the town].
→ to honor는 〈목적〉을 나타내는 부사적 용법의 to부정사
→ [ ]는 선행사 everything을 수식하는 목적격 관계대명사절로, 선행사가 -thing으로 끝나는 부정대명사인 경우 주로 관계대명사 that을 사용함.
→ had done은 주절의 과거 시점(was erected)보다 더 이전에 일어난 일을 나타내는 과거완료

03 무엇이 보이나요? P. 62

정답 1 ④ 2 image, another object 3 ②

문제해설 1 vague는 '흐릿한, 모호한'을 의미하므로 '분명하지 않은'을 의미하는 ④ unclear와 바꿔 쓸 수 있다.
① 믿을 수 없는 ② 익숙한 ③ 독특한 ⑤ 정확한

2 파레이돌리아는 사람들로 하여금 다른 물체에서 사람이나 사물의 이미지를 보게 만드는 현상이다.
사람이 다른 물체에서 어떤 사람이나 사물의 이미지를 보는 현상

3 (A) 파레이돌리아 현상에 관해 설명한 다음, 이에 대한 예시로 성모 마리아의 이미지가 보이는 치즈 샌드위치를 언급하고 있으므로, For example이 적절하다.
(B) 빈칸 앞에서 백만 년 전 부모의 얼굴을 인식할 수 없었던 아기들이 부모와의 강한 유대감을 형성하지 못했기 때문에 생존율이 낮았다는 내용이 언급되었는데, 이는 우리의 두뇌 속에 인간의 얼굴을 식별하는 능력이 갖춰져 있다는 빈칸 뒤 내용의 이유에 해당하므로, 빈칸에는 For this reason이 적절하다.

본문

① Some people claim to have found a smiling face / on the surface of Mars. ② Others say / that they have seen images of animals / in clouds. ③ Why is this?

④ The phenomenon / that causes people to see / the image of a person or a thing / in another object / is known as pareidolia. ⑤ It starts / when our brains perceive a vague image / as being more significant / than it really is. ⑥ There have been many instances / of this type of phenomenon. ⑦ For example, / in America / there was a grilled cheese sandwich / that people claimed / had an image of the Virgin Mary / on it. ⑧ And / in Singapore, / there was an event / that became known as / the "monkey tree phenomenon." ⑨ People from all around the country / came to view a tree / that seemed to contain / an image of a monkey god.

⑩ So / why does this happen? ⑪ Some scientists believe / that pareidolia is a trait / that we developed / through evolution / to help us survive. ⑫ A million years ago, / babies who were unable to recognize their parents' faces / smiled at them less / and therefore didn't develop strong bonds. ⑬ This made it less likely / that they'd survive. ⑭ For this reason, / the ability to identify the human face / is hardwired / in our brains. ⑮ So, / because we can recognize faces / with only minimal details, / we sometimes interpret random shapes and patterns / as faces. ⑯ If you ever see a face / looking back at you / from an unexpected place, / don't panic. ⑰ It's probably / just a result of evolution!

해석

① 어떤 사람들은 화성의 표면에서 미소 짓는 얼굴을 발견했다고 주장한다. ② 또 다른 사람들은 구름 속에서 동물의 이미지를 보았다고 한다. ③ 이것은 왜 그럴까?

④ 사람들로 하여금 다른 물체에서 사람이나 사물의 이미지를 보게 만드는 현상은 파레이돌리아라고 알려져 있다. ⑤ 그것은 우리의 뇌가 어떤 희미한 이미지를 실제보다 더 의미 있는 것으로 인식할 때 시작된다. ⑥ 이런 유형의 현상의 많은 사례가 있었다. ⑦ 예를 들어, 미국에는 성모 마리아의 이미지가 그 위에 있다고 사람들이 주장하는, 그릴에 구운 치즈 샌드위치가 있었다. ⑧ 그리고 싱가포르에서는 '원숭이 나무 현상'이라고 알려지게 된 사건이 있었다. ⑨ 전국 여기저기에서 사람들이 원숭이 신의 이미지를 담고 있는 것처럼 보이는 나무를 구경하기 위해 왔다.

⑩ 그렇다면 이런 일이 왜 생기는 걸까? ⑪ 몇몇 과학자들은 파레이돌리아가 우리가 생존하는 데 도움이 되도록 진화 과정을 거치면서 발달시킨 특징이라고 믿는다. ⑫ 백만 년 전, 부모의 얼굴을 인식할 수 없었던 아기들은 부모를 향해 덜 웃었고, 그래서 강한 유대감을 형성하지 못했다. ⑬ 이것은 그들이 살아남을 확률을 더 적게 만들었다. ⑭ 이러한 이유로, 인간의 얼굴을 식별하는 능력은 우리의 두뇌 속에 갖춰져 있는 것이다. ⑮ 따라서, 우리가 아주 적은 세부 사항만으로도 얼굴을 인식할 수 있기 때문에, 우리는 종종 임의의 형상과 무늬를 얼굴이라고 해석하는 것이다.
⑯ 만일 뜻밖의 장소에서 당신을 쳐다보는 얼굴을 발견한다면, 당황하지 마라. ⑰ 그것은 그저 진화의 결과일 뿐이다!

구문해설

④ The phenomenon [that **causes** people **to see** the image ...] is known as pareidolia.
S V

→ [ ]는 선행사 The phenomenon을 수식하는 주격 관계대명사절
→ cause + 목적어 + to-v: …로 하여금 ~하게 하다

⑦ For example, in America there was a grilled cheese sandwich [that **people claimed** had an image of the Virgin Mary on *it*].
→ [ ]는 선행사 a grilled cheese sandwich를 수식하는 주격 관계대명사절이며, people claimed가 관계사절 내에 삽입됨.
→ it은 a grilled cheese sandwich를 가리킴.

⑪ ... pareidolia is a trait [that we developed through evolution **to *help*** us *survive*].
→ [ ]는 선행사 a trait를 수식하는 목적격 관계대명사절
→ to help는 〈목적〉을 나타내는 부사적 용법의 to부정사
→ help + 목적어 + 동사원형: …가 ~하는 것을 돕다

⑬ This made **it** less likely [that they'd survive].
→ it은 가목적어, 명사절 [ ]가 진목적어

⑯ If you ever see a face [looking back at you] from an unexpected place, don't panic.
→ [ ]는 a face를 뒤에서 수식하는 현재분사구

04 어휘 P. 64

정답 ④ 변형문제 **1** ② **2** ⓑ **3** happiness

문제해설 글의 흐름상 '선택 항목이 더 많아질수록, 사람들은 더 무력해진다'라는 의미가 되어야 하므로, ④의 relieved를 paralyzed 등으로 바꿔야 한다.

변형문제

1 선택할 수 있는 것이 많아질수록 행복감은 덜해진다는 내용이므로 제목으로는 ② '폭넓은 선택의 모순'이 적절하다.
① 똑똑한 소비자 되기
③ 무료 견본 뒤에 숨은 심리학
④ 사람들이 인생에서 더 많은 선택권을 원하는 이유

⑤ 여러분은 선택권이 많을수록, 더 행복해진다

2 지문은 선택 항목의 수와 행복감의 관계에 대한 내용으로, 이를 보여주는 연구와 그 결과를 제시하고 있다. 따라서 사람들의 감정에 영향을 미치는 다른 요소들에 대해 언급한 ⓑ는 전체 흐름과 무관하다.

3 사람들은 고를 수 있는 많은 선택 항목을 원하는 것처럼 보이지만, 그것들을 가지는 것이 항상 행복을 가져오는 것은 아니다.

본문

① The overabundance of options / in today's marketplace / gives you more freedom of choice. ② However, / there may be a price to pay / in terms of happiness. ③ According to research by psychologists David Myers and Robert Lane, / all this choice often makes people depressed. ④ (They were followed by Barry Schwartz, / who found other factors that influence people's emotions.) ⑤ Researchers gave some shoppers / 24 choices of jams to taste / and others / only 6 choices. ⑥ Those who had fewer choices / were happier with the tasting. ⑦ Even more surprisingly, / the ones with a smaller selection / purchased jam 31% of the time, / while those with a wider range of choices / only purchased jam 3% of the time. ⑧ The ironic thing about this / is that people nearly always say / they want more choices. ⑨ Yet, / the more options they have, / the more paralyzed they become. ⑩ Savvy restaurant owners provide fewer choices. ⑪ This allows customers to feel more relaxed, / prompting them to choose easily / and leave more satisfied with their choices.

해석

① 오늘날 시장에서 선택 항목의 과잉은 당신에게 더 많은 선택의 자유를 준다. ② 그러나 행복의 관점에서는 치러야 할 대가가 있을지도 모른다. ③ 심리학자 데이비드 마이어스와 로버트 레인의 연구에 따르면 모든 이러한 선택은 자주 사람들을 우울하게 만든다. ④ (그들에 뒤이어 배리 슈워츠는 사람들의 감정에 영향을 미치는 다른 요소들을 발견했다.) ⑤ 연구자들이 어떤 쇼핑객들에게는 24개의 잼을 맛보게 했고 다른 사람들에게는 오직 6개만 맛보게 했다. ⑥ 더 적은 선택 항목을 가진 사람들이 맛볼 때 더 행복했다. ⑦ 훨씬 더 놀랍게도, 더 넓은 범위의 선택 사항을 가진 사람들 중 오직 3%만이 잼을 구매한 반면, 더 적은 선택 사항을 가진 사람들은 전체 경우 중 31%가 잼을 구매했다. ⑧ 이에 관해 얄궂은 점은 사람들이 거의 항상 더 많은 선택 항목을 원한다고 말한다는 것이다. ⑨ 그러나 선택 항목이 더 많아질수록 그들은 더 무력해진다. ⑩ 사리에 밝은 레스토랑 사장들은 더 적은 선택 항목을 제공한다. ⑪ 이것은 고객들이 더 편안함을 느끼게 하고, 그들이 쉽게 선택하고 그 선택에 더 만족한 채 (레스토랑을) 떠나도록 한다.

구문해설

③ ..., all this choice often **makes people depressed**.
→ make+목적어+목적격보어(형용사): (목적어)가 …하게 하다

④ They were followed by Barry Schwartz, **who** found other factors that influence people's emotions.
→ who는 Barry Schwartz를 부연 설명하는 계속적 용법의 주격 관계대명사(=and he)

⑨ Yet, **the more** options they have, **the more** paralyzed they become.
→ the+비교급 ..., the+비교급 ~: …할수록, 더 ~해지다

⑪ This **allows** customers **to feel** more relaxed, [*prompting* them *to choose* easily and *leave* more satisfied with their choices].
→ allow+목적어+to-v: (목적어)가 …하게 해주다

→ [ ]는 〈연속동작〉을 나타내는 분사구문(= and it prompts....)
→ prompt+목적어+to-v: (목적어)가 …하도록 하다

Review Test

P. 66

A 1 ⓑ 2 ⓐ 3 ⓓ 4 ⓔ 5 ⓒ B 1 erected 2 identify 3 perceive 4 differentiate C 1 ⑤ 2 ④ 3 ③ 4 ② D 1 이것은 그들이 살아남을 확률을 더 적게 만들었다. 2 선택 항목이 더 많아질수록 그들은 더 무력해진다. 3 그들은 외모만 똑같았던 게 아니라 인생까지도 비슷한 과정을 거쳤다. 4 마을 사람들은 읽을 책을 빌리고 다음번에 도서관이 도착하면 책을 반납하면 된다. E 1 prompting them to choose easily 2 a tree that seemed to contain 3 if the town would change its name

해석

A

1 모호한: ⓑ 분명히 진술되거나 보이거나 느껴지지 않는
2 거래: ⓐ 주로 상호 이익을 위한 합의
3 자료: ⓓ 책을 만드는 데 사용되는 사실, 정보, 또는 생각
4 현상: ⓔ 관찰될 수 있는 어떤 것
5 선택: ⓒ 한 집단에서 어떤 것을 선택하는 행위

B

1 그 작곡가의 죽음 후에, 그를 기리기 위해 동상이 세워졌다.
2 기술자들이 네트워크 오류의 원인을 확인하려고 노력하고 있다.
3 아기들은 태어나기 전부터 감각 정보를 인식하기 시작한다.
4 당신은 어떻게 저 두 종의 새를 구별하세요?

C

1 안전벨트를 매는 것은 자동차 충돌로 부상을 입을 확률을 줄이는 데 중요한 요소이다.
① 정확한 ② 미지의 ③ 호의적인 ④ 이동하는 ⑤ 중요한

2 그 우주선의 임무는 멀리 떨어진 행성들을 탐사하고 그것들에 대한 데이터를 수집하는 것이다.
① 사실이 아닌 ② 지속적인 ③ 직접적인 ④ 멀리 떨어진 ⑤ 즉각적인

3 우리는 그 직책에 믿을 수 있고 똑똑한 사람을 찾고 있다.
① 심각하지 않은 ② 부정적인 ③ 믿을 수 있는 ④ 얄궂은 ⑤ 이상한

4 현대의 통신과 수송 체계 때문에, 세상은 점점 더 작아지고 있다.
① 원천 ② 수송 ③ 인식 ④ 해석 ⑤ 진화

SECTION 06

01 1 ⑤ 2 ③ 3 prime-numbered, natural predators
02 1 ① 2 (A) neither (B) nor 3 ①
03 1 ④ 2 Lake Chad has shrunk by nearly 95 percent since 1963. 3 ②
04 ① 변형문제 1 ⑤ 2 we have enough physical strength to do so 3 ②

01 17년마다 나타나요 P. 70

정답 1 ⑤ 2 ③ 3 prime-numbered, natural predators

문제해설 1 (A) 수식하는 앞의 명사 insects와 수동 관계에 있으므로 과거분사 known이 적절하다.
(B) 동사 avoid는 목적어로 동명사를 취하므로 encountering이 와야 한다.
(C) 'A에게 B를 생각나게 하다'는 「remind A of B」로 나타낸다.

2 매미들이 생활 주기를 소수로 맞춰 한꺼번에 나타나는 것은 천적들이 매미를 한꺼번에 잡아먹지 못하게 하고 천적들과 마주치는 것을 피하기 위해서라고 했으므로, 빈칸에는 ③ '자신의 종족을 보존하는'이 가장 적절하다.
① 자신의 포식자를 만나는 ② 자신의 몸집을 조절하는
④ 자신의 적과 잘 지내는 ⑤ 자신의 천적들을 잡아먹는

3 미국의 일부 지역에서, 매미는 그들의 천적들로부터 스스로를 보호하려고 소수의 생활 주기를 가진다.

본문
① Every 17 years / in the eastern United States, / an amazing natural phenomenon occurs / — the area is invaded / by billions of insects / known as "17-year cicadas." ② A similar occurrence can be witnessed / in the southern part of the country, / where "13-year cicadas" and "7-year cicadas" are found.
③ Incredibly, / these cicada species all fit into / the pattern of prime numbers. ④ So, / why do cicadas appear / all at once at prime-numbered intervals? ⑤ This is actually the cicada's way / of preserving its own species. ⑥ First, / with the calculation / that natural predators cannot eat / billions of cicadas / at once, / cicadas appear all at the same time. ⑦ Also, / by basing their life cycles on prime numbers, / they ensure / that their life cycles are different from / those of their natural predators. ⑧ This allows cicadas to avoid encountering predators / for long periods of time. ⑨ For instance, / if the cycle of the cicada is 17 years / and that of a natural predator / is 3 years, / they can only meet / once every 51 years. ⑩ The sound of billions of cicadas / singing at once / reminds some people of a horror movie. ⑪ But / in some parts of North America, / people are comforted by the fact / that they won't have to hear them again / for another 17 years.

해석 ① 미국 동부에서는 17년마다 놀라운 자연 현상이 발생한다. 그 지역은 '17년 매미'로 알려진 곤충 수십억 마리의 침입을 받는다. ② 비슷한 사건이 이 나라의 남부에서도 목격되는데, 그곳에서는 '13년 매미'와 '7년 매미'가 발견된다. ③ 놀랍게도, 이 매미 종들은 모두 소수(素數)의 패턴에 들어맞는다. ④ 그렇다면, 매미들은 왜 소수 간격으로 한꺼번

에 나타나는 걸까? ⑤ 이것은 사실 자신의 종족을 보존하는 매미의 방식이다. ⑥ 첫째로, 천적이 한꺼번에 수십억 마리의 매미를 먹을 수 없다는 계산하에, 매미들은 모두 동시에 나타난다. ⑦ 또한 그들의 생활 주기를 소수에 기반을 둠으로써, 그들은 자신들의 생활 주기가 천적의 생활 주기와 다르도록 한다. ⑧ 이것은 매미들이 오랜 기간 동안 포식자들을 마주치지 않게 해준다. ⑨ 예를 들어, 매미의 주기가 17년이고 천적의 주기가 3년이라면, 그들은 51년마다 한 번만 만날 수 있다.

⑩ 동시에 울어대는 수십억 마리의 매미 소리는 일부 사람들에게 공포영화를 연상시킨다. ⑪ 하지만 북미의 일부 지역에서, 사람들은 그들을 17년 동안 다시 듣지 않아도 될 거라는 사실에 위안을 받는다.

구문해설

② A similar occurrence can be witnessed in the southern part of the country, [where "13-year cicadas" and "7-year cicadas" are found].
→ [ ]는 선행사 the southern part of the country를 부연 설명하는 계속적 용법의 관계부사절

⑦ ..., they ensure [that their life cycles are different from **those** of their natural predators].
→ [ ]는 ensure의 목적어로 쓰인 명사절
→ those는 life cycles를 대신하는 대명사

⑩ The sound (S) of billions of cicadas [singing at once] reminds (V) some people of a horror movie.
→ [ ]는 billions of cicadas를 뒤에서 수식하는 현재분사구

⑪ ..., people are comforted by the fact [that they won't have to hear them again for another 17 years].
→ the fact와 [ ]는 동격 관계로, [ ]는 the fact의 내용을 구체적으로 설명하는 명사절

02 그날은 일급비밀! P. 72

정답 1 ① 2 (A) neither (B) nor 3 ①

문제해설

1 디데이라는 용어를 설명하고 그것이 쓰이는 예를 들고 있으므로, 주제로는 ① '디데이라는 용어는 어떻게 쓰이는가'가 가장 적절하다.
② 연합군의 노르망디 침공 ③ 시간을 알리는 다양한 방법
④ 디데이라는 용어가 사용된 최초의 시기 ⑤ 시간을 기록하는 것의 중요성

2 'A도 B도 아닌'이라는 뜻은 상관접속사 「neither A nor B」를 써서 나타내므로, 빈칸 (A)와 (B)에는 각각 neither와 nor가 들어가야 한다.

3 이 글은 디데이라는 용어가 군대 안팎에서 어떤 경우에 쓰이는지를 설명하는 내용인데, 노르망디 침공을 기념하는 프로그램을 준비하고 있다는 ①번 문장은 흐름에 맞지 않는다.

본문

① When an important event is being planned, / the day on which it is scheduled to occur / is sometimes referred to as "D-Day." ② In the military, / this term refers to the day / on which a certain operation / will be carried out. ③ The most famous D-Day took place / during World War II. ④ On June 6, 1944, / Allied forces landed at Normandy, France, / to free mainland

Europe / from the Nazis. ⑤ However, / this was neither the first / nor the last military operation / to be designated as D-Day. ⑥ (To celebrate the anniversary of the invasion, / Normandy is organizing a program of events / commemorating D-Day.) ⑦ In addition, / the term is commonly used / outside of the military / whenever the date of an event / needs to be kept a secret. ⑧ It is also sometimes used / if the date has not yet been decided. ⑨ Along with "D-Day," / the term "H-Hour" is used / to refer to the exact hour / at which the event will take place. ⑩ Numbers with plus or minus signs / can be used / to refer to certain times / before or after D-Day or H-Hour. ⑪ For example, / H-4 means four hours before H-Hour, / while D+5 means five days after D-Day. ⑫ By using these terms, / the timing of an event can be talked about / both easily and secretly.

해석 ① 중요한 일이 계획되고 있을 때, 그것이 발생할 예정인 날짜는 때때로 '디데이'라고 말해진다. ② 군대에서, 이 용어는 특정 작전이 수행될 날짜를 나타낸다. ③ 가장 유명한 디데이는 제2차 세계대전 중에 발생했다. ④ 1944년 6월 6일에, 연합군은 나치로부터 유럽 본토를 해방시키기 위해 프랑스의 노르망디에 상륙했다. ⑤ 그러나, 이것은 디데이로 지정된 첫 번째 (군사 작전)도 마지막 군사 작전도 아니었다. ⑥ (그 침공 기념일을 기념하기 위해, 노르망디는 디데이를 기념하는 행사 프로그램을 준비하고 있다.) ⑦ 게다가, 그 용어는 어떤 일의 날짜가 비밀로 유지되어야 할 때는 언제든지 군대 밖에서도 흔히 사용된다. ⑧ 그것은 때때로 날짜가 아직 정해지지 않았을 때에도 사용된다. ⑨ '디데이'와 함께, '에이치아워'라는 용어도 일이 발생할 정확한 시간을 나타내기 위해 사용된다. ⑩ 플러스와 마이너스 표시가 있는 숫자는 디데이 또는 에이치아워 전이나 후의 특정 시간을 나타내는 데 사용될 수 있다. ⑪ 예를 들어, H-4는 에이치아워 4시간 전을 의미하는 반면, D+5는 디데이 5일 후를 의미한다. ⑫ 이 용어들을 사용함으로써, 어떤 일의 시기가 쉽고도 은밀히 이야기될 수 있다.

구문해설 ① When an important event **is being planned**, the day (S) [on which it is scheduled to occur] is sometimes *referred to* as (V) "D-Day."

→ is being planned는 '…되고 있다, …당하고 있다'의 의미를 나타내는 현재진행형 수동태
→ [ ]는 선행사 the day를 수식하는 목적격 관계대명사절
→ refer to A as B: A를 B라고 부르다

⑦ ..., the term is commonly used outside of the military **whenever** the date of an event needs to be kept a secret.

→ whenever는 '…할 때는 언제든지'를 의미하는 복합관계부사

⑫ By using these terms, the timing of an event can be talked about **both** easily **and** secretly.

→ 「both A and B」는 'A와 B 둘 다'를 의미하는 상관접속사

03 아프리카의 줄어드는 호수 P. 74

정답 **1** ④ **2** Lake Chad has shrunk by nearly 95 percent since 1963. **3** ②

문제해설 1 차드 호수 지역의 연간 강수량은 감소하고 있다고만 했을 뿐 얼마인지는 언급되지 않았으므로 ④ '차드 호수 지역의 연간 강수량은 얼마인가?'라는 질문에는 답할 수 없다.

① 차드 호수는 지금까지 얼마나 줄어들었나?
② 지금 차드 호수는 얼마나 큰가?
③ 차드 호수가 줄어들고 있는 주요 원인들은 무엇인가?
⑤ 차드 호수의 지리적 특징은 무엇인가?

2 밑줄 친 the change는 맨 처음 언급된, 차드 호수가 1963년 이래 95퍼센트 가까이 줄어들었다는 사실을 의미한다.

3 빈칸 앞 문장에서 더 많은 사람들이 물 수요를 충족하기 위해 차드 호수에 의존하고 있다고 했으므로, 빈칸에는 ② '사람들에게 소중한 수원'이 들어가는 것이 가장 적절하다.

① 외국인들을 위한 완벽한 휴양지
③ 야생동물들의 중요한 자연 서식지
④ 사람들이 이윤을 창출하는 유용한 방법
⑤ 지역 사업을 위한 유명 관광지

본문

① Reports from NASA researchers indicate / that Lake Chad has shrunk / by nearly 95 percent / since 1963. ② Once the fourth-largest body of water in Africa, / it stretched across 9,650 square miles; / now it covers a surface area / of just 520 square miles. ③ What's worse, / projections show / that this trend will continue, / leaving the lake as little more than a "puddle" / in a few years.

④ The reports explain / that a range of factors / are most likely responsible for the change. ⑤ First of all, / global warming over the last few decades / has played a part, / with the region / where the lake is located / experiencing consistent drops in rainfall levels / over this time. ⑥ Secondly, / the particular geographical features of the lake / have contributed to the problem. ⑦ The fact / that the lake is very shallow / means / that its water has evaporated / more quickly / than that of deeper lakes. ⑧ The final reason / is excessive use of water / for drinking and farming. ⑨ The population in the region / has increased dramatically / in recent years, / meaning / many more people are relying on the lake / to fill their water needs. ⑩ The lake has traditionally been / a precious source of water / for people across six countries / — Sudan, Chad, Niger, Nigeria, Cameroon / and the Central African Republic. ⑪ Today, / it is believed to be depended on / by around 20 million people.

⑫ Unfortunately, / the researchers are not optimistic / about the future. ⑬ They expect global warming to get worse / and believe / competition over water resources / will become more intense. ⑭ Moreover, / while the lake may be able to sustain human populations / for a while longer, / the rich wildlife surrounding the lake / is expected to die out / in the near future.

해석

① 나사(NASA) 연구원들의 보고는 차드 호수가 1963년 이래로 95퍼센트 가까이 줄어들었다는 것을 보여준다. ② 한때 아프리카에서 네 번째로 큰 수역이었던 그곳은 9,650 평방 마일에 걸쳐 펼쳐져 있었는데, 지금은 겨우 520평방 마일의 표면적밖에 차지하지 않는다. ③ 더 심각하게는, 이러한 추세가 계속되어, 몇 년 안에 호수는 '물웅덩이'에 지나지 않게 될 것으로 추정된다.

④ 보고는 다양한 요인들이 그 변화의 원인인 것 같다고 설명한다. ⑤ 우선, 지난 수십 년에 걸친 지구 온난화가 일조하여, 그 호수가 위치한 지역은 이 시기 동안에 지속적인 강우량 감소를 겪었다. ⑥ 둘째로, 그 호수 특유의 지리적 특

징이 그 문제의 한 원인이 되었다. ⑦ 호수가 매우 얕다는 사실은 그것의 물이 깊은 호수의 물보다 더 빨리 증발한다는 것을 뜻한다. ⑧ 마지막 이유는 식수와 농업을 위한 과도한 물의 사용이다. ⑨ 그 지역의 인구는 최근 몇 년 동안 급격히 증가했는데, 이는 더 많은 사람들이 그들의 물 수요를 충족하기 위해 그 호수에 의존하고 있다는 것을 의미한다. ⑩ 그 호수는 전통적으로 수단, 차드, 니제르, 나이지리아, 카메룬, 그리고 중앙 아프리카 공화국, 이 여섯 국가의 사람들에게 소중한 수원이 되어 왔다. ⑪ 오늘날, 약 2천만 명의 사람들이 그 호수에 의존하고 있다고 여겨진다. ⑫ 안타깝게도, 연구원들은 미래에 대해 낙관적이지 않다. ⑬ 그들은 지구 온난화가 더 악화될 것이라고 예상하며, 수자원에 대한 경쟁이 더 치열해질 것이라고 믿는다. ⑭ 게다가, 호수가 잠깐 동안은 더 인구를 부양할 수 있을지도 모르지만, 호수 주위의 풍부한 야생 생물은 가까운 미래에 멸종될 것으로 예상된다.

구문해설 ② [Once the fourth-largest body of water in Africa], it stretched across 9,650 square miles; ....

→ 명사구 [ ]와 it은 동격 관계

③ **What's worse**, projections show that this trend will continue, [leaving the lake as *little more than* a "puddle" ...].

→ what's worse: 더욱 나쁜 것은

→ [ ]는 〈연속동작〉을 나타내는 분사구문

→ little more than: …에 지나지 않는, …와 마찬가지인

⑤ ... has played a part, **with the region** [where the lake is located] **experiencing** consistent drops in rainfall levels ....

→ with+(대)명사+현재분사: …가 ~한 채로[하면서]

→ [ ]는 선행사 the region을 수식하는 관계부사절

⑦ The fact [that the lake is very shallow] means [that its water **has evaporated** more quickly than *that* of deeper lakes].

→ The fact와 첫 번째 [ ]는 동격 관계로, [ ]는 The fact의 내용을 구체적으로 설명하는 명사절

→ 두 번째 [ ]는 means의 목적어로 쓰인 명사절

→ has evaporated는 〈계속〉을 나타내는 현재완료

→ that은 앞에 나온 water를 대신하는 대명사

04 요약문 완성 P. 76

정답 ① 변형문제 **1** ⑤ **2** we have enough physical strength to do so **3** ②

문제해설 어린 시절에는 다양한 팀 스포츠에 참여하지만 성인이 되면서 체력이 저하되어 팀 스포츠를 기피하게 된다는 내용이다.

→ 성인들은 팀 스포츠를 피하는 경향이 있는데, 이는 나이가 들면서 그들의 체력 수준이 변하기 때문이다.

변형문제

1 어린 시절과는 달리 성인이 된 뒤에는 체력의 저하로 인해 팀 스포츠에 참여하는 것을 기피하게 된다는 내용이므로, 글의 주제로는 ⑤ '나이가 어떻게 사람들의 스포츠 참여에 영향을 주는가'가 가장 적절하다.

① 성인들을 위한 운동의 건강상의 이점　② 아이들이 스포츠를 하도록 권장하는 방법
③ 시간이 흐르면서 신체에 생기는 변화　④ 대부분의 성인들이 스포츠를 즐기지 않는 이유

2 주어는 we, 동사는 have이며, 목적어인 명사구 enough physical strength를 형용사적 용법의 to부정사구가 뒤에서 수식하는 어순으로 we have enough physical strength to do so라고 쓰는 것이 적절하다.

3 (A) 문맥상 최고 수준에서 '경쟁하다'가 자연스러우므로 compete가 적절하다. compare는 '비교하다'라는 의미이다.
(B) 문맥상 충돌이 잦은 팀 스포츠에 '참여하기'를 그만둔다는 의미가 되어야 적절하므로 participating이 알맞다. anticipate는 '기대하다'라는 뜻이다.
(C) 문맥상 성인들을 위한 팀 스포츠를 '조직하기'가 더 어려워진다는 내용이 자연스러우므로 organize가 되어야 한다. recognize는 '알아보다, 인식하다'라는 의미이다.

본문

① Our childhood years are often spent / testing our physical limits / through all kinds of team sports. ② By the time we reach high school, / we may even engage in / two or three different team sports / at once. ③ At that age, / we have enough physical strength / to do so. ④ But / by the time we become adults, / even though the majority of us still enjoy playing sports, / very few of us have the ability / to compete at the elite level. ⑤ We find / that we don't have the physical strength / that we used to. ⑥ Naturally, / we stop participating in / team sports with frequent collisions, / such as football, basketball, and soccer, / and we move towards sports / that involve less stress on the body / and risk of physical injury. ⑦ Many adults get involved in / individual sports, / instead. ⑧ Thus, / it becomes more difficult / to organize team sports / for adults.

해석

① 우리의 어린 시절은 종종 온갖 종류의 팀 스포츠를 통해 우리의 신체적 한계를 시험하며 보내진다. ② 고등학생이 될 무렵에, 우리는 한 번에 두세 개의 다른 팀 스포츠에 참여하기도 한다. ③ 그 나이 때에는, 우리는 그렇게 할 수 있는 충분한 체력을 가지고 있다. ④ 그러나 성인이 되는 시기가 되면, 비록 우리 중 대다수가 여전히 스포츠를 즐긴다 하더라도, 극히 소수의 사람들만이 최고 수준에서 경쟁할 수 있는 능력을 가진다. ⑤ 우리는 과거에는 있었던 체력이 (현재에는) 없다는 것을 알게 된다. ⑥ 자연스럽게 우리는 미식축구나 농구, 축구와 같은 잦은 충돌이 있는 팀 스포츠에 참여하는 것을 그만두고, 신체에 스트레스와 신체적 부상의 위험을 덜 주는 스포츠로 옮겨간다. ⑦ 많은 성인들은 대신에 개인 스포츠에 참여한다. ⑧ 그래서, 성인들을 위한 팀 스포츠를 조직하는 것은 더욱 어려워진다.

구문해설

① **Our childhood years** **are** often **spent testing** our physical limits ....
(S: Our childhood years / V: are ... spent)
→ 「spend+시간+v-ing」는 '…하는 데 시간을 보내다'라는 의미이며, spend의 목적어에 해당하는 시간이 주어로 쓰인 수동태 문장임.

④ ..., **even though** the majority of us still enjoy playing sports, very few of us have the ability *to compete* at the elite level.
→ even though: 비록 …일지라도, …라고 하더라도
→ to compete는 the ability를 수식하는 형용사적 용법의 to부정사

⑤ We find [that we don't have the physical strength {that we **used to** (**have**)}].

→ [ ]는 find의 목적어로 쓰인 명사절

→ { }는 선행사 the physical strength를 수식하는 목적격 관계대명사절

→「used to+동사원형」은 '(과거에는) …이었다'라는 의미로 과거의 상태를 나타내며, 앞에 나온 동사의 반복을 피하기 위해 used to 다음에 have가 생략됨.

Review Test P. 78

A **1** ① B **1** indicates **2** collision **3** preserving **4** comforted C **1** ③ **2** ④ **3** ② **4** ⑤ D **1** 그 호수 특유의 지리적 특징이 그 문제의 한 원인이 되었다. **2** 이 용어들을 사용함으로써, 어떤 일의 시기가 쉽고도 은밀히 이야기될 수 있다. **3** 호수 주위의 풍부한 야생 생물은 가까운 미래에 멸종될 것으로 예상된다. **4** 고등학생이 될 무렵에, 우리는 한 번에 두세 개의 다른 팀 스포츠에 참여하기도 한다. E **1** it is scheduled to occur **2** the lake as little more than a "puddle" **3** This allows cicadas to avoid

해석 **A**

① 얕은: 매우 깊은

② 목격하다: 어떤 일이 일어나는 것을 보다

③ 줄어들다: 크기나 양이 더 작아지다

④ 한계: 그 너머로는 어떤 것이 존재하지 않는 지점

⑤ 경쟁하다: 활동이나 대회에서 이기려고 애쓰다

B

1 그 그래프는 여성이 남성보다 더 오래 사는 경향이 있음을 나타낸다.

2 그 축구 선수는 다른 선수와의 충돌로 이마를 다쳤다.

3 그 단체는 멸종 위기 종을 보존하는 데 전념한다.

4 그녀는 외로울 때면 항상 음악으로 자신을 위로했다.

C

1 법률 분야에서 용어를 명확히 정의하는 것은 매우 중요하다.

① 간격 ② 먹이 ③ 용어 ④ 기념일 ⑤ 작전

2 도시 범죄율의 계속되는 증가는 사람들을 걱정하게 만들었다.

① 숨겨진 ② 변동이 심한 ③ 강박적인 ④ 계속되는 ⑤ 경쟁력 있는

3 병원의 접수원이 건강 검진에 대해 상기시키려고 나에게 전화를 걸었다.

① 야기하려고 ② 상기시키려고 ③ 관찰하려고 ④ 침략하려고 ⑤ 방해하려고

4 자신의 팀이 우승하지 않는 선수들도 시합에 참여한 것에 대해 메달을 받을 것이다.

① 지원한 ② 제공한 ③ 지연시킨 ④ 관리한 ⑤ 참여한

SECTION 07

01 1 ① 2 ⑤ 3 that they believed could turn any metal into gold 4 ③
02 1 ⑤ 2 ⑤ 3 ② 4 increased, hunger
03 1 ② 2 ② 3 the influence of Puritanism on Dutch culture
04 ② 변형문제 1 ① 2 ⓐ sending ⓑ wrote it down 3 caught in a bad storm

01 미신일까? 과학일까? P. 82

정답 1 ① 2 ⑤ 3 that they believed could turn any metal into gold 4 ③

문제해설 1 연금술의 개념과 그것이 발전해온 역사에 대한 내용이므로, 주제로는 ① '연금술의 역사'가 가장 적절하다.
② 연금술의 다양한 용도 ③ 현자의 돌이란 무엇인가
④ 왜 과학자들은 연금술을 믿지 않는가 ⑤ 화학은 연금술과 어떻게 다른가

2 문맥상 토대를 '놓다'가 적절하므로 '…을 놓다, 두다'의 의미인 타동사 lay(-laid-laid)의 과거형 laid가 쓰여야 어법에 맞다. lay는 '…에 놓여 있다'라는 의미의 자동사 lie(-lay-lain)의 과거형이다.

3 주격 관계대명사절 내에 「주어+believe」 형태의 어구가 삽입된 that they believed could turn any metal into gold로 쓰는 것이 적절하다.

4 ③ 연금술이 전문적인 학문으로 살아남은 곳은 이집트라고 했다.

본문

① Alchemy in the Middle Ages / was a mixture / of science, philosophy, and mysticism. ② It was based on the belief / that all matter is composed of four elements: / earth, air, fire, and water. ③ It was thought that / with the right combination of these elements, / any substance might be formed, / including precious metals / and remedies to cure diseases and prolong life. ④ The dream of alchemists / was to find the "philosopher's stone," / a mysterious substance / that they believed / could turn any metal into gold.
⑤ Alchemy originated in ancient times, / evolving independently / in China, India, and Greece. ⑥ In each of these places, / the practice ultimately degenerated into superstition, / but it migrated to Egypt / and survived there / as a scholarly discipline. ⑦ In medieval Europe, / alchemy was revived / when 12th-century scholars / translated Arabic works into Latin. ⑧ The rediscovered writings of Aristotle / also played a role. ⑨ By the end of the 13th century, / it was discussed seriously / by leading philosophers, scientists, and theologians. ⑩ Eventually, / the practice of alchemy / laid the foundation / for the development of chemistry as a scientific discipline.

해석 ① 중세 시대의 연금술은 과학, 철학, 그리고 신비주의의 혼합물이었다. ② 그것은 모든 물질이 흙, 공기, 불, 물의 4원소로 이루어져 있다는 믿음에 기초했다. ③ 이 원소들을 알맞게 조합하면, 귀금속과 병을 치료하고 수명을 연장시키는 약을 포함하여 어떤 물질이든 만들어질 수 있다고 생각되었다. ④ 연금술사들의 꿈은 어떤 금속이든 금으로 바꿀 수 있다고 그들이 믿었던 신비한 물질인 '현자(賢者)의 돌'을 찾는 것이었다.

⑤ 연금술은 고대에 생겨났고, 중국, 인도, 그리스에서 독립적으로 발달했다. ⑥ 이곳들에서 (연금술의) 관습은 결국 미신으로 쇠퇴했지만, 이집트로 넘어가 그곳에서 전문적인 학문으로 살아남았다. ⑦ 중세 유럽에서 연금술은 12세기 학자들이 아랍어 작품들을 라틴어로 번역하면서 부흥했다. ⑧ 재발견된 아리스토텔레스의 글들도 한몫했다. ⑨ 13세기 말 즈음에는, 연금술이 주요 철학자, 과학자, 그리고 신학자들에 의해 진지하게 논의되었다. ⑩ 결국, 연금술의 관습은 과학적인 학문으로서의 화학의 발달을 위한 토대를 마련했다.

구문해설 ④ The dream of alchemists was **to find** the "philosopher's stone," a mysterious substance [that {they believed} could turn any metal into gold].

→ to find 이하는 주격보어로 쓰인 명사적 용법의 to부정사구

→ the "philosopher's stone"과 a mysterious substance는 동격 관계

→ [ ]는 선행사 a mysterious substance를 수식하는 주격 관계대명사절

→ { }는 관계사절 내에 삽입된 어구

⑤ Alchemy originated in ancient times, [evolving independently in China, India, and Greece].

→ [ ]는 〈연속동작〉을 나타내는 분사구문

02 당신이 배고픈 이유 P. 84

정답 **1** ⑤ **2** ⑤ **3** ② **4** increased, hunger

문제해설

1 그렐린을 조절하는 약물로 비만인들이나 암 환자들을 도울 가능성에 대해서는 언급되었으나, 그렐린 자체로 ⑤ '질병을 치료할 가능성'이 있다는 언급은 없다.

① 배고픔과의 관계 ② 증가하는 시기

③ 식욕에 대한 영향 ④ 생성되는 곳

2 문맥상 식욕을 유발하는 그렐린을 '감소시키는' 약물이 비만인 사람들을 돕는다는 내용이 적절하므로 ⑤ increase를 decrease 등으로 바꿔야 한다.

3 그렐린 수치를 조절하는 약물은 비만인 사람들과 극도로 마른 암 환자들의 체중을 조절하도록 도울 수 있다고 했으므로, 빈칸에는 ② '체중 조절 문제에 대한 실행 가능한 해결책'이 들어가는 것이 적절하다.

① 뇌 외부에서 생성되는 천연 자극제

③ 비만인 사람들이 체중을 줄이는 데 도움이 되는 효과적인 방법

④ 암 환자들의 고통을 경감시키는 데 도움이 되는 약

⑤ 위장 접합술을 받은 사람들을 위한 해답

4 체중을 줄이기 위해 노력하는 사람들은 배고픔을 유발하는 천연 호르몬인 그렐린의 증가된 수치를 경험한다.

본문

① A new scientific breakthrough / may explain / why people get hungry / at mealtimes, / why dieters struggle to maintain weight loss, / and why stomach surgery is an effective treatment / for dangerously overweight patients. ② The answer is ghrelin, / a naturally occurring hormone / that causes hunger / and slows the body's fat-burning capacity.

③ New research indicates / that dieters experience / increased production of ghrelin / when they lose weight. ④ This drives them to eat, / forcing them to put the weight back on. ⑤ In patients / who have received a surgical operation / called a gastric bypass, / however, / ghrelin levels remain low, / so they do not have the same hunger pains. ⑥ Ghrelin is one of many substances / produced naturally in the body / that pass messages / between the brain and the digestive system. ⑦ But / it is the first natural appetite stimulant / found to be produced / outside the brain / — it is produced by specialized cells / in the stomach. ⑧ Since it occurs / outside the brain, / it may be an easier target / for scientists searching for a way / to control appetite.
⑨ The hope is / that drugs that decrease or block ghrelin / may be developed, / which would help obese people to lose weight / and keep it off. ⑩ Likewise, / drugs that boost ghrelin levels / may lead dangerously thin cancer patients / to recover their appetite. ⑪ In short, / ghrelin could be the key / to finding workable solutions / to weight control problems.

해석 ① 한 새로운 과학적 발견이 사람들이 왜 끼니때에 배가 고프게 되는지, 왜 다이어트를 하는 사람들이 체중이 감량된 상태를 유지하기 위해 애쓰는지, 그리고 왜 위 수술이 위험할 정도로 과체중인 환자들에게 효과적인 치료법인지를 설명해 줄지도 모른다. ② 그 답은 그렐린으로, 배고픔을 유발하고 신체의 지방 연소 능력을 떨어뜨리는 자연적으로 발생하는 호르몬이다. ③ 새로운 연구는 다이어트를 하는 사람들이 체중을 감량할 때 증가된 그렐린 생성을 경험한다는 것을 보여준다. ④ 이것은 그들로 하여금 먹게 만들어 다시 체중이 늘어나게 한다. ⑤ 그러나, 위장 접합술이라고 불리는 외과 수술을 받은 환자들에게서는 그렐린 수치가 낮게 유지되고, 따라서 그들은 동일한 배고픔의 고통을 느끼지 않는다.
⑥ 그렐린은 신체 내에서 자연적으로 생성되는, 뇌와 소화기 계통 사이에서 메시지를 전달하는 많은 물질 중 하나이다. ⑦ 그러나 그것은 뇌의 외부에서 생성된다고 알려진 최초의 천연 식욕 자극제이며, 그것은 위장 내의 분화된 세포들에 의해 생성된다. ⑧ 뇌 외부에서 생성되기 때문에, 그것은 식욕을 통제하는 방법을 찾는 과학자들에게는 (연구하기) 더 쉬운 대상일지도 모른다.
⑨ 기대하는 일은 그렐린을 감소시키거나 차단하는 약물이 개발되어, 비만인 사람들이 체중을 감량하고 그것을 유지하는 것을 도와줄지도 모른다는 것이다. ⑩ 마찬가지로, 그렐린 수치를 높이는 약물은 위험할 정도로 마른 암 환자들이 식욕을 회복하게 할지도 모른다. ⑪ 요컨대, 그렐린은 체중 조절 문제에 대한 실행 가능한 해결책을 찾는 데 열쇠가 될 수 있을 것이다.

구문해설 ② The answer is ghrelin, a naturally occurring hormone [that causes hunger ...].
→ ghrelin과 a naturally occurring hormone은 동격 관계
→ [ ]는 선행사 a naturally occurring hormone을 수식하는 주격 관계대명사절

④ This **drives** them **to eat**, [**forcing** them **to put** the weight back on].
→ drive와 force는 둘 다 목적격보어로 to부정사를 취하는 동사임.
→ [ ]는 〈부대상황〉을 나타내는 분사구문

⑥ Ghrelin is one of many substances [produced naturally in the body] [that pass messages between the brain and the digestive system].
→ 첫 번째 [ ]는 many substances를 수식하는 과거분사구

→ 두 번째 [ ]는 선행사 many substances를 수식하는 주격 관계대명사절

⑦ But it is the first natural appetite stimulant [found to be produced outside the brain] ....

→ [ ]는 the first natural appetite stimulant를 수식하는 과거분사구

⑨ The hope is [that drugs {that decrease or block ghrelin} may be developed, {**which** would help obese people *to lose* weight and (*to*) *keep* it *off*}].

→ [ ]는 주격보어 역할을 하는 명사절

→ 첫 번째 { }는 선행사 drugs를 수식하는 주격 관계대명사절

→ 두 번째 { }는 계속적 용법의 주격 관계대명사절로 which의 선행사는 앞의 절(drugs ... may be developed) 전체임.

→「help+목적어+to-v」는 '…가 ~하도록 돕다'라는 의미이며, 목적격보어로 to lose와 (to) keep ... off가 and로 연결된 병렬구조

03 활짝 열린 창문 P. 86

정답 **1** ② **2** ② **3** the influence of Puritanism on Dutch culture

문제해설 **1** 네덜란드 창문의 장점을 언급하고 있는 주어진 문장의 these windows는 ② 앞에서 언급한 their large windows를 가리키며, ② 뒤의 문장들에서 창문의 다른 장점을 추가로 설명하고 있으므로, 주어진 문장은 ②에 들어가는 것이 적절하다.

2 (A) '…가 ~한[된] 채로'를 의미하는 「with+(대)명사+분사」 구문에서, 분사의 의미상의 주어 the interior lights와 turn이 수동 관계이므로 과거분사 turned가 와야 한다.

(B) see의 목적어 역할을 하는 간접의문문을 이끌며, 의문사절 내에서 주어 역할을 하는 what이 적절하다.

(C) prove의 목적어로 문장 성분을 모두 갖춘 완전한 절이 온 것으로 보아, 명사절을 이끄는 접속사 that이 알맞다.

3 네덜란드 집들은 왜 크고 가려지지 않은 창문을 가지고 있는가?

→ 그것은 네덜란드 문화에 대한 청교도주의의 영향 때문이다.

본문

① The most notable feature / of Dutch homes / is their large windows, / which are traditionally left uncovered / both during the day / and through the night. ② One advantage of these windows is / that they allow homes / to be flooded with natural light. ③ More interestingly, / they also create / an unusually high level of visibility / between the people inside of the house / and those passing by outside. ④ At night, / with the interior lights turned on, / anyone standing on the street / can enjoy an unobstructed view of the rooms within. ⑤ And / a person standing inside / can press his or her nose / against the window / and see what is going on outside.
⑥ The reason for these uncovered windows / can be traced back to / the influence of Puritanism on Dutch culture. ⑦ Virtuous people, / in their eyes, / have nothing to hide / and therefore /

have no reason / to draw their curtains. ⑧ Large, uncovered windows, / in other words, / show exactly what's happening inside the home / and prove that there is nothing wrong going on. ⑨ These days, / many things are changing / in the Netherlands, / including windows. ⑩ Some people are installing vertical blinds / that make it difficult / for outsiders to look in. ⑪ However, / there are plenty of places in the country / where uncovered windows are still popular. ⑫ So, / if you ever visit the Netherlands, / keep your eyes open. ⑬ You may get an interesting look at / the private lives of the Dutch.

해석 ① 네덜란드 집의 가장 눈에 띄는 특징은 큰 창문들인데, 그것들은 전통적으로 낮 동안과 밤새 가려지지 않은 채로 있다. ② 이 창문들의 한 가지 장점은 집이 자연광으로 가득 차게 해준다는 것이다. ③ 더욱 흥미롭게도, 그것들은 집 안의 사람들과 밖에 지나가는 사람들 간에 대단히 높은 수준의 가시성도 만든다. ④ 밤에는 실내등이 켜진 채로, 길거리에 서 있는 사람은 누구나 집 내부에 있는 방의 훤히 보이는 광경을 즐길 수 있다. ⑤ 그리고 내부에 서 있는 사람은 창문에 자신의 코를 대고 바깥에서 무슨 일이 일어나고 있는지를 볼 수 있다.

⑥ 이러한 가려지지 않은 창문에 대한 이유는 네덜란드 문화에 대한 청교도주의의 영향으로 거슬러 올라갈 수 있다. ⑦ 그들의 눈에는, 도덕적인 사람들은 숨길 것이 없으며, 따라서 커튼을 칠 이유가 없다. ⑧ 다시 말해서, 크고 가려지지 않은 창문들은 집 안에서 무슨 일이 일어나고 있는지를 정확하게 보여주고, 어떤 나쁜 일도 일어나고 있지 않다는 것을 증명한다.

⑨ 요즘, 네덜란드에서는 창문을 포함하여 많은 것들이 변화하고 있다. ⑩ 어떤 사람들은 밖에 있는 사람들이 안을 들여다보기 어렵게 만드는 수직 블라인드를 설치하고 있다. ⑪ 그러나, 그 나라에는 가려지지 않은 창문들이 여전히 인기 있는 장소가 많다. ⑫ 그러니, 만약 당신이 네덜란드를 방문한다면, 눈을 크게 뜨고 살펴보아라. ⑬ 당신은 네덜란드 사람들의 사생활의 흥미로운 모습을 보게 될지도 모른다.

구문해설 ① ... is their large windows, [which are traditionally left uncovered **both** during the day **and** through the night].

→ [ ]는 선행사 their large windows를 부연 설명하는 계속적 용법의 주격 관계대명사절

→ both A and B: A와 B 둘 다

③ ..., they also create an unusually high level of visibility between the people inside of the house and those [passing by outside].

→ those는 앞에 나온 명사의 반복을 피하기 위해 사용된 지시대명사로 the people을 대신함.

→ [ ]는 those를 수식하는 현재분사구

⑩ Some people are installing vertical blinds [that make **it** difficult *for outsiders* **to look in**].

→ [ ]는 선행사 vertical blinds를 수식하는 주격 관계대명사절

→ it은 make의 가목적어, to look in이 진목적어이며, for outsiders는 to부정사의 의미상의 주어

⑪ However, there are plenty of places in the country [where uncovered windows are still popular].

→ [ ]는 선행사 plenty of places를 수식하는 관계부사절

04 이어질 글의 순서 P. 88

정답 ② 변형문제 **1** ① **2** ⓐ sending ⓑ wrote it down **3** caught in a bad storm

문제해설 병에 든 메시지의 최초이자 가장 잘 알려진 사례로 콜럼버스의 메시지를 소개하는 (B)가 가장 먼저 오고, 콜럼버스가 메시지를 병에 넣어 바다로 보낸 이유를 설명하는 (A)로 이어진 후, 그가 메시지를 병에 넣어 바다로 보낸 후 오랜 시간이 지나서야 이 병이 발견되었다는 내용의 (C)로 연결되는 것이 가장 자연스럽다.

변형문제

1 병에 든 메시지의 최초이자 가장 유명한 사례인 콜럼버스의 메시지를 소개하는 글이므로, 제목으로는 ① '병에 담긴 유명한 메시지'가 적절하다.

② 오랫동안 잃어버렸던 보물 찾기 ③ 증가하는 해양 쓰레기 문제

④ 콜럼버스가 신세계를 발견한 방법 ⑤ 메시지를 병에 넣어 보내지 말아야 하는 이유

2 ⓐ 전치사 of의 목적어로 동명사 putting과 병렬구조를 이루는 것이므로, 동명사 sending이 와야 한다.

ⓑ 「동사+부사」 형태의 동사구가 목적어로 대명사를 취한 경우, 대명사는 반드시 동사와 부사 사이에 위치해야 하므로 wrote it down의 어순이 알맞다.

3 그의 배가 심한 폭풍에 휘말렸기 때문에, 콜럼버스는 병에 든 메시지를 이용했다.

본문

① You have probably heard of / putting a message in a bottle / and sending it across the sea. ② Unfortunately, / it is impossible / to tell / where the bottle will wash up / or how long it will take the sea / to deliver it there.

③ (B) One of the earliest and / most famous bottled messages / was sent by Christopher Columbus. ④ In 1493, / he was returning to Spain / to announce his discovery / to the king and queen, / and his ship became caught in a bad storm.

⑤ (A) Because he was still / more than a thousand miles away from Europe, / Columbus was afraid / that he would never live / to share his news. ⑥ So, / he took a piece of paper / and wrote it down.

⑦ (C) He put it in a wooden bottle / and tossed it into the ocean. ⑧ It was found / more than 300 years later / off the coast of Morocco / by the captain of an American ship.

해석 ① 당신은 아마 메시지를 병에 넣어 바다로 보내는 것에 대해 들어본 적이 있을 것이다. ② 안타깝게도, 그 병이 어디에서 떠밀려 올라올지나 바다가 그것을 그곳으로 배달하는 데 얼마나 걸릴지 아는 것은 불가능하다.

③ (B) 가장 초기의 그리고 가장 유명한 병에 든 메시지 중 하나는 크리스토퍼 콜럼버스가 보낸 것이었다. ④ 1493년에 그는 자신이 발견한 것을 왕과 왕비에게 알리려고 스페인으로 돌아가고 있었는데, 그의 배가 심한 폭풍에 휘말리게 되었다.

⑤ (A) 그는 아직도 유럽에서 천 마일 이상 떨어져 있었기 때문에, 콜럼버스는 그가 살아서 자신의 소식을 나눌 수 없을까 봐 두려웠다. ⑥ 그래서 그는 종이를 꺼내 그것을 적었다.

⑦ (C) 그는 그것을 나무 병에 넣었고 바다로 던졌다. ⑧ 그것은 300년도 더 지난 뒤에 한 미국 선박의 선장에 의해 모로코 해변에서 발견되었다.

구문해설 ① You **have** probably **heard** of putting a message in a bottle and sending it across the sea.
→ have heard는 〈경험〉을 나타내는 현재완료

② Unfortunately, **it** is impossible **to tell** [where the bottle will wash up] or [how long *it will take* the sea *to deliver* it there].
→ it은 가주어, to tell 이하가 진주어
→ 두 개의 [ ]는 모두 tell의 목적어 역할을 하는 간접의문문으로 「의문사+주어+동사」의 어순임.
→ it takes+사람[사물]+시간+to-v: …가 ~하는 데 얼마의 시간이 걸리다

⑤ ..., Columbus was afraid that he would never live **to share** his news.
→ to share는 〈결과〉를 나타내는 부사적 용법의 to부정사

Review Test

P. 90

A **1** ⓔ **2** ⓐ **3** ⓒ **4** ⓑ **5** ⓓ B **1** unobstructed **2** operation **3** migrated **4** announced C **1** ③ **2** ② **3** ③ **4** ③ D **1** 내부에 서 있는 사람은 바깥에서 무슨 일이 일어나고 있는지를 볼 수 있다. **2** 콜럼버스는 그가 살아서 자신의 소식을 나눌 수 없을까 봐 두려워했다. **3** 그것은 뇌의 외부에서 생성된다고 알려진 최초의 천연 식욕 자극제이다. **4** 연금술은 고대에 생겨났고, 중국, 인도, 그리스에서 독립적으로 발달했다. E **1** all matter is composed of **2** make it difficult for outsiders **3** forcing them to put the weight

해석

A

1 미신: ⓔ 이성이나 지식에 근거하지 않은 믿음
2 부흥시키다: ⓐ 어떤 것을 다시 인기 있게 하다
3 치료(약): ⓒ 질병 또는 부상에 대한 치료
4 식욕: ⓑ 먹거나 마시고자 하는 욕구
5 도덕적인, 고결한: ⓓ 강한 도덕심을 지닌

B

1 각 객실은 풍경의 탁 트인 조망을 제공한다.
2 브라이언은 그 사고 후에 눈 수술을 받았다.
3 암세포가 신체의 다른 장기들로 전이되었다.
4 그 도시에 새로운 공항이 건설될 것이라는 사실이 발표되었다.

C

1 나는 썩은 사과를 쓰레기통에 던졌다.
① 해고했다 ② 묶었다 ③ 던졌다 ④ 재배했다 ⑤ 건넜다

2 나쁜 식습관 때문에 비만인 아동의 수가 증가하고 있다.
① 영리한 ② 비만인 ③ 버려진 ④ 고립된 ⑤ 유망한

3 레오나르도 다빈치는 여러 뛰어난 미술 작품을 남겼다.
① 믿을 수 있는 ② 이용 가능한 ③ 뛰어난 ④ 유능한 ⑤ 자격이 없는

4 그 수업에서 그녀는 자기표현 능력을 향상시키길 원했다.
① 역할 ② 쟁점 ③ 능력 ④ 책임 ⑤ 중요성

SECTION 08

01 1 ⑤ 2 ④ 3 ④ 4 unique bond, together
02 1 ③ 2 ⓐ was invited ⓑ performing 3 ④
03 1 ② 2 expensive, ship 3 ② 4 ④
04 ④ 변형문제 1 ⑤ 2 ③ 3 attractive, unattractive

01 우리는 가족이에요 P. 94

정답 1 ⑤ 2 ④ 3 ④ 4 unique bond, together

문제해설

1 하마 오웬과 거북이 음제의 독특한 우정을 소개하는 글이므로, 제목으로는 ⑤ '오웬과 음제 사이의 특이한 우정'이 가장 적절하다.

① 구조된 거북이 이야기 ② 오웬이 그의 친부모를 만났을 때
③ 세계 최고의 동물 보호 구역 ④ 몸바사의 세계적으로 유명한 동물원

2 ④는 음제를 가리키고, 나머지는 모두 오웬을 가리킨다.

3 음제가 처음에는 오웬을 '경계했다'는 내용의 문장이다. wary는 '경계하는, 조심하는'의 의미이므로 '의심하는'의 의미의 ④ suspicious와 바꿔 쓸 수 있다.

① 자랑스러워하는 ② 비판적인 ③ 참을성 있는 ⑤ 동정 어린

4 오웬과 음제는 모든 것을 함께 하며 독특한 유대를 형성했다.

본문

① Sometimes / true friendship can be found / in the most unlikely circumstances. ② Such is / the case of Owen and Mzee, / a hippopotamus and a tortoise / who formed a unique bond.
③ After a devastating tsunami, / Owen, a baby hippo, / was orphaned / and lost in the Indian Ocean. ④ Luckily, / he was rescued and taken to an animal sanctuary / near Mombasa. ⑤ There, / he was placed / in an enclosure / with a cohabitant, / a 130-year-old tortoise named Mzee.
⑥ At first, / Mzee was wary of Owen, / who imitated the tortoise's behavior / as if he were Mzee's own child. ⑦ As time passed, / however, / he grew used to the hippo / and began to teach him / what to eat / and where to sleep. ⑧ Soon, / they became inseparable companions / who did everything together, / and they even developed / their own system of vocal communication.
⑨ Due to their astonishing behavior, / Owen and Mzee became worldwide celebrities. ⑩ They've been featured in films / and are the subject of two bestselling picture books, / one of which has been translated / into 13 languages.

해석

① 때때로 진정한 우정은 가장 예상 밖의 상황에서 발견될 수 있다. ② 독특한 유대를 형성한 하마와 거북이인 오웬과 음제의 경우가 그렇다.
③ 엄청난 쓰나미가 일어난 후에, 아기 하마인 오웬은 고아가 되었고, 인도양에서 미아가 되었다. ④ 운 좋게도, 그는 구조되어 몸바사 근처에 있는 동물 보호 구역으로 보내졌다. ⑤ 그곳에서, 그는 동거자로 130살 된 음제라는 이름의

거북이와 함께 울타리를 친 곳에 넣어졌다.

⑥ 처음에 음제는 오웬을 경계했는데, 오웬은 마치 자신이 음제의 새끼라도 되는 것처럼 그 거북이의 행동을 모방했다. ⑦ 그러나 시간이 지남에 따라, 음제는 그 하마에게 익숙해졌고, 그에게 무엇을 먹어야 하고 어디서 잠을 자야 할지를 가르쳐주기 시작했다. ⑧ 곧 그들은 모든 것을 함께 하는 떨어질 수 없는 친구가 되었고, 심지어 자신들만의 음성 의사소통 체계를 만들기도 했다.

⑨ 그들의 놀라운 행동으로 인해, 오웬과 음제는 세계적인 유명 인사가 되었다. ⑩ 그들은 영화에 출연했고, 두 권의 베스트셀러 그림책의 소재인데, 그중 하나는 13개의 언어로 번역되었다.

구문해설 ② Such(C) is(V) the case of Owen and Mzee(S), a hippopotamus and a tortoise [who formed a unique bond].

→ 보어인 Such가 문두로 나와서 주어와 동사가 도치됨.

→ [ ]는 선행사 a hippopotamus and a tortoise를 수식하는 주격 관계대명사절

⑤ ... in an enclosure with a cohabitant, [a 130-year-old tortoise {named Mzee}].

→ a cohabitant와 [ ]는 동격 관계

→ { }는 a 130-year-old tortoise를 수식하는 과거분사구

⑥ ... Owen, [who imitated the tortoise's behavior **as if** he **were** Mzee's own child].

→ [ ]는 선행사 Owen을 부연 설명하는 계속적 용법의 주격 관계대명사절

→ 「as if + 가정법 과거」는 '마치 …인 것처럼'이라는 뜻으로, 주절과 같은 시점의 일을 가정함.

02 위대한 음악 신동 P. 96

정답 1 ③ 2 ⓐ was invited ⓑ performing 3 ④

문제해설 1 (A) 평생 장애를 가졌음에도 '불구하고' 그 무엇도 그의 바이올린 연주를 막을 수 없었다는 내용이 되어야 자연스러우므로 '…이지만, …에도 불구하고'의 뜻을 나타내는 양보의 접속사 Though가 와야 한다.

(B) 연주하는 '동안' 앉아 있다는 내용이 되어야 자연스러우므로 '…하는 동안'의 의미를 나타내는 접속사 while이 적절하다.

2 ⓐ 문맥상 펄만이 '초대를 받은' 것이므로 수동태인 was invited로 쓰는 것이 알맞다.

ⓑ 문맥상 〈부대상황〉을 나타내는 분사구문이 되어야 적절한데, 분사의 의미상의 주어인 펄만이 연주를 하는 주체이므로, 능동의 의미를 나타내는 현재분사 performing으로 쓰는 것이 알맞다.

3 ④ '언제 첫 콘서트를 열었는지'에 대한 언급은 없었다.

① 어디에서 태어났는지

② 몇 살 때 소아마비에 걸렸는지

③ 어떤 사건이 그를 유명하게 만들었는지

⑤ 누구와 *쉰들러 리스트* 음악을 작업했는지

본문

① Itzhak Perlman is considered / one of the greatest classical violinists / in history. ② Born in Israel in 1945, / Perlman decided to become a violinist / when he was just three years old. ③ He began practicing intensely every day, / but before he could realize his goal, / he was faced with / the toughest challenge of his life. ④ At age four, / Perlman was stricken with polio.
⑤ Though disabled for life, / nothing could stop him / from playing the violin. ⑥ Over time / he learned / how to walk with crutches, / but to this day / he remains seated / while performing.
⑦ He attended the Music Academy of Tel Aviv, / where his teachers immediately recognized his talent. ⑧ In 1958 / he was invited to the United States / to appear on the Ed Sullivan Show.
⑨ This television performance made him an instant superstar. ⑩ Since then, / Perlman has traveled nonstop, / performing with almost every symphony orchestra / as well as great musicians like Yo-Yo Ma and Placido Domingo. ⑪ He also worked with composer John Williams / on the score for *Schindler's List*. ⑫ His amazing onstage presence speaks eloquently / on behalf of the disabled, / and his commitment to their welfare / is an important part of his life.

해석

① 이작 펄만은 역사상 가장 훌륭한 클래식 바이올린 연주자 중 한 명으로 여겨진다. ② 1945년 이스라엘에서 태어난 펄만은 겨우 세 살이었을 때 바이올린 연주자가 되기로 결심했다. ③ 그는 매일 열심히 연습하기 시작했지만, 자신의 목표를 달성하기 전에 인생에서 가장 힘든 시련에 맞닥뜨렸다. ④ 네 살 때, 펄만은 소아마비에 걸렸다.
⑤ 평생 장애를 가졌음에도 불구하고, 그 무엇도 그가 바이올린을 연주하는 것을 막을 수 없었다. ⑥ 시간이 지나면서 그는 목발을 짚고 걷는 법을 배웠지만, 지금까지도 연주하는 동안에는 그는 앉아 있어야 한다. ⑦ 그는 텔아비브의 음악 학교에 다녔는데, 그곳에서 선생님들이 즉시 그의 재능을 알아보았다. ⑧ 1958년에 그는 미국에 초청받아 에드 설리번 쇼에 출연했다. ⑨ 이 텔레비전 공연은 순식간에 그를 슈퍼스타로 만들었다. ⑩ 그 이후로 펄만은 요요마와 플라시도 도밍고 같은 훌륭한 음악가뿐만 아니라 거의 모든 교향악단과 함께 연주하면서, 쉼 없이 (공연을) 다녔다.
⑪ 그는 또한 *쉰들러 리스트*의 배경 음악을 위해서 작곡가 존 윌리엄스와 함께 작업하기도 했다. ⑫ 그의 놀라운 무대 위에서의 존재는 장애인들을 대표하여 감동적으로 말하며, 장애인들의 복지를 위해 헌신하는 것은 그의 인생의 중요한 일부분이다.

구문해설

② [Born in Israel in 1945], Perlman decided to become a violinist ....
→ [ ]는 과거분사로 시작하는 수동형 분사구문

⑤ [Though disabled for life], nothing could **stop** him **from playing** the violin.
→ [ ]는 의미를 명확하게 하기 위해 접속사를 생략하지 않은 분사구문으로 〈양보〉를 나타냄.
→ stop+목적어+from+v-ing: …가 ~하는 것을 막다

⑦ He attended the Music Academy of Tel Aviv, [where his teachers immediately recognized ...].
→ [ ]는 선행사 the Music Academy of Tel Aviv를 부연 설명하는 계속적 용법의 관계부사절

⑩ Since then, Perlman **has traveled** nonstop, [performing with almost every symphony orchestra *as well as* great musicians ...].
→ has traveled는 〈계속〉을 나타내는 현재완료
→ [ ]는 〈부대상황〉을 나타내는 분사구문
→ A as well as B: B뿐만 아니라 A도

03 우주에서도 맛있게!

P. 98

정답 1 ② 2 expensive, ship 3 ② 4 ④

문제해설 1 우주에서 우주비행사들이 식량 조달을 위해 수경 재배로 작물을 기르는 것에 관한 글이므로, 주제로는 ② '우주에서 재배되는 수경 재배 식품'이 적절하다.

① 우주 식품을 먹는 방법 ③ 우주비행사들은 우주에 있는 동안 무엇을 먹는가

④ 수경 재배 채소를 기르는 방법 ⑤ 우주에서 농작물을 재배하는 것의 어려움

2 식품을 우주로 운송하는 것은 몹시 비싸다.

3 우주로 식품을 운송하는 비용 문제를 해결하기 위해 우주비행사들이 직접 식품을 재배할 수 있는 방법을 과학자들이 개발하고 있다고 했으므로, 빈칸에는 ② '운송 비용을 절감하다'라는 내용이 들어가는 것이 적절하다.

① 식품의 영양을 향상시키다 ③ 불필요한 인력을 줄이다

④ 지구의 다양한 식물을 보호하다 ⑤ 우주비행사들에게 더 나은 환경을 제공하다

4 우주에서 수경 재배로 자란 식물 중에 콩과 같은 일부 식물은 단백질 함량이 더 높았다고 했으므로, ④는 글의 내용과 일치하지 않는다.

본문

① What do astronauts eat / when they're floating around / in space? ② As it turns out, / there are lots of space foods / made here on Earth. ③ However, / it's very expensive / to ship enough of this food / into space, / especially for astronauts / who will be in space / for many months. ④ To solve this problem, / scientists are developing ways / by which food can be grown by the astronauts themselves / once they're in space, / thus eliminating the cost of shipping.

⑤ You may think / it's impossible to grow food / without soil or sunlight, / but in fact / this is already being done / here on Earth / with hydroponics. ⑥ Hydroponic crops are raised / in artificial environments / such as green houses, / where artificial light / and substances like charcoal and special chemical mixtures / help them grow. ⑦ At first, / scientists worried / that plants would have problems growing in space / and wouldn't yield / as much food as on Earth. ⑧ However, / not only did hydroponic plants in space / grow faster than here on Earth, / but some of them, / such as beans, / also had a higher protein content.

⑨ The nutrition of these foods / is obviously very important, / but scientists aren't ignoring the taste factor, / either. ⑩ NASA recently funded / the development of 200 different recipes / using hydroponically grown foods / with the intention of enhancing their flavor / as well as their nutrition levels. ⑪ Initial taste tests have met / with great success. ⑫ Perhaps someday / astronauts will be able to dine on hydroponic meals / that are truly out of this world.

해석 ① 우주비행사들은 우주에서 떠다닐 때 무엇을 먹는가? ② 알고 보면, 이곳 지구에서 만들어지는 많은 우주 식품이 있다. ③ 그렇지만 충분한 양의 이 식품을 우주로 운송하는 것은 비용이 매우 많이 드는데, 몇 달씩 우주에 가 있을 우주비행사의 경우에 특히 그렇다. ④ 이 문제를 해결하기 위해서, 과학자들은 우주비행사들이 우주에 있을 때 그들에 의해 식품이 재배되는 방법을 개발하고 있는데, 이렇게 해서 운송 비용을 절감할 수 있다.

⑤ 당신은 흙이나 햇빛 없이 식품을 재배하는 것이 불가능하다고 생각할지 모르지만, 사실 이것은 수경 재배법으로 이미 이곳 지구에서도 행해지고 있다. ⑥ 수경 재배 작물은 온실과 같은 인공적인 환경에서 재배되는데, 그곳에서는 인공조명과 숯이나 특수한 화학 배합물 같은 물질들이 작물이 자라는 것을 돕는다. ⑦ 처음에, 과학자들은 식물들이 우주에서 자라는 데에 문제가 있을 것이며, 지구에서만큼 많은 식품을 생산하지는 못할 거라고 걱정했다. ⑧ 하지만, 우주에서 수경 재배 식물들은 이곳 지구에서보다 더 빨리 자랐을 뿐만 아니라, 그중 콩과 같은 일부 식물은 단백질 함량이 더 높았다.

⑨ 이들 식품의 영양도 분명 매우 중요하지만, 과학자들은 맛이라는 요소도 무시하지 않는다. ⑩ 나사(NASA)는 수경 재배 식품의 영양 수준뿐만 아니라 맛을 향상시키려는 의도를 가지고, 최근 수경 재배로 길러진 식품들을 이용한 200가지의 다양한 조리법 개발에 자금을 투자했다. ⑪ 초기의 맛보기 테스트는 큰 성공을 거두었다. ⑫ 아마도 언젠가 우주비행사들은 진짜로 이 세상의 것이 아닌 수경 재배 식품들로 식사를 할 수 있게 될 것이다.

구문해설

③ However, **it**'s very expensive **to ship** enough of this food into space, ...
→ it은 가주어, to ship 이하가 진주어

④ **To solve** this problem, scientists are developing ways [by which food can be grown ...], [thus eliminating the cost of shipping].
→ To solve는 〈목적〉을 나타내는 부사적 용법의 to부정사
→ 첫 번째 [ ]는 선행사 ways를 수식하는 목적격 관계대명사절
→ 두 번째 [ ]는 〈연속동작〉을 나타내는 분사구문

⑥ Hydroponic crops are raised in artificial environments such as green houses, [where artificial light and substances ... **help** *them* **grow**].
→ [ ]는 선행사 artificial environments를 부연 설명하는 계속적 용법의 관계부사절
→ help+목적어+동사원형: …가 ~하도록 돕다
→ them은 Hydroponic crops를 가리킴.

⑦ At first, scientists worried that plants would **have problems growing** in space and wouldn't yield *as much* food *as* on Earth.
→ have a problem+v-ing: …하는 데 문제가 있다
→ as+형용사의 원급+as ...: …만큼 ~한

⑧ However, *not only* (부정어구) *did* (조동사) *hydroponic plants in space* (주어) *grow* (동사원형) faster than here on Earth, **but** some of them, ..., **also** had a higher protein content.
→ not only A but also B: A뿐만 아니라 B도
→ 부정어구인 not only가 문두에 나와 주어와 동사의 어순이 도치됨. 부정어구로 인해 도치된 문장의 경우, 동사가 일반동사이면 「부정어구+do[does/did]+주어+동사원형」의 어순으로 씀.

04 주어진 문장의 위치 P. 100

정답 ④ 변형문제 **1** ⑤ **2** ③ **3** attractive, unattractive

문제해설 주어진 문장은 '이러한 증거에도 불구하고' 유권자들이 자신들의 편견을 인지하지 못했다는 후속 연구에 대해 언급하고 있다. 따라서 주어진 문장은 증거의 구체적 내용을 언급하는 문장과 후속 연구를 설명하는 문장 사이인 ④에 들어가는 것이 가장 적절하다.

변형문제

1 (A) be aware 다음에 주어(physical attractiveness)와 동사(is playing)로 이루어진 절이 이어지고 있으므로, 명사절을 이끄는 접속사 that이 와야 한다.
(B) votes는 셀 수 있는 명사의 복수형이므로 many가 적절하다. much는 셀 수 없는 명사와 함께 쓰인다.
(C) 동사 deny의 목적어로 문장 성분을 모두 갖춘 완전한 절이 왔으므로 접속사 that이 적절하다. what 다음에는 불완전한 절이 온다.

2 bias는 '편견'을 의미하는 단어이므로 '편견, 선입견'을 의미하는 ③ prejudice로 바꿔 쓸 수 있다.
① 재능 ② 불안 ④ 균형 ⑤ 만족

3 어떤 캐나다 연방 선거에서, 매력적인 후보자들이 매력적이지 않은 후보자들보다 더 많은 표를 받았다.

본문

① According to researchers, / we automatically assign favorable traits, / including honesty, kindness, talent, and intelligence, / to good-looking individuals. ② Moreover, / we aren't even aware / that physical attractiveness is playing a role / when we make these judgments. ③ I believe / this unconscious assumption / that "good-looking equals good" / can have some scary consequences. ④ For example, / according to a study of the 1974 Canadian federal elections, / "attractive" candidates received / over two and a half times as many votes / as "unattractive" ones. ⑤ In spite of this evidence / of favoritism towards attractive politicians, / it was demonstrated by follow-up research / that voters were unaware of their bias. ⑥ In fact, / 73 percent of the surveyed voters / strongly denied / that physical appearance had influenced their votes; / only 14 percent even acknowledged / the possibility of such influence. ⑦ While voters can deny / that attractiveness affects electability, / evidence has shown / the troubling presence of this bias.

해석 ① 연구원들에 따르면, 우리는 무의식적으로 정직, 친절, 재능, 그리고 지성을 포함하는 좋은 특성들을 외모가 뛰어난 사람들에게 부여한다고 한다. ② 게다가, 우리는 이러한 판단을 내릴 때 신체적인 매력이 한몫한다는 사실을 인식조차 하지 못한다. ③ 나는 '외모가 뛰어난 것이 좋은 것이다.'라는 이 무의식적인 가정이 몇 가지 무서운 결과를 가져올 수 있다고 믿는다. ④ 예를 들어, 1974년 캐나다 연방 선거에 관한 한 연구에 따르면, '매력적인' 후보자들이 '매력적이지 않은' 후보자들보다 2.5배 넘는 더 많은 표를 받았다고 한다. ⑤ 매력적인 정치인들을 향한 이 편애의 증거에도 불구하고, 유권자들이 자신들의 편견을 인식하지 못했다는 것이 후속 연구에 의해 입증되었다. ⑥ 실제로, 조사에 참여한 유권자들 중 73퍼센트가 신체적인 외모가 자신의 투표에 영향을 주었다는 사실을 강하게 부인했고, 14퍼센트만이 그런 영향력의 가능성 정도나마 인정했다. ⑦ 유권자들은 매력이 선출 가능성에 영향을 준다는 사실을 부인할 수는 있겠지만, 증거가 이 편견의 꺼림칙한 존재를 드러내 왔다.

구문해설 ③ I believe [(that) this unconscious assumption {that "good-looking equals good"} can have some scary consequences].

S′ = V′

→ [ ]는 believe의 목적어 역할을 하는 명사절로, 접속사 that이 생략됨.

→ { }는 this unconscious assumption의 내용을 구체적으로 설명하는 동격의 명사절

④ ..., "attractive" candidates received over **two and a half times as many** votes **as** "unattractive" *ones*.

→ 배수사+as+형용사의 원급+as ...: …보다 몇 배 더 ~한

→ ones는 앞에 나온 candidates를 대신하는 부정대명사

⑤ **In spite of** this evidence of favoritism ..., *it* was demonstrated by follow-up research [that voters were unaware of their bias].

→ in spite of: …에도 불구하고 (= despite)

→ it은 가주어, [ ]가 진주어

⑥ In fact, 73 percent of the surveyed voters strongly denied [that physical appearance **had influenced** their votes]; ....

→ [ ]는 denied의 목적어로 쓰인 명사절

→ had influenced는 주절의 과거 시점(denied)보다 더 이전에 일어난 일을 나타내는 과거완료

Review Test

P. 102

A 1 ① B 1 wary 2 unaware 3 artificial 4 imitated C 1 ③ 2 ② 3 ① 4 ② D 1 1958년에 그는 미국에 초청받아 에드 설리번 쇼에 출연했다. 2 평생 장애를 가졌음에도 불구하고, 그 무엇도 그가 바이올린을 연주하는 것을 막을 수 없었다. 3 우주에서 수경 재배 식물들은 이곳에서보다 더 빨리 자랐을 뿐만 아니라, 그중 일부는 단백질 함량이 더 높았다. 4 '매력적인' 후보자들이 '매력적이지 않은' 후보자들보다 2.5배 넘는 더 많은 표를 받았다. E 1 He grew used to the hippo 2 plants would have problems growing 3 one of which has been translated

해석 **A**

① 처음의: 끝에 존재하거나 발생하는

② 유대: 사람이나 사물을 결합하는 밀접한 관계

③ 자금을 대다: 어떤 목적을 위해 돈 또는 자원을 제공하다

④ 편견: 무언가를 지지하거나 반대하는 공정하지 않은 경향

⑤ 복지: 개인 또는 집단의 건강, 행복, 부

B

1 아이들은 항상 낯선 사람을 경계해야 한다.

2 경찰은 그 범인의 행방을 알지 못했다.

3 로라는 파티를 위해 꽃병에 인조 꽃을 꽂았다.

4 많은 작가들이 셰익스피어의 문체와 기법을 모방했다.

C

1 낙엽이 호수 표면에 떠 있었다.

① 매달렸다 ② 수송했다 ③ 떠 있었다 ④ 가라앉았다 ⑤ 도망쳤다

2 소방관들이 현장에 도착해서 그 건물에서 한 남자를 구조했다.

① 예약했다 ② 구조했다 ③ 응답했다 ④ 해결했다 ⑤ 기록했다

3 그 전화기의 최신 모델은 향상된 배터리 수명을 특징으로 한다.

① 향상된 ② 감소한 ③ 관여하는 ④ 설치된 ⑤ 할인된

4 저희 팀을 대표하여 이 상을 받게 되어 영광입니다.

① 무리 ② 편 ③ 비용 ④ 추구 ⑤ 존재

SECTION 09

01 **1** ⑤ **2** so that guests can order there **3** ①

02 **1** ③ **2** ② **3** be stopped for economic and environmental reasons

03 **1** ② **2** ④ **3** ④ **4** wasn't interested in math[mathematics]

04 ④ 변형문제 **1** ② **2** to know what makes their employees satisfied with their jobs **3** ⑤

01 암흑 속의 식사 P. 106

정답 **1** ⑤ **2** so that guests can order there **3** ①

문제해설 **1** ⑤ 고객을 안내하는 종업원 역시 시각 장애인이라고 했다.

2 '…하기 위해, …하도록'의 의미를 나타내는 「so that …」 구문을 활용하여 so that guests can order there로 쓰는 것이 적절하다.

3 어두운 곳이므로 ① '아무도 당신을 볼 수 없어서' 식사 예절에 대해 불평하지 않을 것이라는 내용이 문맥상 적절하다.

② 여종업원들이 당신을 도와줘서 ③ 음식이 정말로 맛있어서

④ 모든 사람이 서로 다른 식탁 예절을 사용해서 ⑤ 당신이 식사를 매우 빨리 마칠 수 있어서

본문

① Eating at the Blindekuh Restaurant in Zurich / is a truly once in a lifetime experience. ② The restaurant's name means / "blind cow" in English. ③ It also refers to a common Swiss saying, / "as dark as the inside of a cow."

④ The theme of the restaurant / is total darkness. ⑤ This idea was created / by the Swiss Association for Blind People, / with the aim of making people aware of / the reality of being sight disabled.

⑥ Guests are greeted in the lobby, / and all their belongings, / including cell phones and illuminated watches, / are stored in lockers. ⑦ The menu is displayed in the lobby / so that guests can order there. ⑧ After ordering, / each group is led / through a tunnel / by a waitress, / who is herself blind, / to a table. ⑨ Eating is tricky but fun, / and using your fingers / to locate all the food / is the best solution. ⑩ Nobody will complain about your manners / as no one can see you!

해석 ① 취리히의 블린데쿠 식당에서 식사하는 것은 정말 일생에 단 한 번뿐인 경험이다. ② 그 식당의 이름은 영어로 '눈먼 소'라는 뜻이다. ③ 그것은 또한 흔히 쓰이는 스위스 속담인 '소의 배 속처럼 어두운'을 나타낸다.

④ 그 식당의 테마는 완전한 어둠이다. ⑤ 이 아이디어는 사람들로 하여금 시각 장애가 있는 것의 현실을 알게 하려는 목적으로 스위스의 맹인 협회에 의해 창안되었다.

⑥ 손님들은 로비에서 맞이되며, 휴대전화와 조명이 있는 시계를 포함한 모든 소지품은 사물함에 보관된다. ⑦ 메뉴는 손님들이 그곳에서 주문할 수 있도록 로비에 전시되어 있다. ⑧ 주문한 후에, 각 그룹은 여종업원에 의해 터널을 통과하여 테이블로 안내되는데, 여종업원 본인도 맹인이다. ⑨ 식사하는 것은 힘들긴 하지만 재미있으며, 모든 음식의 위치를 알기 위해서는 손가락을 이용하는 것이 가장 좋은 해결책이다. ⑩ 아무도 당신을 볼 수 없으므로, 어느 누구도 당신의 식탁 예절에 대해 불평하지 않을 것이다!

구문해설 ① [Eating at the Blindekuh Restaurant in Zurich] (S) **is** (V) a truly once in a lifetime experience.

→ 동명사구인 [ ]가 문장의 주어이므로 수 일치하여 단수형 동사 is가 옴.

⑧ ..., each group (A) is **led** through a tunnel by a waitress, [who is herself blind], **to** a table (B).

→ 「lead A to B」는 'A를 B로 이끌다, 안내하다'라는 의미임. A(목적어)에 해당하는 말인 each group이 주어로 쓰인 수동태 문장임.

→ [ ]는 선행사 a waitress를 부연 설명하는 계속적 용법의 주격 관계대명사절

02 원자력 산업에 대한 의견 P. 108

정답 **1** ③ **2** ② **3** be stopped for economic and environmental reasons

문제해설 **1** 뒤에서 'I believe that further development of nuclear power, which you support, ...'라고 한 것으로 보아 your special report는 원자력 개발을 지지하는 내용이었다는 것을 유추할 수 있다.

2 ② 앞의 명사 an environmental threat를 선행사로 하는 주격 관계대명사 that이나 which가 와야 알맞다. what은 선행사를 포함하는 관계대명사이다.

3 원자력 에너지의 개발은 경제적인 이유와 환경적인 이유로 중단되어야 한다.

본문

To the Editor

① After reading your special report / on the nuclear power industry / published on August 14, 2018, / I would like to make some comments.

② I believe / that further development of nuclear power, / which you support, / is not the best way / to go forward / and should in fact be stopped. ③ First of all, / when the costs of dealing with nuclear waste / are examined, / nuclear power is found to be very expensive. ④ Secondly, / nuclear waste from power plants / is an environmental threat / that will be around / for a very long time. ⑤ High-level nuclear waste / remains deadly / for 250,000 years.

⑥ For these important reasons, / I think / the government should start reducing energy consumption / through investment in energy conservation measures, / such as housing insulation / and the development of energy-efficient appliances, cars, and machines. ⑦ Investment in research and development / of renewable energy from the sun, the wind, and waves / would be my second policy recommendation. ⑧ It's time for the government / to come up with ways / to end the use of non-renewable, pollution-creating energy sources.

Michael Bowles
New York

해석

편집자님께

① 2018년 8월 14일에 게재된 원자력 산업에 대한 당신의 특집 보도를 읽고 난 후, 저는 몇 가지 의견을 말하고 싶습니다.

② 저는 당신이 지지하는 원자력의 추가 개발은 나아가야 할 최선의 길이 아니며, 사실 중단되어야 한다고 생각합니다. ③ 첫째로, 핵폐기물의 처리 비용을 검토해 봤을 때, 원자력이 매우 비싼 것으로 나타납니다. ④ 둘째로, 발전소에서 배출되는 핵폐기물은 아주 오랫동안 주변에 남아 있게 될 환경 위협 요소입니다. ⑤ 고준위 핵폐기물은 250,000년 동안 치명적인 상태로 남아 있습니다.

⑥ 이런 중요한 이유로, 저는 정부가 주택 단열과 에너지 절약형 가전제품, 자동차, 기계의 개발과 같은 에너지 보존책들에 투자함으로써 에너지 소비를 줄이기 시작해야 한다고 생각합니다. ⑦ 태양과 바람, 파도를 이용한 재생 가능한 에너지를 연구 개발하는 데 투자하는 것이 저의 두 번째 정책 추천안입니다. ⑧ 정부가 재생 불가능하며 오염을 일으키는 에너지원의 사용을 중단할 방법들을 모색할 때입니다.

마이클 보울즈
뉴욕

구문해설

① After reading your special report on the nuclear power industry [published on August 14, 2018], ...

→ [ ]는 your ... industry를 수식하는 과거분사구

② I believe that further development of nuclear power, [which you support], is not the best way [to go forward] and should in fact be stopped.

→ 첫 번째 [ ]는 문장 중간에 삽입된 계속적 용법의 목적격 관계대명사절

→ 두 번째 [ ]는 the best way를 수식하는 형용사적 용법의 to부정사구

⑧ **It's time for** the government **to come up with** ways to end the use ....
→ it's time+for+(대)명사+to-v: …가 ~할 때이다

03 노벨상 대신 필즈 메달! P. 110

정답 1 ② 2 ④ 3 ④ 4 wasn't interested in math[mathematics]

문제해설 **1** 알프레드 노벨이 노벨 상을 제정했다는 내용에 이어, 그가 다양한 분야의 상을 만들었으나 수학을 위한 상은 만들지 않았다는 내용인 (B)가 오고, 수학상을 만들지 않은 이유에 대해 언급한 (A)가 이어지고, 결과적으로 이유에 상관없이, 노벨상에 수학분야가 없어서 같은 목적을 이루기 위한 여러 다른 상들이 만들어지게 되었다는 내용인 (C)로 이어지는 것이 자연스럽다.

2 필즈 메달을 받은 수학자들이 잘 알려지지 않은 이유를 설명하는 내용이므로, 그들이 수학 분야 밖에서 찬사를 받는 일이 '거의 없다'는 내용이 되어야 자연스럽다. 따라서 ④ often을 seldom 등으로 고쳐야 한다.

3 ④ 수상자들의 나이는 40세 미만으로 제한된다고 했다.

4 노벨이 수학을 위한 상을 제정하지 않은 이유는 무엇인가?
→ 그것은 단지 그가 수학에 관심이 없었기 때문이었다.

본문

① Swedish chemist Alfred Nobel, / the inventor of dynamite, / established the Nobel Prizes / in his will. ② (B) Although he created a prize / for a number of different fields, / he did not create one / for mathematics. ③ (A) It has been rumored / that this was because / Nobel and a famous mathematician / once fell in love with the same woman, / but the truth is / that Nobel simply wasn't interested in math. ④ (C) Regardless of the reason, / the absence of a Nobel Prize for mathematics / has inspired the creation of several other awards / to serve the same purpose. ⑤ The most famous of these / is the Fields Medal.

⑥ Named for John Charles Fields, / a Canadian mathematician, / the medal was first awarded / in 1936. ⑦ Four years earlier, / Fields had died, / leaving money in his will / to establish the award. ⑧ Along with $15,000, / each winning mathematician / has the honor of knowing / that he or she has attained the highest honor / in the field of math. ⑨ The Fields Medal is awarded / every four years / and is restricted to mathematicians / under the age of 40. ⑩ This is because / it is intended to serve / as an inspiration / to do even greater work / in the future. ⑪ The location of the awarding ceremony varies, / as it is held / wherever the International Congress of the International Mathematical Union meeting / is taking place that year.

⑫ Whereas many Nobel Prize winners have been quite famous, / few of the people / who have received the Fields Medal / are well-known, / as mathematicians seldom achieve acclaim / outside of their field. ⑬ But / by winning such a prestigious award, / they are able to enjoy their moment / in the spotlight.

해석 ① 다이너마이트의 발명가인 스웨덴의 화학자 알프레드 노벨은 그의 유언을 통해 노벨상을 제정했다. ② (B) 그는 서로 다른 여러 분야를 위한 상을 제정했지만, 수학을 위한 상은 제정하지 않았다. ③ (A) 이는 노벨과 어떤 유명한 수학자가 한때 동일한 여성과 사랑에 빠졌었기 때문이라는 소문이 있어 왔지만, 사실은 노벨이 단지 수학에 관심이 없었다는 것이다. ④ (C) 이유에 상관없이, 수학을 위한 노벨상의 부재는 동일한 목적을 이루기 위한 여러 다른 상의 제정을 고무시켜왔다. ⑤ 이 중 가장 유명한 것이 필즈 메달이다.

⑥ 캐나다의 수학자인 존 찰스 필즈의 이름을 따서 명명된 그 메달은 1936년에 처음으로 수여되었다. ⑦ 그보다 4년 전에 필즈는 사망하면서, 상을 제정하기 위해 그의 유언에서 돈을 남겼다. ⑧ 15,000달러와 함께, 수상하는 각 수학자는 자신이 수학 분야에서 가장 높은 명예를 얻었다는 것을 알게 되는 영광을 차지한다. ⑨ 필즈 메달은 4년마다 수여되며, 40세 미만의 수학자들로 제한되어 있다. ⑩ 이것은 그것이 미래에 훨씬 더 위대한 일을 할 수 있는 영감으로서 작용하도록 의도되었기 때문이다. ⑪ 시상식의 장소는 다양한데, 그것이 그 해 국제 수학 연맹의 국제 대회가 열리는 곳에서 개최되기 때문이다.

⑫ 많은 노벨상 수상자들이 꽤 유명한 데 반해, 필즈 메달을 받은 사람들 중 잘 알려진 사람은 거의 없는데, 수학자들이 그들의 분야 밖에서 찬사를 받는 일이 드물기 때문이다. ⑬ 그러나 이런 권위 있는 상을 받음으로써, 그들은 주목을 받는 순간을 즐길 수 있다.

구문해설 ③ It *has been rumored* [that this was because Nobel ... the same woman], ...

→ It은 가주어, 명사절 [ ]가 진주어

→ has been rumored는 〈계속〉의 의미를 나타내는 현재완료 수동태

⑤ The most famous of these (S) is (V) the Fields Medal.

→ the + 최상급 + of + 복수명사: … 중에서 가장 ~한 것

⑥ [Named for John Charles Fields, a Canadian mathematician], the medal was first awarded in 1936.

→ [ ]는 과거분사로 시작하는 수동형 분사구문

→ John Charles Fields와 a Canadian mathematician은 동격 관계

⑦ Four years earlier, Fields had died, [leaving money in his will **to establish** the award].

→ [ ]는 〈부대상황〉을 나타내는 분사구문

→ to establish는 〈목적〉을 나타내는 부사적 용법의 to부정사

⑪ ..., **as** it is held [wherever the International Congress of the International Mathematical Union meeting is taking place that year].

→ as는 〈이유〉를 나타내는 접속사

→ [ ]는 '…하는 곳은 어디든지'의 의미를 나타내는 복합관계부사절

⑫ ..., few of the people [who have received the Fields Medal] are well-known, ...

→ [ ]는 선행사 the people을 수식하는 주격 관계대명사절

04 무관한 문장 P. 112

정답 ④ 변형문제 **1** ② **2** to know what makes their employees satisfied with their jobs **3** ⑤

문제해설 이 글은 고객 경험과 회사 실적에 큰 영향을 끼친다는 점에서 직원들의 직업 만족도는 중요하다는 것이 주요 내용이므로, 제품의 가격과 가치에 대한 내용인 ④는 글의 흐름과 무관하다.

변형문제

1 회사들이 직원들의 직업 만족도를 높이려고 하는 이유에 대한 내용이므로 제목으로 ② '직원 만족도가 중요한 이유'가 가장 적절하다.
① 소비자 행동의 수수께끼
③ 직업 만족도를 높이는 비결
④ 생산성 향상: 행복한 고객들에게 집중하라
⑤ 직원들이 지켜야 하는 고객 서비스 원칙

2 it은 가주어이고 for companies는 to부정사의 의미상의 주어이다. 그 뒤에 진주어인 to부정사구를 배열하되 know의 목적어 자리에 의문사 what으로 시작하는 간접의문문을 넣는다.

3 ⑤ 직원들의 직업 만족도가 높으면 생산성도 높아지고, 고객의 경험과 회사 실적에도 영향을 미친다고 했다.
직원 만족도를 증가시키는 것은 만족스러운 직원들이 더 열심히 일할 가능성이 높고 고객들을 향한 그들의 태도가 회사 실적에 영향을 미치기 때문에 중요하다.

본문

① Companies would like to enhance employee contentment on the job / for several reasons. ② Job satisfaction increases productivity / because happy employees work harder, / allowing them to produce more at a lower cost. ③ Moreover, / in many service organizations, client satisfaction / often depends directly on the attitudes of employees, / who are the company's face for customers. ④ Because people's purchasing patterns are affected / by how they feel during the buying experience, / happy employees matter. ⑤ When workers are dissatisfied, / their unhappiness makes the customer's experience worse; / as a result, consumers buy less, / and company performance suffers. ⑥ (In other words, / when a product costs more, / but is worth it, / its value becomes acceptable to the consumer.) ⑦ Clearly, / it is important for companies to know / what makes their employees satisfied with their jobs.

해석 ① 회사들은 몇 가지 이유들로 직업에 있어서 직원 만족도를 높이고 싶어 한다. ② 행복한 직원들은 열심히 일하기 때문에 직업 만족도는 생산성을 높이며, 그들로 하여금 더 낮은 비용에 더 많이 생산하게 한다. ③ 게다가, 많은 서비스 조직에서 고객 만족은 종종 고객에 대한 회사의 얼굴인 직원들의 태도에 직접적으로 달려 있다. ④ 사람들의 구매 패턴이 구매 경험 동안 그들의 기분이 어떠한지에 의해 영향을 받기 때문에, 행복한 직원들은 중요하다. ⑤ 직원들이 불만족할 때, 그들의 불행은 고객의 경험을 나쁘게 만든다. 결과적으로, 고객들은 덜 사게 되고, 회사의 실적은 더 나빠진다. ⑥ (즉 다시 말해, 어떤 제품이 값이 더 나가지만, 그럴 만한 가치가 있을 때, 그것의 가치는 소비자에게 용인된다.) ⑦ 분명히, 회사가 무엇이 자사의 직원들이 자기 일에 만족하게 하는지를 아는 것은 중요하다.

구문해설 ② Job satisfaction increases productivity because happy employees work harder, [**allowing** them **to produce** more at a lower cost].
→ [ ]는 〈부대상황〉을 나타내는 분사구문
→ allow+목적어+to-v: (목적어)가 …하게 해주다

④ Because people's purchasing patterns are affected by [how they feel during the buying experience], happy employees matter.
→ [ ]는 전치사 by의 목적어로 쓰인 간접의문문으로, 「의문사+주어+동사」의 어순임.

Review Test

P. 114

A **1** ⓓ **2** ⓒ **3** ⓐ **4** ⓔ **5** ⓑ B **1** located **2** industry **3** field **4** association C **1** ⑤ **2** ① **3** ③ **4** ④ D **1** 각 그룹은 여종업원에 의해 터널을 통과하여 테이블로 안내되는데, 여종업원 본인도 맹인이다. **2** 아무도 당신을 볼 수 없으므로, 어느 누구도 당신의 식탁 예절에 대해 불평하지 않을 것이다. **3** 정부가 재생 불가능한 에너지원의 사용을 중단할 방법들을 모색할 때이다. **4** 사람들의 구매 패턴은 구매 경험 동안 그들이 어떻게 느끼는지에 의해 영향을 받는다. E **1** as dark as the inside of a cow **2** It is intended to serve as **3** not the best way to go forward

해석 **A**

1 치명적인: ⓓ 죽음을 야기하거나 치명적인 결과를 가져올 수 있는
2 소지품: ⓒ 누군가가 소유한 물건들
3 한정하다: ⓐ 어떤 것의 범위를 제한하다
4 향상시키다: ⓔ 무언가의 품질이나 가치를 높이다
5 보존: ⓑ 천연 자원을 낭비하지 않기 위해 주의 깊게 사용하는 것

B

1 조사관들은 그 비행기의 엔진에서 결함 부위를 찾아냈다.
2 출판 산업은 디지털 시대에 살아남기 위해 고군분투하고 있다.
3 제시카는 심리학 분야에서 꽤 유명하다.
4 협회의 회원들은 연회비를 내야 한다.

C

1 팀은 열심히 공부해서 그 나라에서 가장 권위 있는 대학 중 하나에 합격했다.
① 우려하는 ② 전념하는 ③ 보증된 ④ 관대한 ⑤ 권위 있는

2 나는 의사가 내 시력을 검사할 수 있도록 왼쪽 눈을 가렸다.
① 검사할 ② 맞이할 ③ 투자할 ④ 출판할 ⑤ 지지할

3 그 영화는 영화제에서 비평가들의 찬사를 받았다.
① 계획 ② 목적 ③ 찬사 ④ 소비 ⑤ 약속

4 나이나 성별에 상관없이 누구나 그 대회에 참가할 수 있다.
① … 때문에 ② 끝없는 ③ …에 따라 ④ 상관없이 ⑤ …에 관하여

SECTION 10

01 1 ⑤ 2 climb, Eiger 3 ④
02 1 What just happened is called the "decoy effect" 2 ⑤ 3 ③
03 1 ② 2 ③ 3 bus, compose, record
04 ③ 변형문제 1 ① 2 ② 3 ③

01 알프스의 노스페이스 P. 118

정답 1 ⑤ 2 climb, Eiger 3 ④

문제해설 1 ⑤ 아이거는 폭풍이 심하고 예측이 불가능하다고 했다.

2 아이거의 북쪽 면을 오르는 것

3 밑줄 친 scale은 '(높고 가파른 곳을) 오르다'라는 의미로 ④ '어떤 것의 꼭대기에 도달하다'가 가장 적절하다.

① 목적 없이 돌아다니다 ② 긍정적인 방향으로 발전하다
③ 어떤 것의 무게를 측정하다 ⑤ 변화 없는 상태로 유지하거나 지속하다

본문

① The 1,800-meter tall north face of the Eiger, / a mountain in the Swiss Alps, / is known as one of the most difficult in the world / to climb; / more than 50 people have lost their lives / attempting to do so / since 1935. ② Despite the extreme dangers, / it is considered one of the greatest challenges / for alpine mountaineers.
③ In 1935, / the first pair of climbers / to attempt to reach its peak / froze to death / at an altitude of 3,000 meters. ④ The next year, / four more climbers died / after bad weather forced them to turn back. ⑤ Year after year, / similar tragedies continued to take the lives of unfortunate climbers. ⑥ Nevertheless, / there were always more brave climbers / willing to test themselves / by attempting to scale the north face.
⑦ There are several reasons / that the Eiger is so difficult / for climbers to conquer. ⑧ It is extremely steep / and full of loose stones / that can easily break off / and fall on climbers. ⑨ At higher altitudes, / avalanches present a similar danger. ⑩ The weather can also be a serious problem; / the Eiger is known for its storms, / which are both terrible and unpredictable. ⑪ Climbers who are able to somehow overcome / all of these obstacles / and reach the top / all make the same vow: / they will never try to do it again. ⑫ Defeating the Eiger / is truly a once in a lifetime experience.

해석

① 스위스의 알프스 산맥에 있는 산인 아이거의 1,800미터 높이의 북쪽 면은 세상에서 가장 오르기 어려운 산 중 하나로 알려져 있다. 1935년 이후로 50명 이상의 사람들이 그것을 시도하다 목숨을 잃었다. ② 극도의 위험에도 불구하고, 그것은 알프스 산악인들에게 가장 위대한 도전 중 하나로 여겨진다.
③ 1935년에, 그곳의 정상에 도달하고자 시도한 최초의 등반가 두 명이 고도 3,000미터에서 동사했다. ④ 그다음해에는 네 명의 등반가들이 악천후로 인해 되돌아와야 했을 때 사망했다. ⑤ 해마다 유사한 비극이 계속해서 운이 나쁜

등반가들의 생명을 앗아갔다. ⑥ 그럼에도 불구하고, 북쪽 면을 오르려고 시도함으로써 자기 자신을 시험하고자 하는 용감한 등반가들이 늘 더 있었다.

⑦ 등반가들이 아이거 산을 정복하기가 그렇게 어려운 데에는 몇 가지 이유가 있다. ⑧ 그곳은 매우 가파르며, 쉽게 떨어져 나와 등반가들 위로 떨어질 수 있는 헐거운 돌들로 가득 차 있다. ⑨ 더 높은 고도에서는, 산사태가 유사한 위험을 야기한다. ⑩ 날씨 또한 심각한 문제가 될 수도 있다. 아이거 산은 그곳의 폭풍으로 유명한데, 그것은 끔찍하면서도 예측 불가능하다. ⑪ 이 모든 장애들을 어떻게든 극복하고 정상에 오를 수 있는 등반가들은 모두 똑같은 맹세를 한다. 다시는 그것을 하려고 하지 않겠다는 것이다. ⑫ 아이거 산을 정복하는 것은 진정으로 평생 단 한 번뿐인 경험이다.

구문해설 ③ In 1935, the first pair of climbers [to **attempt to reach** its peak] froze to death ....

→ [ ]는 the first pair of climbers를 수식하는 형용사적 용법의 to부정사구

→ 「the first+명사+to-v」는 '처음으로 …한 ~'라는 의미로 자주 쓰임.

→ attempt+to-v: …하는 것을 시도하다

⑦ There are several reasons [that the Eiger is so difficult **for climbers** *to conquer*].

→ [ ]는 선행사 several reasons를 수식하는 관계부사절로, 관계부사 why 대신 that이 쓰임.

→ for climbers는 to부정사의 의미상의 주어

⑩ ...; the Eiger is known for its storms, [which are **both** terrible **and** unpredictable].

→ [ ]는 선행사 its storms를 부연 설명하는 계속적 용법의 주격 관계대명사절

→ 「both A and B」는 'A와 B 둘 다'를 의미하는 상관접속사

⑪ Climbers(S) [who are able to somehow **overcome** all of these obstacles and **reach** the top] all make(V) the same vow(O): ....

→ [ ]는 선행사 Climbers를 수식하는 주격 관계대명사절

→ overcome과 reach는 and에 의해 연결된 병렬구조

02 세 번째 선택사항의 비밀! P. 120

정답 **1** What just happened is called the "decoy effect" **2** ⑤ **3** ③

문제해설 **1** 주어로는 명사절을 이끄는 관계대명사 what을 이용한 What just happened를 쓰고, 동사로는 수동태 is called를 써서 What just happened is called the "decoy effect"의 어순으로 써야 한다.

2 세 번째 미끼 상품이 원래의 두 가지 선택사항 중 하나를 더 나아 보이게 한다는 것이 문맥상 적절하므로, 빈칸에는 ⑤ '비교했을 때 더 좋아 보인다'가 적절하다.

① 인기 있어 보인다 ② 세트의 일부가 된다

③ 미끼 상품의 역할을 한다 ④ 그것의 사소한 결함을 개선한다

3 미끼 효과는 세 번째 선택사항의 도입이 이전의 선택사항들 중 하나를 더 호감 가게 만들 때 발생한다.

본문

① Imagine / you're making dinner plans / with a friend. ② There's a restaurant with delicious food / that you want to go to. ③ But it takes 15 minutes to walk there, / and you're quite hungry. ④ Your friend suggests another restaurant. ⑤ Its food is average, / but it's right across the street. ⑥ You might have a very hard time deciding / between these two options. ⑦ Both have a good point and a bad point. ⑧ But then / your friend suggests a third place. ⑨ It also has great food, / but it's a 20-minute subway ride away. ⑩ Suddenly, / your decision is clear. ⑪ A 15-minute walk / doesn't sound so bad! ⑫ So you decide to go to the first place.

⑬ What just happened / is called the "decoy effect" / in marketing. ⑭ When consumers need to decide / between two products, / marketers will sometimes introduce an undesirable third option. ⑮ The purpose of this third option is / simply to make / one of the two original choices / look better / in comparison. ⑯ For example, / if a company's product's weak point is its high price, / it might introduce a third "decoy" product / with an even higher price. ⑰ This will make the first product / seem like a smarter choice / to consumers.

해석

① 당신이 친구와 함께 저녁 식사 계획을 세우고 있다고 상상해보라. ② 당신이 가고 싶은 맛있는 음식을 파는 음식점이 있다. ③ 그런데 거기까지는 걸어서 15분이 걸리고, 당신은 상당히 배가 고프다. ④ 당신의 친구가 다른 음식점을 제안한다. ⑤ 그곳의 음식은 보통이지만, 바로 길 건너편에 있다. ⑥ 당신은 이 두 가지 선택사항 중에서 결정하기가 매우 힘들지도 모른다. ⑦ 둘 다 장점과 단점이 있다. ⑧ 그런데 그때 당신의 친구가 세 번째 장소를 제안한다. ⑨ 그곳도 음식은 훌륭하지만, 지하철로 20분 거리에 있다. ⑩ 갑자기, 당신의 결정은 분명해진다. ⑪ 15분 걸어가는 것이 그렇게 나쁘지 않은 것 같다! ⑫ 그래서 당신은 첫 번째 장소에 가기로 결정한다.

⑬ 방금 일어난 일은 마케팅에서 '미끼 효과'라고 불린다. ⑭ 소비자가 두 가지 상품 중에서 결정해야 할 때, 마케팅 담당자들은 때때로 달갑지 않은 세 번째 선택사항을 제시할 것이다. ⑮ 이 세 번째 선택사항의 목적은 단지 원래의 두 가지 선택사항 중 하나가 비교했을 때 더 좋아 보이게 만드는 것이다. ⑯ 예를 들어, 한 회사의 상품의 약점이 높은 가격이라면, 그 회사는 훨씬 더 높은 가격의 세 번째 '미끼' 상품을 내놓을지도 모른다. ⑰ 이것은 소비자들에게 첫 번째 상품이 더 현명한 선택인 것처럼 보이게 만들 것이다.

구문해설

② There's a restaurant with delicious food [that you want to go to].

→ [ ]는 선행사 a restaurant with delicious food를 수식하는 목적격 관계대명사절

③ But **it takes** 15 minutes **to walk** there, and you're quite hungry.

→ it takes + 시간 + to-v: …하는 데 얼마의 시간이 걸리다

⑥ You might **have a** very **hard time deciding** between these two options.

→ have a hard time + v-ing: …하느라 힘든 시간을 보내다

⑮ The purpose of this third option is simply **to *make*** one of the two original choices *look* better in comparison.

→ to make 이하는 주격보어 역할을 하는 명사적 용법의 to부정사구

→ 사역동사(make) + 목적어 + 동사원형: …을 ~하게 하다

03 존 레논은 살아 있다 P. 122

정답 1 ② 2 ③ 3 bus, compose, record

문제해설 1 존 레논 교육 순회버스가 이스트뷰 고등학교를 방문한 내용을 알리는 기사이므로, 제목으로는 ② '레논 버스가 마을에 오다'가 적절하다.

① 존 레논이 사랑한 버스 ③ 스타들이 레논 버스에 모이다
④ 존 레논과 그의 고등학교 추억 ⑤ 고등학교 음악 교육의 현실

2 존 레논 교육 순회버스는 음악을 통해 자신을 표현하려는 청소년들을 가르치고자 한다고 했으므로 ③은 글의 내용과 일치하지 않는다.

3 버스에서의 수업에 참가한 학생들은 음악을 작곡하고 녹음하고 제작하는 방법에 대해 배웠다.

본문

① The Lennon Bus Comes to Town

② It's been more than 40 years / since the Beatles, / one of the most popular rock bands ever, / broke up. ③ But / this amazing band continues to have an effect on / younger generations. ④ Yesterday, / the John Lennon Educational Tour Bus made a stop / at Eastview High School.

⑤ John Lennon, / of course, / was one of the greatest rock musicians / of all time. ⑥ Tragically, / he was killed in 1980. ⑦ Eighteen years later, / the John Lennon Educational Tour Bus was established / to continue working towards / the musician's dream of teaching youngsters / to express themselves through music.

⑧ A handful of lucky Eastview High School students were selected / to attend a special lesson / given on the bus, / which is really a mobile recording studio. ⑨ The topic of the lesson was / how to mix vocals with drums and horns. ⑩ The students met with a team of producers and engineers / who showed them / not only how to compose an original song / but also how to record and produce one.

⑪ Since its founding, / the Lennon Bus has taught similar lessons / to millions of young students, / targeting schools with music programs / that are struggling / due to budget cuts.

⑫ The head of the Lennon Bus program stressed / that even though many of the students were born / after John Lennon's death, / they still love his legendary music.

⑬ Eastview High School senior Ryan Castleton / summed up his experience this way: / "It gave me a lot of confidence / in my musical ability. ⑭ And / it was a lot of fun, / too!"

해석

① 레논 버스가 마을에 오다

② 역대 가장 인기 있는 록밴드 중 하나인 비틀즈가 해체한 지 40년이 넘었다. ③ 그러나 이 놀라운 밴드는 젊은 세대들에게 계속해서 영향을 미치고 있다. ④ 어제, 존 레논 교육 순회버스가 이스트뷰 고등학교에 정차했다.

⑤ 존 레논은 물론 역대 가장 훌륭한 록 음악가 중 한 명이었다. ⑥ 비극적이게도, 그는 1980년에 살해당했다. ⑦ 18년 후, 존 레논 교육 순회버스가 음악을 통해 자신을 표현하려는 청소년들을 가르치고자 한 그 음악가의 꿈을 향해 계속해서 노력하고자 설립되었다.

⑧ 소수의 운 좋은 이스트뷰 고등학교 학생들이 선발되어 버스에서 진행되는 특별 수업에 참여했는데, 그 버스는 실

제로 이동식 녹음실이다. ⑨ 수업의 주제는 보컬을 드럼과 호른과 함께 믹싱 녹음하는 방법이었다. ⑩ 학생들은 독창적인 곡을 작곡하는 방법뿐만 아니라 곡을 녹음하고 제작하는 방법도 가르쳐준 제작자와 기술자 팀과 만났다.

⑪ 설립 이래로, 레논 버스는 예산 삭감 때문에 고전하고 있는 음악 프로그램을 가진 학교들을 대상으로 삼으며, 수백만의 어린 학생들에게 유사한 수업을 가르쳐왔다. ⑫ 레논 버스 프로그램의 책임자는 비록 학생들 상당수가 존 레논의 사망 이후에 태어났지만 그들은 여전히 그의 전설적인 음악을 사랑한다고 강조했다.

⑬ 이스트뷰 고등학교의 졸업반 학생인 라이언 캐슬톤은 그의 경험을 이렇게 요약했다. "그것은 제 음악적 능력에 있어서 저에게 많은 자신감을 주었어요. ⑭ 그리고 그것은 정말 재미있기도 했고요!"

구문해설 ② ... the Beatles, [one of the most popular rock bands ever], broke up.

→ the Beatles와 [ ]는 동격 관계

⑧ ... students were selected **to attend** a special lesson [given on the bus], [which is really a mobile recording studio].

→ to attend는 〈결과〉를 나타내는 부사적 용법의 to부정사

→ 첫 번째 [ ]는 a special lesson을 뒤에서 수식하는 과거분사구

→ 두 번째 [ ]는 선행사 the bus를 부연 설명하는 계속적 용법의 주격 관계대명사절

⑩ The students met with a team of producers and engineers [who showed them **not only** how to compose an original song **but also** how to record and produce one].

→ [ ]는 선행사 a team of producers and engineers를 수식하는 주격 관계대명사절

→ not only A but also B: A뿐만 아니라 B도

⑪ ..., the Lennon Bus has taught similar lessons to millions of young students, [targeting schools with music programs {that are struggling ...}].

→ [ ]는 〈동시동작〉을 나타내는 분사구문

→ { }는 선행사 music programs를 수식하는 주격 관계대명사절

04 빈칸 추론 P. 124

정답 ③ 변형문제 **1** ① **2** ② **3** ③

문제해설 자신에게 중요한 것을 고려해서 목표를 세워야 한다고 했으므로 빈칸에는 ③ '여러분 자신만의 가치'가 적절하다.

① 여러분의 도덕적 임무 ② 엄격한 기한

④ 부모의 지도 ⑤ 인력 시장의 동향

변형문제

1 자기가 해야만 하는 것이 아니라, 자기 자신에게 중요한 것을 고려해서 목표를 세워야 한다는 내용이므로 글의 요지로는 ①이 적절하다.

2 주어진 문장은 어떤 것이 목표를 고수하기 어렵게 만든다는 내용인데, 이는 문맥상 자기가 해야 하는 것 또는 남들이 그래야 한다고 생각하는 것을 목표로 하면 그것이 실제로는 우리에게 중요한 일이 아니기 때문에 목표 달성이 어려워진다는 의미이다. 따라서 주어진 문장은 ②에 들어가는 것이 적절하다.

3 (A) enough가 부사로 쓰일 때는 형용사나 부사 뒤에서만 수식하므로 hard enough가 적절하다.
(B) 절에서 보어 역할을 하는 명사절이 와야 하므로 선행사를 포함하는 관계대명사 what이 적절하다.
(C) 문맥상 목적을 나타내야 하므로 부사적 용법의 to부정사 to get이 적절하다.

본문

① It's hard enough to stick with goals / you want to accomplish, / but sometimes we make goals / we're not even thrilled about in the first place. ② We set resolutions / based on what we're supposed to do, / or what others think we're supposed to do, / rather than what really matters to us. ③ This makes it nearly impossible / to stick to the goal. ④ For example, / reading more is a good habit, / but if you're only doing it / because you feel like / that's what you're supposed to do, / not because you actually want to learn more, / you're going to have a hard time reaching the goal. ⑤ Instead, / make goals based / on your own values. ⑥ Now, / this isn't to say / you should read less. ⑦ The idea is to first consider / what matters to you, / then figure out / what you need to do / to get there.

해석

① 여러분이 성취하고자 하는 목표를 고수하는 것만으로도 충분히 어려운데, 때때로 우리는 심지어 애초부터 우리가 열광하지도 않는 목표를 세우기도 한다. ② 우리는 우리에게 실제로 중요한 것이 아니라 우리가 해야 하는 것, 또는 다른 사람들이 우리가 해야만 한다고 생각하는 것에 기초하여 결심을 하게 된다. ③ 이것은 목표를 고수하는 것을 거의 불가능하게 만든다. ④ 예를 들어, 더 많은 독서를 하는 것은 좋은 습관이지만, 여러분이 실제로 더 배우기를 원해서가 아니라 단지 그것이 여러분이 해야 하는 것이라고 느끼기 때문에 그것을 하고 있다면, 여러분은 목표에 도달하는 데 어려움을 겪을 것이다. ⑤ 대신에, 여러분 자신만의 가치에 기초하여 목표를 세워라. ⑥ 자, 이것은 여러분이 독서를 더 적게 해야 한다고 말하려는 것이 아니다. ⑦ 방법은 우선 여러분에게 무엇이 중요한지 고려하고, 그러고 나서 그것에 도달하기 위해 여러분이 무엇을 해야 하는지 파악하는 것이다.

구문해설

② We set resolutions based on **what** we*'re supposed to do*, or **what** [others think] we're supposed to do, rather than **what** really matters to us.
→ 세 개의 what은 선행사를 포함하는 관계대명사
→ [ ]는 명사절에 삽입되어, '다른 사람이 생각하기에'라는 의미임.
→ be supposed to-v: …하기로 되어 있다, …해야 한다

④ ..., you're going to **have a hard time reaching** the goal.
→ have a hard time v-ing: …하는 데 어려움을 겪다

Review Test

P. 126

A 1 ⓑ 2 ⓓ 3 ⓒ 4 ⓔ 5 ⓐ B 1 undesirable 2 targets 3 resolution 4 accomplish C 1 ③ 2 ② 3 ⑤ 4 ① D 1 등반가들이 아이거 산을 정복하기가 그렇게 어려운 데에는 몇 가지 이유가 있다. 2 당신은 이 두 가지 선택사항 중에서 결정하기가 매우 힘들지도 모른다. 3 수업의 주제는 보컬을 드럼과 호른과 함께 믹싱 녹음하는 방법이었다. 4 방법은 여러분에게 무엇이 중요한지 고려하고, 그러고 나서 그것에 도달하기 위해 무엇을 해야 하는지 파악하는 것이다. E 1 The Eiger is known for its storms 2 attended a special lesson given on the bus 3 what you're supposed to do

해석 A

1 시도하다: ⓑ 무언가를 하려고 노력하다

2 비극(적인 사건): ⓓ 큰 슬픔을 야기하는 사건

3 장애(물): ⓒ 진척을 방해하는 것

4 이동식의: ⓔ 한 장소에서 다른 장소로 이동할 수 있는

5 봉우리, 정상: ⓐ 산의 꼭대기

B

1 몇몇 의사들은 전자 기기의 과도한 사용이 우리 건강에 미치는 바람직하지 않은 영향을 우려한다.

2 그 잡지는 20대와 30대 초반의 독신 여성을 대상으로 한다.

3 그는 월급의 절반을 저축하겠다는 굳은 결심을 했다.

4 이 이야기는 사람들이 그들의 역경을 극복하고 목표를 이루도록 격려했다.

C

1 지난주 수요일 축구 경기에서 한국이 일본을 이겼다.

① 고군분투했다 ② 드러냈다 ③ 이겼다 ④ 간과했다 ⑤ 비교했다

2 평균적인 미국 십대는 한 달에 5,000건의 문자 메시지를 보낸다.

① 이전의 ② 평균적인 ③ 가파른 ④ 본래의 ⑤ (가격이) 적당한

3 우리 회사를 법률적으로 설립하기 위해서는, 시의 허락을 받아야 한다.

① 필요로 하기 ② 영향을 주기 ③ 피하기 ④ 약속하기 ⑤ 설립하기

4 정장에 결함이 있었기 때문에 손님은 그것을 반품했다.

① 결함 ② 미끼 ③ 선택사항 ④ 지도, 안내 ⑤ 규모

SECTION 11

01 1 ⑤ 2 The greater the area of skin touching the glass 3 (1) T (2) T (3) F

02 1 ⑤ 2 ② 3 green, red

03 1 Intelligence levels, increasing 2 ③ 3 ④ 4 ③

04 ④ 변형문제 1 ② 2 ⑤ 3 Recycling or composting, landfills

01 손가락과 유리잔 사이

P. 130

정답 1 ⑤ 2 The greater the area of skin touching the glass. 3 (1) T (2) T (3) F

문제해설 1 우리가 손가락으로 유리 같은 미끄러운 물질을 어떻게 잡을 수 있는가에 대한 내용이므로 주제로는 ⑤ '우리 손가락이 미끄러운 물건들을 잡는 방법'이 적절하다.

① 우리 손가락의 감각 세포

② 마찰의 정의와 그 역할

③ 땀이 우리 몸에 중요한 이유

④ 다양한 물질 속의 서로 다른 분자들

2 「The+비교급 ..., the+비교급 ~: …할수록, 더 ~하다」 구문을 활용해 배열한다. 여기서 touching the glass는 skin을 수식하는 현재분사구이므로, skin 뒤에 배열한다.

3 (1) 유리의 분자들과 우리 손가락의 분자들 간의 마찰은 우리가 유리잔을 잡도록 도와준다.

(2) 우리 지문의 융선은 우리가 유리잔을 잡고 있을 때 땀 때문에 평평해진다.

(3) 우리 몸은 매끄러운 물질을 감지하면 즉시 우리 손가락에 땀을 배출한다.

→ 우리 몸이 매끄러운 물질을 감지하고 땀을 배출하기까지 걸리는 시간은 테스트를 받는 개인과 물체의 무게에 따라 단 몇 초 또는 20초까지 될 수 있다고 했다.

본문

① Glass is a slippery material, / so why doesn't it slip / right through our fingers / when we hold it? ② It is partly due to the friction / between molecules in the glass and molecules in our skin. ③ The greater the area of skin touching the glass, / the stronger the friction. ④ Researchers recently discovered / that our fingers actually adapt to slippery materials / by increasing the contact area. ⑤ Surprisingly, / they do this / by using sweat.

⑥ The adaptation involves small changes / on the outer layer of our skin, / where our fingerprints are located. ⑦ The ridges of our fingerprints help us / hold onto rough materials, / but they can't help with smooth materials like glass. ⑧ So when our body senses a smooth material, / it releases a little bit of sweat onto the skin. ⑨ The sweat causes the ridges to flatten, / which allows more skin to touch the glass / and increases the amount of friction. ⑩ As a result, / we can easily keep a firm grip on the glass.

⑪ Scientists researching this unusual process / have found that / it doesn't happen immediately. ⑫ Sometimes it takes only a few seconds to start / and other times / it can take as long as 20 seconds, / depending on the individual being tested / and the weight of the object.

해석 ① 유리는 미끄러운 물질인데, 그러면 우리가 그것을 잡을 때, 그것은 왜 우리의 손가락 사이로 바로 미끄러지지 않는가? ② 그것은 부분적으로 유리 속 분자들과 우리 피부 속 분자들 사이의 마찰력 때문이다. ③ 유리잔에 닿는 피부의 면적이 더 커질수록, 마찰도 더 강해진다. ④ 연구원들은 최근에 우리의 손가락이 접촉 면적을 증가시킴으로써 실제로 미끄러운 물질들에 적응한다는 것을 발견했다. ⑤ 놀랍게도, 그것들(손가락들)은 땀을 이용함으로써 이렇게 한다. ⑥ 이 적응은 우리 피부의 바깥층에 작은 변화들을 수반하는데, 그 층에 지문이 있다. ⑦ 우리 지문의 융선은 우리가 거친 물질을 잡도록 도와주지만, 유리 같은 매끄러운 물질을 잡는 것은 도와줄 수 없다. ⑧ 그래서 우리의 몸이 매끄러운 물질을 감지하면, 우리 몸은 피부에 약간의 땀을 배출한다. ⑨ 땀은 융선들이 평평해지게 하고, 이는 더 많은 피부가 유리에 접촉하게 해 마찰의 양을 증가시킨다. ⑩ 결과적으로, 우리는 유리를 쉽게 꽉 붙잡을 수 있다.
⑪ 이러한 특이한 과정을 조사하는 과학자들은 이 과정이 즉시 일어나지 않는다는 것을 발견했다. ⑫ 테스트를 받는 개인과 물체의 무게에 따라, 때로는 시작되는 데 몇 초만 걸리기도 하고 다른 때는 20초까지도 걸릴 수 있다.

구문해설

⑥ The adaptation involves small changes on the outer layer of our skin, [where our fingerprints are located].
→ [ ]는 the outer layer of our skin을 부연 설명하는 계속적 용법의 관계부사절

⑨ The sweat **causes** the ridges **to flatten**, *which* allows more skin to touch the glass and increases the amount of friction.
→ cause+목적어+to-v: (목적어)가 …하게 만들다
→ which는 앞 절을 부연 설명하는 계속적 용법의 주격 관계대명사
→ 관계대명사절의 동사 allows와 increases가 접속사 and로 병렬 연결됨.

02 왜 하필 녹색일까? P. 132

정답 **1** ⑤ **2** ② **3** green, red

문제해설

1 의사들이 녹색 수술복을 입는 이유를 과학적으로 설명하는 글이므로, 제목으로는 ⑤ '의사의 수술복에 숨겨진 과학'이 적절하다.
① 잔상이란 무엇인가? ② 색의 상징적 사용
③ 우리의 눈은 어떻게 색상을 보는가 ④ 눈의 피로를 예방하는 방법

2 수술이 출혈을 동반한다는 내용에 이어, 의사들이 오랫동안 붉은 피를 보면 추상체가 피로해진다는 내용인 (A)가 오고, 피로해진 눈으로 흰색 수술복을 보면 빨간색의 보색인 녹색 잔상을 보게 된다는 (C)가 이어지고, 이 잔상이 의사들의 시야를 혼란시켜 집중력을 떨어뜨린다는 내용인 (B)로 이어지는 것이 자연스럽다.

3 수술하는 동안 의사들이 흰색 수술복을 입으면, 그들의 피로해진 추상체에는 빨간색의 보색인 녹색 잔상이 남을 수 있다.

본문

① Why do doctors wear green gowns / instead of white coats / during surgery? ② There is actually a scientific reason.
③ Our eyes' retina is made up of / two types of receptor cells / — rods and cones. ④ Rods are sensitive to weak light / and can sense low levels of light. ⑤ Cones are sensitive to stronger light / and can interpret color. ⑥ But cones get fatigued / from looking at strong colors / for a long time. ⑦ When fatigued cones see a white surface, / they are left / with an afterimage. ⑧ An afterimage refers to the complementary color / that you sometimes see / after you look away / from a strong color.

⑨ Medical surgeries are normally accompanied by bleeding. ⑩ (A) When doctors look at red blood for a long time, / their cones become fatigued. ⑪ (C) So if they look at other doctors / wearing white coats, / they see a green afterimage, / as green is the complementary color of red. ⑫ (B) This afterimage confuses the doctors' vision / and lowers their concentration. ⑬ Thus, / to prevent this, / doctors wear green gowns / during surgery.

해석 ① 왜 의사들은 수술하는 동안 흰색 수술복 대신 녹색 수술복을 입을까? ② 거기에는 사실 과학적인 이유가 있다. ③ 우리 눈의 망막은 간상체와 추상체라는 두 가지 수용체 세포로 구성되어 있다. ④ 간상체는 약한 빛에 민감하고, 낮은 단계의 빛을 감지할 수 있다. ⑤ 추상체는 더 강한 빛에 민감하고, 색깔을 감지할 수 있다. ⑥ 그러나 오랫동안 강한 색들을 보고 있으면 추상체가 피로해진다. ⑦ 피로해진 추상체가 하얀 표면을 보면, 잔상이 남게 된다. ⑧ 잔상이란 당신이 강한 색에서 눈길을 돌렸을 때 때때로 보게 되는 보색을 말한다.

⑨ 의학적인 수술은 대개 출혈을 동반한다. ⑩ (A) 의사들이 오랜 시간 동안 붉은 피를 보면, 그들의 추상체가 피로해진다. ⑪ (C) 그래서 만약 그들이 흰색 수술복을 입고 있는 다른 의사들을 보면, 그들은 녹색 잔상을 보게 되는데, 이는 녹색이 빨간색의 보색이기 때문이다. ⑫ (B) 이 잔상은 의사들의 시야를 혼란시켜 그들의 집중력을 떨어뜨린다. ⑬ 그래서, 이것을 막기 위해서 의사들은 수술하는 동안 녹색 수술복을 입는다.

구문해설 ⑧ An afterimage refers to <u>the complementary color</u> [that you sometimes see ...].

→ [ ]는 선행사 the complementary color를 수식하는 목적격 관계대명사절

⑪ So if they look at <u>other doctors</u> [wearing white coats], they see a green afterimage, ...

→ [ ]는 other doctors를 수식하는 현재분사구

⑬ Thus, **to prevent** this, doctors wear green gowns during surgery.
→ to prevent는 〈목적〉을 나타내는 부사적 용법의 to부정사

03 똑똑해지는 사람들 P. 134

정답 **1** Intelligence levels, increasing **2** ③ **3** ④ **4** ③

문제해설 **1** <u>지능 수준</u>이 각 세대에서 <u>증가해</u>오고 있다.

2 (A) 대대로 사람의 지능이 높아지는 '플린 효과'의 원인으로 길어진 학교 교육 기간과 향상된 영양을 제시한 빈칸 앞의 내용과, 그 이유에 설득력 있는 근거가 있지는 않다는 빈칸 뒤의 내용은 서로 상반되므로, 역접의 연결사인 However가 오는 것이 알맞다.
(B) 컴퓨터의 사용이 지능을 향상시켰을 것이라는 내용에 이어, 스마트폰과 같은 새로운 기계의 사용도 추상적인 사고를 요구한다는 내용을 추가로 언급하고 있으므로, 첨가를 나타내는 What's more가 오는 것이 알맞다.

3 주어진 문장은 오늘날 아이들이 많은 양의 정보를 제공받고 더 복잡한 문제에 직면한다는 내용으로, ④ 앞의 문장에서 언급된 사회의 복잡성 증가로 인해 나타나는 결과에 해당하므로, 주어진 문장은 ④의 위치에 들어가는 것이 가장 적절하다.

4 ③ '복잡한 교육'은 플린 효과의 원인으로 언급되지 않았다.
① 길어진 학교 교육 ② 향상된 영양
④ 증가된 컴퓨터 사용 ⑤ 새로운 기계들의 사용

본문

① Did you know / that you're probably smarter / than your parents? ② That's because / intelligence levels have been increasing / from one generation to the next. ③ New Zealand political scientist James R. Flynn / discovered this surprising fact / through an analysis of data / on IQ scores. ④ It showed / that they go up / on average by three points / per decade. ⑤ Known as the "Flynn effect," / this interesting phenomenon / has left many wondering / what its causes might be.

⑥ A longer period of schooling is one important reason / put forward, / and improved nutrition is another. ⑦ However, / neither reason has compelling support. ⑧ For instance, / Flynn actually discovered / that the IQ scores of American children rose / even when time spent in school / stayed constant. ⑨ Moreover, / studies show / that intellectual impairment is only caused / by significant malnutrition. ⑩ A more general explanation / may be the increased complexity of society. ⑪ These days, / children are provided with / a huge amount of information / and are facing more complex problems. ⑫ The increased use of computers / also probably helps to boost / their logical thinking and intellectual creativity. ⑬ What's more, / new gadgets they're using / — such as smartphones — / demand more abstract reasoning, / which their parents often lack. ⑭ It seems / that the increasing sophistication of modern life / may stimulate a more complex mind. ⑮ There is, / at the moment, / no clear understanding / of what exactly is boosting intelligence. ⑯ Although it is still uncertain, / it is likely / that all of these factors combine and interact / to make each generation smarter / than the last. ⑰ Perhaps / we will need to wait a few generations / to find individuals / who are smart enough / to work out this puzzle precisely!

해석

① 아마도 당신이 부모님보다도 더 똑똑할지도 모른다는 것을 알고 있었는가? ② 그것은 지능 수준이 한 세대에서 다음 세대로 이동하며 증가해오고 있기 때문이다. ③ 뉴질랜드의 정치학자인 제임스 R. 플린은 IQ 지수에 관한 자료 분석을 통해 이 놀라운 사실을 발견했다. ④ 그 분석은 그것들이 평균적으로 10년에 3점씩 오른다는 것을 보여주었다. ⑤ '플린 효과'로 알려진 이 흥미로운 현상은 많은 이들에게 그것의 원인들이 무엇인지를 궁금하게 했다.

⑥ 더 긴 학교 교육 기간이 제기되는 하나의 중요한 이유이며, 향상된 영양이 또 다른 이유이다. ⑦ 그러나, 둘 중 어느 이유에도 설득력 있는 근거가 있지는 않다. ⑧ 예를 들어, 플린은 실제로 학교에서 보낸 시간이 변함없이 유지되었던 때조차도 미국 아동들의 IQ 지수가 올랐다는 것을 발견했다. ⑨ 게다가, 연구들은 지적 장애는 현저한 영양 실조에 의해서만 발생된다는 것을 보여준다. ⑩ 더 일반적인 설명은 사회의 증가된 복잡성일지도 모른다. ⑪ 오늘날 아이들은 엄청난 양의 정보를 제공받고, 더 복잡한 문제들을 직면하고 있다. ⑫ 증가된 컴퓨터 사용 또한 아마도 그들의 논리적인 사고와 지적 창의력을 신장시키는 데 도움이 된다. ⑬ 게다가, 그들이 사용하고 있는 스마트폰과 같은 새로운 기계들은 더욱 추상적인 사고를 필요로 하는데, 이는 그들의 부모들에게는 대개 결여되어 있다. ⑭ 아마 증가하고 있는 현대 생활의 복잡성이 더 복잡한 사고방식을 자극하는 것 같다.

⑮ 현재로서는 정확히 무엇이 지능을 향상시키고 있는지에 관한 확실한 이해는 없다. ⑯ 여전히 불확실하지만, 이 모든 요인들이 결합하고 상호작용해서 각 세대를 이전 세대보다 더 똑똑하게 만드는 것 같다. ⑰ 아마도 우리는 이 수수

께끼를 정확하게 풀어낼 만큼 충분히 똑똑한 사람들을 찾기 위해 몇 세대를 기다려야 할 것 같다!

구문해설 ② That's because intelligence levels **have been increasing** from one generation to the next.

→ have been increasing은 과거에 시작된 일이 현재에도 진행 중임을 나타내는 현재완료 진행형

⑥ A longer period of schooling is one important reason [put forward], and improved nutrition is another.

→ [ ]는 one important reason을 뒤에서 수식하는 과거분사구

⑬ ...— demand more abstract reasoning, [which their parents often lack].

→ [ ]는 선행사 abstract reasoning을 부연 설명하는 계속적 용법의 목적격 관계대명사절

⑯ ..., **it** is likely [that all of these factors combine and interact *to make* each generation smarter than the last].

→ it은 가주어, [ ]가 진주어

→ to make는 〈결과〉를 나타내는 부사적 용법의 to부정사

⑰ Perhaps we will need to wait a few generations **to find** individuals [who are *smart enough to work out* this puzzle precisely]!

→ to find는 〈목적〉을 나타내는 부사적 용법의 to부정사

→ [ ]는 선행사 individuals를 수식하는 주격 관계대명사절

→ 형용사+enough+to-v: …하기에 충분히 ~한

04 도표 P. 136

정답 ④ 변형문제 **1** ② **2** ⑤ **3** Recycling or composting, landfills

문제해설 오스트리아의 '폐기물 에너지화' 비율은 30%로, 7%인 미국의 4배 이상이므로 5배 이상이라고 한 ④는 도표의 내용과 일치하지 않는다.

변형문제

1 (A) 의문사 how가 이끄는 명사절의 동사가 와야 하므로, managed가 적절하다.

(B) 뒤의 과거분사 used를 수식해야 하므로, 부사 commonly가 적절하다.

(C) 비교 대상이 the percentage of "Energy from waste"이므로, 단수 지시대명사 that이 적절하다.

2 문맥상 account for는 '(부분 · 비율을) 차지하다'라는 의미로 ⑤ '어느 정도의 양을 나타냈다'가 가장 적절하다.

① …로 여겼다

② 사람들이 어디에 있는지 말했다

③ 설명했다

④ 어떤 것의 원인이었다

3 2011년에, 이 도표의 유럽 국가들은 폐기물 처리에서 '재활용 또는 퇴비화'의 비율이 가장 높았던 반면에, 미국은 매립지에 고형 폐기물을 묻는 고형 폐기물 처리 기법을 가장 많이 사용했다.

본문

① The above graph shows / how the United Sates managed solid waste / compared to five European nations in 2011. ② The United States had lower percentages / of "Recycling or composting" and "Energy from waste," / and a higher percentage of "Landfilled" / than the five European nations. ③ Burying solid waste in landfills / was the most commonly used solid waste management technique / in the United States, / accounting for 69 percent of total solid waste disposal. ④ On the other hand, / "Landfilled" took up zero (or statistically insignificant) percent in Germany, the Netherlands and Austria, / and just 1 percent in Belgium and Sweden respectively. ⑤ Among the five European nations, / Austria recorded the lowest percentage / of "Energy from waste," / which was more than five times / that of the United States. ⑥ The United States recycled or composted about a quarter of its total solid waste, / but Sweden recycled or composted half of its total solid waste.

해석

① 위의 그래프는 2011년에 유럽 5개국과 비교해서 미국이 고형 폐기물을 어떻게 처리했는지를 보여 준다. ② 미국은 유럽 5개국보다 '재활용 또는 퇴비화'와 '폐기물 에너지화' 비율이 더 낮았고, '매립' 비율이 더 높았다. ③ 매립지에 고형 폐기물을 묻는 것은 미국에서 가장 흔히 사용되는 고형 폐기물 처리 기법이었는데, 전체 고형 폐기물 처리의 69퍼센트를 차지했다. ④ 반면, '매립'은 독일, 네덜란드, 그리고 오스트리아에서 0(또는 통계적으로 무의미한) 퍼센트를, 그리고 벨기에와 스웨덴에서는 각각 1퍼센트만 차지했다. ⑤ 오스트리아는 유럽 5개국 가운데 가장 낮은 '폐기물 에너지화' 비율을 기록했는데, 그것은 미국의 5배가 넘었다. ⑥ 미국은 전체 고형 폐기물의 약 4분의 1을 재활용하거나 퇴비화했지만, 스웨덴은 전체 고형 폐기물의 절반을 재활용하거나 퇴비화했다.

구문해설

③ [Burying solid waste in landfills]_S was_V the most commonly used solid waste management technique in the United States, **accounting** for 69 percent of total solid waste disposal.

→ [ ]는 동명사구 주어로 단수 취급하여 단수 동사 was가 쓰임.

→ accounting 이하는 〈부대상황〉을 나타내는 분사구문

⑤ ..., Austria recorded the lowest percentage of "Energy from waste," **which** was more than five times that of the United States.

→ which는 the percentage of "Energy from waste"를 부연 설명하는 계속적 용법의 주격 관계대명사

Review Test

P. 138

A 1 ⓔ 2 ⓓ 3 ⓐ 4 ⓒ 5 ⓑ B 1 sensitive 2 extended 3 accompanied 4 stimulate C 1 ⑤ 2 ③ 3 ④ 4 ⑤ D 1 유리잔에 닿는 피부의 면적이 더 커질수록, 마찰도 더 강해진다. 2 이 모든 요인들이 상호작용해서 각 세대를 이전 세대보다 더 똑똑하게 만드는 것 같다. 3 매립지에 고형 폐기물을 묻는 것은 미국에서 가장 흔히 사용되는 고형 폐기물 처리 기법이었다. 4 그것은 지능 수준이 한 세대에서 다음 세대로 이동하며 증가해오고 있기 때문이다. E 1 who are smart enough to work out 2 wondering what its causes might be 3 There is no clear understanding

해석 **A**

1 꽉 붙잡음: ⓔ 무언가에 대한 강하고 확고한 잡음

2 적응: ⓓ 그것이 새로운 상황에 적합하도록 행동을 변화시키는 행위

3 집중(력): ⓐ 생각을 집중시키는 행위

4 추상적인: ⓒ 물리적이거나 구체적이지 않은

5 장애: ⓑ 사람의 능력이 줄어들거나 약화된 상태

B

1 이 식물은 온도 변화에 민감하다.

2 신년 휴일 동안 그 음식점은 연장 영업을 한다.

3 7세 미만의 아동은 어른과 동반해야 한다.

4 경제 성장은 에너지 소비를 활성화하는 경향이 있다.

C

1 신제품 출시는 그 회사가 매출을 신장시키는 데 도움을 주었다.
① 감소하는 ② 도달하는 ③ 투자하는 ④ 모방하는 ⑤ 신장시키는

2 애완동물의 행동의 의미를 이해하는 것은 어려울 수 있다.
① 비판하는 ② 활용하는 ③ 이해하는 ④ 부인하는 ⑤ 방출하는

3 야간 근무 후에, 그는 너무 피곤해서 영화에 집중할 수 없었다.
① 지속적이어서 ② 향상되어서 ③ 위치해서 ④ 피곤해서 ⑤ 만족스러워서

4 고데기를 이용해서 그녀는 그녀의 곱슬머리를 펼 수 있었다.
① 감지할 ② 치료할 ③ 재활용할 ④ 예방할 ⑤ 펼

SECTION 12

01 **1** ③ **2** ⑤ **3** change, process, information
02 **1** ② **2** through these passageways that the majority of diseases enter the body **3** ② **4** ④
03 **1** center, empty, outer surface **2** ⑤ **3** ①
04 ④ 변형문제 **1** ④ **2** making → made **3** ③

01 같은 사람이 아니라고? P. 142

정답 **1** ③ **2** ⑤ **3** change, process, information

문제해설 **1** 사람들이 모든 변화를 인식하지는 못한다는 사실과 그 이유를 설명하는 글이므로, 제목으로는 ③ '변화: 우리는 왜 그것들을 항상 알아채지 못하는가'가 가장 적절하다.

① 뇌는 무엇에 집중할지 어떻게 결정하는가 ② 주변의 사물들을 보는 새로운 방법들
④ 집중하는 것은 당신이 생각하는 것보다 더 쉽다 ⑤ 낯선 사람을 돕는 일의 뜻밖의 결과

2 As a result로 시작하는 주어진 문장은 결과적으로 많은 정보가 스쳐 지나간다는 내용이므로, 그 이유에 해당하는 내용 뒤에 와야 한다. 따라서 뇌가 감지하는 정보를 다 처리할 수 없기 때문에 집중할 대상을 선택한다는 내용 다음인 ⑤에 들어가는 것이 가장 적절하다.

3 뇌는 그것이 감지하는 모든 정보를 처리할 수는 없기 때문에 사람들이 모든 변화를 알아챌 수는 없다.

본문

① While walking down the street, / a woman is approached by a stranger. ② He asks for directions, / and they start to have a conversation. ③ Suddenly, / two men carrying a large piece of wood / walk between them. ④ During the interruption, / the stranger walks away / and is replaced by a different man. ⑤ After the wood is gone, / he continues the conversation. ⑥ What just happened? ⑦ Well, / the two men were conducting a scientific experiment. ⑧ And here's the amazing part — / the woman didn't even notice / that the person she was talking to / had changed! ⑨ This phenomenon is known as "change blindness." ⑩ In certain situations, / people don't notice changes / however large they are. ⑪ The reason is / that it is impossible / for the brain to process / every single piece of information / it detects. ⑫ Therefore, / it must choose what to focus on. ⑬ As a result, / a lot of information gets passed by. ⑭ In other words, / when changes occur in things / we aren't focusing on, / we tend not to notice them!

해석

① 길을 걷고 있는데, 한 여성에게 낯선 사람이 다가간다. ② 그가 길을 묻자, 그들은 대화를 시작한다. ③ 갑자기, 커다란 나무 토막을 운반하는 두 남성이 그들 사이를 지나간다. ④ 중단된 동안에, 그 낯선 사람은 가버리고 그는 다른 남성으로 교체된다. ⑤ 나무가 지나간 뒤, 그는 대화를 계속한다. ⑥ 방금 무슨 일이 있었는가? ⑦ 자, 두 남자는 과학 실험을 하는 중이었다. ⑧ 그리고 놀라운 점은, 여성이 자신이 대화하고 있던 사람이 바뀌었다는 사실을 알아채지 못했다는 것이다! ⑨ 이 현상은 '변화맹'이라고 알려져 있다. ⑩ 특정 상황에서, 사람들은 변화가 아무리 크다고 하더라도 그것을 알아채지 못한다. ⑪ 그 이유는 뇌가 감지하는 모든 정보를 처리하기는 불가능하기 때문이다. ⑫ 그래서, 그것은 무엇에 집중할지 선택해야만 한다. ⑬ 결과적으로, 많은 정보가 스쳐 지나간다. ⑭ 다시 말해서, 우리가 집중하지 않고 있는 것들에 변화가 생길 때, 우리는 그것들을 알아채지 못하는 경향이 있다!

구문해설

③ Suddenly, two men [carrying a large piece of wood] walk between them.
→ [ ]는 two men을 뒤에서 수식하는 현재분사구

⑧ ...— the woman didn't even notice [that the person {(that[who(m)]) she was talking to} **had changed**]!
→ [ ]는 notice의 목적어 역할을 하는 명사절
→ { }는 선행사 the person을 수식하는 목적격 관계대명사절로, 관계대명사 that[who(m)]이 생략됨.
→ had changed는 주절의 과거 시점보다 더 이전에 일어난 일을 나타내는 과거완료 시제

⑩ In certain situations, people don't notice changes [however large they are].
→ [ ]는 '아무리 …할지라도'의 의미를 나타내는 복합관계부사절

⑪ ... **it** is impossible *for the brain* **to process** every single piece of information [(that) it detects].

→ it은 가주어, to process가 진주어, for the brain은 to부정사의 의미상의 주어
→ [ ]는 선행사 every single piece of information을 수식하는 목적격 관계대명사절로, information과 it 사이에 관계대명사 that이 생략됨.

02 당신의 소중한 코를 위해 P. 144

정답 1 ② 2 through these passageways that the majority of diseases enter the body 3 ② 4 ④

문제해설 1 코를 씻어내는 데 사용하는 제품인 '네티'를 홍보하는 글이므로, 글의 목적으로는 ②가 가장 적절하다.

2 '~하는 것은 바로 …이다'의 의미를 나타내는 「it is ... that ~」 강조 구문이 쓰인 문장으로, 강조하고자 하는 내용인 through these passageways를 it is와 that 사이에 쓰고 나머지를 that 뒤에 배열한다.

3 문맥상 증가된 오염 물질 수치가 자연적 방어를 '막다'는 의미이므로, clog up은 '막다, 차단하다'라는 뜻의 ② block으로 바꿔 쓸 수 있다.
① 패배시키다 ③ 강화하다 ④ 초래하다 ⑤ 발달시키다

4 '네티'가 알레르기나 호흡기 감염을 완화하는 방법이 된다고 했으므로, ④ '알레르기나 호흡기 감염이 그것의 부작용이다.'는 글의 내용과 일치하지 않는다.
① 사람들이 쉽게 호흡할 수 있도록 도와준다.
② 일종의 액체를 사용한다.
③ 콧속 통로에서 박테리아와 바이러스를 깨끗이 청소해준다.
⑤ 약국에서 판매된다.

본문

① Do you suffer from / nasal congestion or respiratory illnesses? ② These problems are more common / than ever / in our modern world, / as the air we breathe / is polluted with / many kinds of chemicals, dust, and pollen. ③ But / now there's a new method of protection / that will let you breathe easily again: / Neti.

④ Neti is a device / that uses saline solution / to safely and effectively clean out / your nasal passageways. ⑤ Doctors have found / that it is through these passageways / that the majority of diseases enter the body, / so keeping them clean / is especially important. ⑥ Ordinarily, / the sinuses are protected / by a filtering system of hair and mucus membranes, / but increased levels of pollutants / can clog up this natural defense. ⑦ When you use Neti, / you'll be sending a gentle stream of saltwater / through your nasal passages, / and this liquid will wash away / bacteria, viruses, or other harmful materials.

⑧ It sounds simple, / but Neti has proven to be highly effective / in fighting off illness. ⑨ So / if you're looking for relief / from a bad case of allergies / or an uncomfortable respiratory tract infection, / Neti is just the product for you. ⑩ Stop by your local pharmacy / and pick one up today.

해석 ① 코 막힘이나 호흡기 질환으로 고생하십니까? ② 이 문제들은 우리가 숨 쉬는 공기가 많은 종류의 화학물질, 먼지, 꽃가루로 오염되어 있기 때문에 어느 때보다 현대 세상에서 더 흔합니다. ③ 하지만 이제 여러분이 다시금 수월하게 숨 쉬게 해줄 새로운 보호 수단이 있습니다. 바로 네티입니다.
④ 네티는 식염수를 사용하여 여러분의 콧속 통로를 안전하고 효과적으로 씻어내는 장치입니다. ⑤ 의사들은 대부분의 질병이 몸속으로 들어오는 것은 바로 이 통로를 통해서임을 발견했으며, 따라서 이를 청결하게 유지하는 것이 특히 중요합니다. ⑥ 보통, 공동(空洞)은 코털과 점막의 여과 시스템에 의해 보호되지만, 높아진 오염 물질 수치가 이 자연 방어를 막아 버릴 수 있습니다. ⑦ 여러분이 네티를 사용하실 때, 코의 통로를 통해 소금물을 살짝 흘려보내게 될 것이며, 이 액체는 박테리아, 바이러스 또는 다른 유해 물질들을 씻어낼 것입니다.
⑧ 단순하게 들리지만, 네티는 질병을 물리치는 데 아주 효과적인 것으로 입증되었습니다. ⑨ 그러므로 여러분이 심한 알레르기나 불편한 호흡기 감염을 완화할 방법을 찾고 계신다면, 네티가 바로 여러분을 위한 제품입니다. ⑩ 오늘 여러분 집 근처 약국을 방문해 하나 구매하십시오.

구문해설 ③ But now there's a new method of protection [that will **let** you **breathe** easily again]: Neti.

→ [ ]는 선행사 a new method of protection을 수식하는 주격 관계대명사절
→ 사역동사 let은 목적격보어로 동사원형을 취하므로 breathe가 옴.

⑤ Doctors have found [that **it is** through these passageways **that** the majority of diseases enter the body], ...
→ [ ]는 have found의 목적어 역할을 하는 명사절
→ 「it is ... that ~」 강조 구문: ~하는 것은 바로 …이다

03 대나무 자전거를 타본 적이 있나요? P. 146

정답 **1** center, empty, outer surface **2** ⑤ **3** ①

문제해설 **1** 무엇이 대나무를 아주 가볍고 구부리기 어렵게 만드는가?
→ 그것은 대나무 줄기의 중심부가 비어 있고, 가장 튼튼한 섬유질이 바깥쪽 표면에 위치해 있기 때문이다.

2 수익의 일부가 더 많은 사람들을 '교육하는 데 사용된다'는 의미가 적절하므로, '…하는 데 사용되다'를 의미하는 「be used+to-v」 구문이 쓰여야 한다. 따라서 ⑤ training을 train으로 고쳐야 한다. 「be used to+v-ing」는 '…하는 데 익숙하다'라는 의미이다.

3 기존의 재료에서 벗어나 대나무라는 새로운 재료를 사용해 자전거를 만든 것을 이야기하고 있으므로, think outside the box의 의미로는 ① '혁신적으로 생각하다'가 적절하다.
② 어떤 것들을 쉽게 받아들이다 ③ 일들을 논리적으로 숙고하다
④ 생각할 다른 장소로 가다 ⑤ 모든 것의 가치를 알아보다

본문 ① What is your bicycle made of? ② Most likely, / it's constructed of some kind of metal. ③ But / not all bikes are made of metal. ④ These days, / some of the best bikes in the world / are being made of bamboo!

⑤ So / why bamboo? ⑥ It's because of the way / its fibers are arranged. ⑦ In wood, / the strongest fibers are packed tightly together / at the center of the tree. ⑧ But / the center of a bamboo stalk / is full of empty spaces, / with the strongest fibers / on the outer surface. ⑨ This is why / bamboo is so light. ⑩ This fiber structure also makes bamboo / both stronger and more difficult to bend / than wood. ⑪ And most importantly, / bamboo easily absorbs / vibrations and impacts.

⑫ When a bicycle designer learned about / the advantages of bamboo, / he realized / that making bamboo bicycle frames / would be a great way / for poor people / to earn a living. ⑬ Since bamboo grows quickly, / it is a cheap and available resource / in many places. ⑭ He started an organization / called Bamboosero, / which travels around the world / teaching people in developing nations / how to make bamboo bicycle frames. ⑮ The frames are sold / for about $700 each, / and part of the profit is used / to train more people / in the art of making bamboo bikes.

⑯ It's amazing / what can happen / when people "think outside the box." ⑰ Cyclists benefit from / the smooth ride and classic beauty / of these unique bicycles, / while the people who make them / are able to support themselves / in a way that doesn't harm the environment.

해석

① 당신의 자전거는 무엇으로 만들어져 있는가? ② 아마도 그것은 일종의 금속으로 구성되어 있을 것이다. ③ 그러나 모든 자전거들이 금속으로 만들어지는 것은 아니다. ④ 오늘날, 세계에서 가장 좋은 자전거 중 일부는 대나무로 만들어지고 있다!

⑤ 그렇다면 왜 대나무인가? ⑥ 그것은 대나무의 섬유질이 배열되어 있는 방식 때문이다. ⑦ 나무에는 가장 튼튼한 섬유질이 나무의 중심부에 빽빽이 채워져 있다. ⑧ 그런데 대나무 줄기의 중심부는 빈 공간으로 가득 차 있으며, 가장 튼튼한 섬유질이 바깥쪽 표면에 위치해 있다. ⑨ 이것이 대나무가 그렇게 가벼운 이유이다. ⑩ 이 섬유질 구조는 또한 대나무를 나무보다 더 강하고 더 구부러지기 어렵게 만든다. ⑪ 그리고 가장 중요한 점은, 대나무는 진동과 충격을 쉽게 흡수한다는 것이다.

⑫ 한 자전거 디자이너가 대나무의 장점에 대해 알게 되었을 때, 그는 대나무 자전거 뼈대를 만드는 것이 가난한 사람들이 생계를 꾸릴 수 있는 아주 좋은 방법이 되리라는 것을 깨달았다. ⑬ 대나무는 빨리 자라기 때문에 저렴하면서도 많은 곳에서 이용 가능한 재료이다. ⑭ 그는 Bamboosero라고 불리는 단체를 시작했는데, 이 단체는 개발 도상국의 사람들에게 대나무 자전거 뼈대를 만드는 법을 가르치며 전 세계를 여행한다. ⑮ 그 뼈대들은 개당 약 700달러에 팔리며, 수익의 일부는 대나무 자전거 제작 기술에 있어 더 많은 사람들을 교육하는 데 사용된다.

⑯ 사람들이 '혁신적으로 생각할' 때 일어날 수 있는 일은 놀랍다. ⑰ 자전거를 타는 사람들은 이 독특한 자전거의 부드러운 승차감과 고전적인 아름다움에서 이익을 얻는 한편, 그것들을 만드는 사람들은 자연을 훼손하지 않는 방법으로 자립할 수 있다.

구문해설

③ But **not all** bikes are made of metal.

→ 「not all ...」은 '모두 …한 것은 아니다'의 의미로 부분 부정을 나타냄.

⑥ It's because of the way [its fibers are arranged].

→ [ ]는 선행사 the way를 수식하는 관계부사절이며, 선행사 the way와 관계부사 how는 함께 쓸 수 없으므로 둘 중 하나만 써야 함.

⑫ ..., he realized [that {making bamboo bicycle frames} would be a great way *for poor people* **to earn** a living].

→ [ ]는 realized의 목적어 역할을 하는 명사절

→ { }는 that절의 주어로 쓰인 동명사구

→ to earn은 a great way를 수식하는 형용사적 용법의 to부정사이며, for poor people은 to부정사의 의미상의 주어

⑭ He started an organization **called Bamboosero**, [which travels around the world {teaching people in developing nations ...}].

→ called Bamboosero는 an organization을 뒤에서 수식하는 과거분사구

→ [ ]는 선행사 an organization called Bamboosero를 부연 설명하는 계속적 용법의 주격 관계대명사절

→ { }는 〈동시동작〉을 나타내는 분사구문

⑯ **It**'s amazing [what can happen when people "think outside the box."]

→ It은 가주어, [ ]가 진주어

04 내용 일치 P. 148

정답 ④ 변형문제 **1** ④ **2** making → made **3** ③

문제해설 특수 효과들이 영화 촬영 중에 제작되었다고 했으므로 ④는 글의 내용과 일치하지 않는다.

변형문제

1 오늘날까지도 사용되는 영화 특수 효과를 제작해 낸 라이데커 형제에 대한 내용이므로, 글의 제목으로는 ④ '특수 효과에서 진전을 이룬 형제'가 가장 적절하다.

① 영화 제작의 발전 ② 특수 효과를 사용한 역사상 최초의 영화

③ 컴퓨터 그래픽을 이용한 영화가 기피되는 이유 ⑤ 영화 내 특수 효과의 증대하는 중요성

2 영화는 리퍼블릭 픽처스에 의해 '만들어지는' 대상이므로 making을 수동의 의미를 나타내는 과거분사 made로 고쳐야 한다.

3 ③은 앞 문장에 나온 라이데커 형제의 특수 효과(= their effects)를 가리키고, 나머지는 모두 라이데커 형제를 가리킨다.

본문

① From the 1930s to the 1950s, / the amazing special effects / in the movies / made by Republic Pictures / were created by the brothers Howard and Theodore Lydecker. ② They specialized in producing extremely realistic effects / on very low budgets. ③ They used carefully constructed models / and insisted / that their effects be created / "in camera." ④ This means / that they were created / during the original filming, / which made their effects believable. ⑤ Since the effects were shot / on the same film stock / as the movie itself, / the quality of the image was very high. ⑥ The Lydeckers also developed / a method of flying model aircraft / that made them look like real planes. ⑦ This technique gave them / total control over the aircraft's movement, / and it is still used today.

해석 ① 1930년대에서 1950년대까지, 리퍼블릭 픽처스에 의해 제작된 영화들의 놀라운 특수 효과는 하워드와 테오도르 라이데커 형제에 의해 만들어졌다. ② 그들은 아주 적은 예산으로 대단히 사실적인 효과를 만들어내는 것이 전문이었다. ③ 그들은 세심하게 구성된 모형을 사용했으며 효과들이 '카메라 안에서' 제작되어야 한다고 주장했다. ④ 이것은 그것들이 원본 촬영 중에 제작되었다는 것을 의미하는데, 이는 그들의 효과를 그럴듯하게 만들어 주었다. ⑤ 특수 효과가 영화 자체와 같은 촬영용 필름에 촬영되었기 때문에, 영상의 품질이 매우 높았다. ⑥ 라이데커 형제는 실제 비행기처럼 보이게 하는 모형 비행기 조종 기법을 또한 개발했다. ⑦ 이 기술은 그들에게 비행기의 움직임에 대한 완전한 통제력을 제공했으며, 오늘날에도 여전히 쓰인다.

구문해설 ③ They ... **insisted** that their effects (**should**) **be created** "in camera."

→ 주장을 나타내는 동사 insist의 목적어로 쓰인 that절의 내용이 '…해야 한다'는 당위성을 나타낼 경우, that절의 동사로는 「(should)+동사원형」이 옴.

④ This means that they were created during the original filming, [which made their effects believable].

→ [ ]는 앞의 that절의 내용을 선행사로 하는 계속적 용법의 주격 관계대명사절

⑥ The Lydeckers also developed a method of flying model aircraft [that made **them** look like real planes].

→ [ ]는 a method of flying model aircraft를 선행사로 하는 주격 관계대명사절

→ them은 앞에 나온 model aircraft를 가리킴. aircraft는 단수명사와 복수명사의 형태가 같음.

Review Test P. 150

A 1 ④ B 1 absorb 2 resources 3 benefit 4 construct C 1 ③ 2 ① 3 ④ 4 ⑤ D 1 그 여성은 자신이 대화하고 있던 사람이 바뀌었다는 사실을 알아채지 못했다. 2 대부분의 질병이 몸속으로 들어오는 것은 바로 이 통로를 통해서이다. 3 사람들이 '혁신적으로 생각할' 때 일어날 수 있는 일은 놀랍다. 4 그들은 그들의 효과들이 '카메라 안에서' 제작되어야 한다고 주장했다. E 1 tend not to notice them 2 will let you breathe easily 3 made them look like real planes

해석 **A**

① 여과하다: 어떤 것이 통과할 때 그것으로부터 원하지 않는 물질을 제거하다

② 중단, 방해: 행동이 멈추도록 하는 어떤 것

③ 원본의: 특정 예술가에 의해 직접 만들어진; 사본이 아닌

④ 오염 물질: 공기, 물, 또는 흙을 깨끗하게 만드는 어떤 것

⑤ 예산: 주어진 기간 동안의 지출 추정치

B

1 냄새를 흡수하도록 냉장고에 베이킹 소다를 넣어 두어라.

2 당신은 아동을 위한 많은 훌륭한 교수 자료를 온라인에서 찾을 수 있다.

3 고용주와 고용인 모두가 유연 근무 시간제로부터 이익을 얻을 수 있다.

4 영어 에세이를 쓸 때는 문법적으로 정확한 문장을 구성하는 것이 중요하다.

C

1 당신의 현재 것을 대체할 새로운 프로필 사진을 선택하십시오.

① 더할 ② 첨부할 ③ 대체할 ④ 업로드할 ⑤ 확인할

2 우리는 의자들을 탁자 주변에 원형으로 배열했다.

① 배열했다 ② 제거했다 ③ 발전시켰다 ④ 생산했다 ⑤ 비교했다

3 팬들은 항상 거리의 스타에게 다가가서 사인이나 사진을 요청한다.

① 실시해서 ② 회피해서 ③ 조직해서 ④ 다가가서 ⑤ 감염시켜서

4 그 식당은 전통 멕시코 요리를 전문으로 한다.

① 판매한다 ② 처리한다 ③ 개시한다 ④ 운영한다 ⑤ 전문으로 한다

MEMO

MEMO

고등 독해의 절대 자신감

READING TUTOR

READING TUTOR의 특징

Fun & Interesting 지루한 독해는 그만! 우린 재미있게 공부한다

High Quality 최신 학습 경향을 반영한 양질의 문제로 독해 실력을 키운다

New & Informative 새로운 정보로 가득한 지문을 통해 배경지식을 넓힌다